Costs of Democracy

Costs of Democracy

Political Finance in India

EDITED BY
DEVESH KAPUR
MILAN VAISHNAV

OXFORD
UNIVERSITY PRESS

OXFORD
UNIVERSITY PRESS

Oxford University Press is a department of the University of Oxford.
It furthers the University's objective of excellence in research, scholarship,
and education by publishing worldwide. Oxford is a registered trademark of
Oxford University Press in the UK and in certain other countries.

Published in India by
Oxford University Press
2/11 Ground Floor, Ansari Road, Daryaganj, New Delhi 110 002, India

ISBN-13 (print edition): 978-0-19-948727-1
ISBN-10 (print edition): 0-19-948727-8

ISBN-13 (eBook): 978-0-19-909313-7
ISBN-10 (eBook): 0-19-909313-X

Typeset in Bembo Std 10.5/13
by Tranistics Data Technologies, Kolkata 700 091
Printed in India by Replika Press Pvt. Ltd

Contents

Figures and Tables

FIGURES

TABLES

Acknowledgements

Five years ago, we first discussed the idea of bringing together a group of scholars who work on the issue of money and politics in India. Each time we raised the topic, we struggled to identify a critical mass of researchers doing empirical work in this area. In 2015, with a push from Simon Chauchard, we finally assembled the group whose work is on display in this volume.

Our biggest thanks go to the contributors whose passion has sustained this project from the outset. It is often said that editing volumes is akin to herding cats but, in this case, no herding was necessary. Each of the contributors was as fired up about this undertaking as we were.

In June 2016, the Center for the Advanced Study of India (CASI) at the University of Pennsylvania and the Carnegie Endowment for International Peace, USA, jointly hosted a workshop where early drafts of the present chapters were first presented. As a collective, we immediately knew that we had the beginnings of an important volume on a subject that has received far too little scholarly attention, in India and across the developing world. We owe special thanks to Juliana Di Giustini, Georgette Rochlin, and Mollie Laffin-Rose of CASI and Rachel Osnos of Carnegie for making the workshop possible. Aidan Milliff and Saksham Khosla served as rapporteurs for the workshop, but also provided enormously helpful comments on each of the chapters.

We are grateful to Oxford University Press, for their support in helping us publish this book. Rebecca Brown and Matthew Lillehaugen at the Carnegie Endowment provided expert research and editorial assistance, and we are extremely grateful to her for her help on all aspects of the volume. Milan would like to acknowledge financial support from the Carnegie Corporation of New York and the Hurford Foundation. This support was truly invaluable.

Last but not least, we would like to thank our families for their forbearance. While we thank them for their support, we would also like to point out that—every once in a while—our crazy ideas do pan out.

Devesh Kapur
Milan Vaishnav
February 2018

Abbreviations

AAP	Aam Aadmi Party
ADMK	Anna Dravida Munnetra Kazhagam
ADR	Association for Democratic Reforms
AEO	Assistant Expenditure Observer
AIADMK	All India Anna Dravida Munnetra Kazhagam
AIC	Akaike Information Criterion
BC	Backward Class
BJP	Bharatiya Janata Party
BMC	Brihanmumbai (Bombay) Municipal Corporation
BSP	Bahujan Samaj Party
CAG	Comptroller and Auditor General
CBI	Central Bureau of Investigation
CEO	Chief Electoral Officer
CIC	Central Information Commission
CII	Confederation of Indian Industry
CLU	Change in Land Use
CMA	Cement Manufacturers' Association of India
CMS	Centre for Media Studies
CPI	Communist Party of India
CPI(M)	Communist Party of India (Marxist)
DK	Dravida Kazhagam
DMK	Dravida Munnetra Kazhagam
DPI	Dalit Panther Iyakkam
DWCRA	Development of Women and Children in Rural Areas
ECI	Election Commission of India
EO	Expenditure Observer

EVR	E.V. Ramasamy
FCRA	Foreign Contributions Regulation Act
FDI	Foreign Direct Investment
FEC	Federal Election Commission
FERA	Foreign Exchange Regulation Act
FIR	First Information Report
FOIA	Freedom of Information Act
FS	Flying Squad
FSI	Floor Space Index
GDP	Gross Domestic Product
IAC	India Against Corruption
IIP	Index of Industrial Production
INC	Indian National Congress
INR	Indian Rupees
IT	Income Tax
LJP	Lok Janshakti Party
MBC	Most Backward Class
MC	Master of ceremonies
MCMC	Markov Chain Monte Carlo
MGNREGA	Mahatma Gandhi National Rural Employment Guarantee Act
MGR	M.G. Ramachandran
MLA	Member of the Legislative Assembly
MLC	Member of the Legislative Council
MNS	Maharashtra Navnirman Sena
MP	Member of Parliament
MRTP	Monopolies and Restrictive Trade Practices
NCP	Nationalist Congress Party
NDA	National Democratic Alliance
NGO	Non-governmental organization
NSS	National Sample Survey
OBC	Other Backward Class
OLS	Ordinary Least Squares
PAC	Political Affairs Committee
PAN	Permanent Account Number
PC	Parliamentary Constituency
PCSE	Panel-corrected Standard Errors
PIL	Public Interest Litigation

PMK	Pattali Makkal Katchi
PT	Pudhiya Tamizhagam
PWA	People's Welfare Alliance
RBI	Reserve Bank of India
RERA	Real Estate Regulatory Authorities
RJD	Rashtriya Janata Dal
RO	Returning Officer
RPA	Representation of the People Act
RPI	Republican Party of India
RTI	Right to Information
SC	Scheduled Caste
SEZ	special economic zone
SHG	Self-Help Group
SRS	Slum Rehabilitation Scheme
SS	Shiv Sena
SST	Static Surveillance Team
ST	Scheduled Tribe
USD	United States Dollar
VCK	Viduthalai Chiruthaigal Katchi
VST	Video Surveillance Team
VVT	Video Viewing Team
YSR	Y.S. Reddy

Introduction

Devesh Kapur and Milan Vaishnav[*]

Worldwide, there is a palpable sense that democracy is under stress. Numerous books and articles lament the democratic 'recession,' 'decline,' or 'retreat' across the globe.[1] The breakdown of democracy in 27 countries between 2000 and 2015 and new constrictions on individual and associational freedoms in several others show just how quickly the post–Cold War state of euphoria over liberal democracy's triumph has faded.[2]

Scholars have pointed to an array of factors that have contributed to this recent stress on democracy, including widening inequalities, stagnant middle-class incomes, limited social mobility, and weak political leadership. To quote Francis Fukuyama, the crux of the problem is that

[*] The authors are grateful to the contributors for helpful comments and to Rebecca Brown for excellent research assistance.

[1] On the 'democratic malaise' infecting Western democracies, see Charles Kupchan, 'The Democratic Malaise: Globalization and the Threat to the West', *Foreign Affairs* 91, no. 1 (January/February 2012): 62–7. For a discussion on the global democratic recession, see Larry Diamond, 'Facing up to the Democratic Recession', *Journal of Democracy* 26, no. 1 (January 2015): 141–55. For a global argument, see Joshua Kurlantzick, *Democracy in Retreat: The Revolt of the Middle Class and the Worldwide Decline of Representative Government* (New Haven: Yale University Press, 2014).

[2] Larry Diamond, 'Democracy in Decline: How Washington Can Reverse the Tide', *Foreign Affairs* 95, no. 4 (July/August 2016): 151–9.

'state capacity in many new and existing democracies has not kept pace with popular demands for democratic accountability.'[3] The emerging gap between the rhetoric and reality of democracy has also fuelled a reconsideration of non-democratic alternatives, namely, the models put forward by authoritarian China and Russia.[4]

Perhaps one of the most damaging attacks on the primacy of democracy is the inability of representative governments to regulate the flood of money in politics.[5] Ironically, the problem is structurally part of democracy itself. It is widely accepted that elections represent the procedural foundations of democracy; indeed, it is impossible to conceive of democracy without them. However, it is equally impractical to imagine elections without financial resources. As American politician and Democratic power broker Jesse Unruh once put it, 'Money is the mother's milk of politics.' Observers have long understood that the sources, amounts, and uses of money for elections have profound political consequences. Indeed, two millennia ago, Plutarch suggested that the corrosive effects of money gradually led to the fall of the Roman republic, writing that: 'The abuse of buying and selling votes crept in and money began to play an important part in determining elections.' In his 1932 study of political financing in the United Kingdom, Germany, and France, James Kerr Pollock warned: 'The relation between money and politics has come to be one of the great problems of democratic government.'[6]

The massive disruptions of the war upended pre-war arrangements in political finance, especially the role of private industry. The changes were underpinned by new laws (for example, public funding of parties in Germany instituted in 1958) and numerous court decisions. However, as is often the case, over time, private interests found new ways to fund parties and candidates. Scandals would occasionally erupt and the resulting public outrage would drive a new round of political

[3] Francis Fukuyama, 'Why is Democracy Performing So Poorly', *Journal of Democracy* 26, no. 1 (January 2015): 12.

[4] Joshua Kurlantzick, *State Capitalism: How the Return of Statism is Transforming the World* (New York: Oxford University Press, 2016).

[5] Pippa Norris and Andrea Abel van Es, eds, *Checkbook Elections? Political Finance in Comparative Perspective* (New York: Oxford University Press, 2016).

[6] James Kerr Pollock, *Money and Politics Abroad* (New York: Knopf, 1932), 1.

finance reforms.[7] While the current angst might be viewed as another 'punctuated equilibria', there are three concomitant trends that make the current scenario different.

First, parties—especially cadre-based parties—have weakened globally, which has increased their dependency on external sources of political finance.[8] Second, income inequalities have grown to levels unprecedented in living memory and the concentration of wealth has, in turn, drawn attention to imbalances in the concentration of power.[9] And third, political polarization appears to be increasing in many democracies, raising the stakes of elections.[10]

In virtually all corners of the world, contesting elections is a costly undertaking—albeit one that has become dramatically more expensive.[11] Data compiled by the United States Federal Election Commission (FEC) indicates that candidates, parties, political action committees, and independent groups spent more than $8.2 billion in the 2011–12 election cycle. This is more than double what these entities spent on races held in 1999–2000 (in nominal terms).[12] Identifying hard numbers on election spending in most developing countries is a

---

[7] Examples include the series of party finance scandals in 1987 in France that forced legislative changes and the mid-1990s scandal in Germany when Chancellor Helmut Kohl's Christian Democratic Union (CDU) party was found to have received dubious donations. For a discussion, see Véronique Pujas and Martin Rhodes, 'Party Finance and Political Scandal in Italy, Spain, and France', *West European Politics* 22, no. 3 (July 1999): 41–63.

[8] For a discussion on the decline of political parties, drawing on the European experience, see Paul F. Witeley, 'Is the Party Over? The Decline of Party Activism and Membership across the Democratic World', *Party Politics* 17, no. 1 (March 2009): 21–44.

[9] Thomas Piketty, *Capital in the Twenty-First Century*, trans. Arthur Goldhammer (Cambridge, MA: Harvard University Press, 2014).

[10] Daniela Giannetti and Kenneth Benoit, eds., *Intra-Party Politics and Co-alition Governments* (New York: Routledge, 2009).

[11] Michael Pinto-Duschinsky, 'Financing Politics: A Global View,' *Journal of Democracy* 13, no. 4 (October 2002): 69–85.

[12] The quoted figures include both congressional and presidential elections. See United States Federal Election Commission, 'FEC Summarizes Campaign Activity of the 2011-2012 Cycle', 27 March 2014, https://www.fec.gov/updates/fec-summarizes-campaign-activity-of-the-2011-2012-election-cycle/.

harder task, but estimates suggest they are increasingly lucrative affairs. In India's 2014 general election, the Centre for Media Studies (CMS) estimated that as much as $5 billion was spent on election-related activities. This was considerably higher than the $2 billion price tag CMS placed on the previous national election in 2009.[13] The story is similar in Brazil, where official political party spending has increased more than tenfold from 2002 to 2014. Since actual expenditure is underreported, the volume of true spending is likely even larger.[14]

The costs of democracy are cause for concern, not simply because of the significance of the material outlays involved, but also due to the broader impacts money can have on political behaviour. In recent decades, the growing concentration of wealth, rising cost of elections, and deepening links between money and political power have raised serious normative concerns, prompting a range of studies about the causes and consequences of money in democratic politics.

To the extent access to financial resources is considered a prerequisite for contesting elections, money can have a powerful 'selection effect' on the candidate pool standing for office, not to mention the characteristics of who is ultimately elected.[15] With regard to impacts on public policy, raising money from supporters can potentially incentivize post-election paybacks in terms of the political manipulation of public policies.[16] Several studies have documented the financial rewards office-holders extract, quantifying the rents afforded those with politi-

[13] Niraj Sheth, 'Corruption Mars Image of Change in India Elections', *Wall Street Journal*, 9 April 2009; Sruthi Gottipati and Rajesh Kumar Singh, 'India Set to Challenge U.S. for Election-Spending Record', *Reuters*, 9 March 2014.

[14] 'Financing Democracy: Funding of Political Parties and Election Campaigns and the Risk of Policy Capture', *OECD Public Governance Reviews,* 2016, http://dx.doi.org/10.1787/9789264249455-en.

[15] Timothy Besley, 'Political Selection', *Journal of Economic Perspectives* 19, no. 3 (Summer 2005): 43–59.

[16] Rui J.P. De Figueiredo Jr. and Geoff Edwards, 'Does Private Money Buy Public Policy? Campaign Contributions and Regulatory Outcomes in Telecommunications', *Journal of Economics and Management Strategy* 16, no. 3 (July 2007): 547–76; Atif Mian, Amir Sufi, and Francesco Trebbi, 'The Political Economy of the US Mortgage Default Crisis', *American Economic Review* 100, no. 5 (December 2010): 1967–98.

cal connections.[17] But perhaps most seriously, even the perception of money 'buying' elections can severely undermine citizens' confidence in the democratic process itself.[18] Finally, rising election costs can contribute to growing inequality. Money allows wealthy individuals or interests to influence electoral politics in their favour, thereby entrenching their wealth and creating a reinforcing cycle in which inequality and public policies interlock. The result, some have argued, is a polity that responds most forcefully to the preferences of the rich.[19]

While there are myriad consequences of money in politics, to date, much of the scholarly literature has focused on advanced industrialized democracies, especially the United States. But the implications of the costs of democracy can be significant for all democracies—new or old, rich or poor. Furthermore, the scholarship on the developing world that does exist shows that models of political finance from industrialized democracies have limited purchase on the problems developing democracies face.

Simply put, money often flows in distinct ways in new and developing democracies. In advanced democracies, there are well-established systems of monitoring and accounting for political finance and complementary systems for prosecuting those involved in alleged improprieties. These systems, though imperfect, likely deter the transfer

[17] Andrew C. Eggers and Jens Hainmueller, 'MPs for Sale? Returns to Office in Postwar British Politics', *American Political Science Review* 103, no. 4 (November 2009): 513–33; Pablo Querubin and James M. Snyder, 'The Control of Politicians in Normal Times and Times of Crisis: Wealth Accumulation by U.S. Congressmen, 1850–1880', *Quarterly Journal of Political Science* 8 (2013): 409–50; Raymond Fisman, Florian Schulz, and Vikrant Vig, 'The Private Returns to Public Office', *Journal of Political Economy* 122, no. 4 (August 2014): 806–62.

[18] Mitchell A. Seligson, 'The Impact of Corruption on Regime Legitimacy: A Comparative Study of Four Latin American Countries', *The Journal of Politics* 64, no. 2 (May 2002): 408–33; Christopher J. Anderson and Yuliya V. Tverdova, 'Corruption, Political Allegiances, and Attitudes Toward Government in Contemporary Democracies', *American Journal of Political Science* 47, no. 1 (January 2003): 91–109.

[19] Larry M. Bartels, *Unequal Democracy: The Political Economy of the New Gilded Age* (Princeton: Princeton University Press, 2008); Martin Gilens, *Affluence and Influence: Economic Inequality and Political Power in America* (Princeton: Princeton University Press, 2012).

of illicit funds to a considerable extent. In less developed countries, poor accountability, weak or partial transparency, and a lack of well-enforced disclosure norms and laws offer a conducive context in which undocumented money can flow. Indeed, numerous accounts from the developing world attest to the fact that illicit campaign finance expenditures often dwarf legal flows by orders of magnitude.[20] Yet because these flows of 'black money' are opaque by definition, we know very little about their relative size or mechanics.

This volume seeks to shed light on the methods, sources, and implications of political finance in a major developing country setting: India. Given its size, lengthy track record of representative government, and global significance, it is hard to conjure a more pertinent example than the world's largest democracy. The following section explains the logic of focusing on India in greater detail before turning to the larger theoretical questions addressed by the chapters in this volume. Next, we briefly review the answers this collection of scholarly research provides, and then conclude with some thoughts about a future research agenda.

INSIGHTS FROM INDIA

The case of India provides a unique lens into how money and politics interact in a developing democratic setting. On its own terms, India is an important case. India is the most populous democracy in the world; it is home to roughly one out of every six voting-age persons residing on the planet. It is also the most enduring democracy in the developing world, which means that it can offer lessons for other countries embarking on a democratic path but have not yet attained the same stage of democratic consolidation. India's remarkably competitive elections—more than 8,000 candidates, representing as many as 464 political parties, contested its general election in 2014—leave no doubt that the stakes of electoral contests are high and the outcomes far from ordained. Embedded within this raucous democratic setting is

---

[20] Daniel W. Gingerich, 'Brokered Politics in Brazil: An Empirical Analysis', *Quarterly Journal of Political Science* 9, no. 3 (2014): 269–300; Kevin Casas-Zamora and Daniel Zovatto, *The Cost of Democracy: Essays on Political Finance in Latin America* (Stockholm: International IDEA, 2016).

tremendous subnational variation. Formally, India is a federation comprising 29 states (and seven union territories, which are administered directly by the central government), and this federal framework allows scholars to leverage variation across India's states while holding institutional design constant.

That there is a growing amount of money involved in Indian elections is a widely held sentiment, but the drivers of this increase are worth enumerating. First, since the opening of the economy in 1991, the size of the economy has grown fivefold and the size of the electorate by more than half. These structural changes have likely had independent effects on election spending. Second, the Indian electoral landscape has grown vastly more competitive. As the one-party dominance of the Congress party began to fray, beginning in the late 1960s, India's political landscape fragmented as political parties proliferated to fill in the vacuum. Whereas the average margin of victory in a parliamentary election was 15 per cent in 1952, that number dipped below 10 per cent in 2009.[21] To place this number in comparative perspective, the average margin of victory in a 2016 US congressional race for a seat in the House of Representatives was 37 per cent. Third, the organizational strength of parties has diminished over time. Sturdy party structures are being replaced by charismatic (often dynastic) political leaders who are increasingly reliant on private funds as opposed to party coffers. For instance, 22 per cent of India's Members of Parliament (MPs) elected in 2014 hail from a political family. Fourth, the overall number of elections has massively expanded. The 73rd and 74th amendments to the Indian constitution, which established a new, three-tier structure of local governance in the early 1990s, created nearly three million locally elected positions. With decentralization came greater fiscal devolution,

---

[21] The margin of victory in India's 2014 general election was more in line with the earlier trend, averaging around 15 per cent. However, the 2014 election was generally recognized to be a 'wave' election in which one political party captured an outright majority of seats in the lower house of Parliament for the first time in three decades. See Milan Vaishnav and Danielle Smogard, 'A New Era in Indian Politics?' Carnegie Endowment for International Peace, 10 June 2014, http://carnegieendowment.org/2014/06/10/new-era-in-indian-politics-pub-55883, accessed 17 October 2017.

which increased the stakes of winning local elections and, in turn, the potential profitability of holding local office.

Faced with this influx of money, India's system of regulating political finance has struggled, which explains why the country fares poorly on most global indicators of political finance regulation. One study on the integrity of political finance regulatory and enforcement mechanisms in 54 countries gave India a score of 31 (out of 100), placing it twelfth from bottom.[22] Another effort, which analysed election management in 125 countries, gave India's election commission high marks overall, but found the country's performance on matters of political finance to be middling—placing it 51 out of 125.[23]

OUR CONTRIBUTION

The contributions in this volume are structured around four central questions: First, what is the institutional and regulatory context governing the flow of money in politics? Second, what are the sources of political finance? Third, what do campaigns spend on and why do they spend such vast sums? Fourth, how does money operate at, and interact with, different levels of government?

As the chapter by Sridharan and Vaishnav points out, India has one of the most well-regarded (and powerful) elections agencies in the world. The Election Commission of India (ECI) is a constitutional body with wide-ranging powers over the conduct of elections. It has deservedly earned global acclaim for ensuring the integrity of elections for more than 850 million voters, and for the equitable participation of the poor and socially marginalized communities. Yet it has struggled mightily to regulate political finance for two key reasons. First, more than a quarter century following India's landmark

[22] The Money, Politics and Transparency Campaign Finance Indicators project relies on the inputs of more than 110 political finance experts around the world. For more information, see https://data.moneypoliticstransparency.org/.

[23] Pippa Norris, Ferran Martinez i Coma, Alessandro Nai, and Max Gromping, 'Perceptions of Electoral Integrity, (PEI-4.5)', Harvard Dataverse, 18 August 2010.

economic reforms, the state continues to have a major role in the economy. Whether through a banking system dominated by the public sector that controls the flow of credit or burgeoning public-sector contracts that allow politicians and bureaucrats to exchange regulatory or policy favours in exchange for financial contributions, the state's reach is sprawling.

Second, while there has been a marked improvement in transparency and disclosure laws, poor enforcement has hampered their effectiveness. Legal loopholes, which the ECI cannot address without enhanced statutory authority, have stymied attempts to sanction candidates and parties whose actions contravene the laws on the books. The regulation of political parties has proven to be exceptionally tricky because the very entity being regulated is also the one making the regulations. The Indian Constitution, save for a 1985 constitutional amendment intended to curb party defections, is entirely silent on the issue of political parties. This has set up a high-stakes showdown between civil society, the judiciary, and accountability institutions, on the one hand, and political parties, on the other, over whether the latter are public or private entities under Indian law.

One of the key sources of money for elections is candidates themselves. The chapter by Sircar argues that there are structural and institutional reasons for the outward display of wealth in Indian electoral campaigns that transcend political culture or levels of economic development. This, in turn, has led to the rise of 'self-financing' candidates for at least two reasons: first, parties are cash-strapped and often depend on wealthy candidates to fill their coffers; and second, money makes candidates competitive (the 'winnability' factor, as it is often referred to in India) as the costs of elections has grown exponentially. Sircar marshals granular data on more than 20,000 parliamentary candidates between 2004 and 2014 to investigate the role of personal wealth and self-financing candidates in Indian elections. Through careful empirical analysis, the author finds that a candidate's liquid wealth, measured in terms of moveable assets, has a strong positive impact on his or her electoral fortunes. This correlation is more complex than it might seem at first glance; Sircar's analyses show that competitive parties select candidates that are far wealthier on average. But even accounting for this selection effect, the wealthiest candidate is more likely to emerge victorious on election day.

Of course, candidates are not the only source of material resources. Drawing on the connection between the regulatory intensity of a sector and its rent extraction potential outlined in the chapter by Sridharan and Vaishnav, the analysis in this volume by Kapur and Vaishnav explores the close relationship that has blossomed between builders in the real estate and construction industry and politics. The authors, building on the economics literature on the 'regulation of entry', develop a series of hypotheses about the construction sector in India, where the state's heavy regulatory footprint is well-documented. Specifically, Kapur and Vaishnav argue that the construction sector should exhibit political business cycle fluctuations consistent with the idea that builders contribute heavily to political campaigns in exchange for regulatory forbearance. Because these flows are opaque, the authors devise a novel empirical strategy that leverages a staggered calendar of state elections and longitudinal data on cement consumption, an indispensable ingredient in any construction project. The booming construction sector in India has limited access to official finance (from banks) and relies heavily on unofficial sources of finance—often from politicians, who also control the rules and regulations in the sector. The authors find that the consumption of cement significantly declines during the month of elections as builders channel cash from their activities into political campaigns. The resulting liquidity constraints slow construction activities, and therefore the demand for cement. The assembled qualitative and quantitative evidence suggests that under-the-table campaign contributions help explain why burdensome regulation persists in India's economy, despite broader negative impacts on the 'ease of doing business.'

However, not all political actors can rely on financial support, licit or otherwise, from business. The chapter by Collins explores the question of financing elections from a very different viewpoint—that of the Viduthalai Chiruthaigal Katchi (VCK), a small political party founded to advocate on behalf of India's Dalits, or low-caste citizens, in the southern state of Tamil Nadu. Collins's intensive fieldwork reveals that the VCK's strategy relies on chains of association with larger, better-financed regional parties. Over successive elections, either one of the two dominant Tamil parties has essentially 'adopted' the VCK, providing monetary support in exchange for a pre-election alliance. Yet the money provided circulates within the larger party's own organization and infrastructure, which still leaves the VCK on the hook to finance their own cadres. This *quid pro quo* provides a short-term lifeline to the minor VCK, but also involves 'broader trade-offs that may affect candidate selection, structure vote canvassing techniques, and even set the terms of democratic participation'.

An insightful chapter by Björkman and Witsoe shifts the focus from raising money to the purposes for which it is spent. The authors examine the role of money in two different locales: urban Mumbai, which is among India's richest political geographies, and rural Bihar, which falls at the other extreme. Fieldwork in both sites suggests that despite many differences between the two locales, money in politics is playing an important role in shaping—and re-shaping—social relationships. In contrast to traditional models of campaign spending, the authors find that money does not flow unidirectionally from the top to the bottom, but rather multidirectionally. The article also upends a second piece of conventional wisdom: so-called 'vote buying' rarely involves the actual buying of anyone's vote. The extant comparative literature has emphasized the importance of a *quid pro quo* or implicit contract in which voters trade their vote for cash, and these contracts are said to be enforced by party machines that possess extensive local networks. In contrast, Björkman and Witsoe find that money plays a role in 'gift giving', rather than 'vote buying', in which the election-time distribution of cash is not a one-off transaction, but rather one element of a layered series of relationships among broker networks. Rather than buying votes per se, cash distribution signals a leader's access to broader, 'translocal' networks.

Gift giving is an important object of campaign spending, but the chapter by Chauchard reminds us that it is not the only (or necessarily most important) one in all instances. Drawing on ethnographic fieldwork in Mumbai over several years, Chauchard shines a spotlight on what campaigns actually spend on and to what extent their resources are oriented towards 'illegal' tactics that could threaten the fairness of elections. While the author finds that gift giving is quite common, 'politics as usual' expenses—such as wage payments to party workers, payments for participating in rallies, or even basic transportation and logistics costs—are important financial priorities for politicians. While the chapter finds that many voters or communities are recipients of costly gifts, campaigns are getting more expensive not due to gift giving alone but thanks to the fact that campaigns are more ambitious, sophisticated, professional, and competitive. The larger takeaway from this chapter is that the widely perceived increase in the cost of elections does not necessarily have one cause but several. Furthermore, the rise in the costs of campaigns cannot solely be attributed to illegitimate or illegal tactics.

Bussell's chapter expertly ties together many of the threads developed by the other chapters and takes a comprehensive look at where the money for elections comes from and what it is spent on. Most notably, her survey in three north Indian states collects first-hand data on politicians operating across the different tiers of a federal system—from national (MPs) to state (members of state legislative assemblies) and local elected bodies. This type of nested and highly granular information on political finance is exceedingly rare. Bussell finds that financial support from political parties to candidates is primarily relevant at the upper echelons; lower-level politicians depend heavily on their own pocketbooks or local fundraising efforts. When asked to discuss their perceptions about the 'most common' sources of funding for politicians, black money is the modal response for national and state-level politicians and remains a popular response for lower-level functionaries as well. Across all tiers of governance, however, politicians report spending a substantial share of campaign funds on 'gift giving,' which accords with the findings of Björkman and Witsoe. When it comes to non-financial assistance, the sources of support vary considerably across levels—suggesting that the identity of influential supporters is not uniform across tiers. For instance, lower-level politicians are more reliant on local associations whereas their counterparts higher up the political hierarchy depend much more on party workers.

The concluding chapter by Kapur, Sridharan, and Vaishnav focuses on the scholarly and policy implications of the analyses found herein. While there has been a flurry of activity in India on issues concerning 'black money' in the economy and in politics, the fundamental landscape remains largely unchanged. Notwithstanding India's dramatic November 2016 demonetization, cash remains the lifeblood of electoral politics. Despite legislative moves intended to increase transparency, we know very little about political contributions and the state of party finances. The authors make the case that reform is not only in the interests of the public, it is also in the interests of parties and contributors themselves. They outline a detailed reform blueprint that marries strict disclosure rules and enhanced regulatory powers for the ECI to a system of public funding. Unless political actors, especially political parties, are required to adhere to higher standards of transparency, new forms of public financing risk augmenting—rather than replacing— privately raised money.

Yet, the authors acknowledge there is much more work to be done by the research community; basic questions about subnational variation in election spending or the impact of political competition remain under-theorized. The numbers cited by Collins in his examination of politics in Tamil Nadu are far larger than what other scholars in this volume have quoted for other locales in India, some of which are also among India's most prosperous pockets. What accounts for this substantial level of variation in the costs of elections across subnational units? Second, greater electoral competition is generally seen as a sign of a healthy democracy. But, as competition leads to greater amounts of money being spent on elections, is there a point at which it might actually undermine democracy in the long run by restricting the prospective candidate pool to wealthy elites?

Taken together, the chapters in this volume shed light on political finance in novel ways. Although unified by a common case, they employ a diversity of methodological tools and draw from varied geographies to develop and test new micro-foundations of the role money plays in democratic elections. In doing so, they provide often surprising new insights on how money and politics interact. For instance, increasing transparency on money flows in politics, while an admirable objective in its own right, will only have a limited impact on curbing corruption without parallel changes in the regulatory architecture governing the economy. Counter-intuitively, black money can have positive consequences in terms of building social networks, providing economic stimulus, and generating employment. Politics, many of the essays suggest, is a business unto itself. Vote buying, though much discussed, is a misnomer; pre-electoral handouts in highly competitive environments have more to do with signalling than forging *quid pro quos* with voters. Furthermore, the flow of money need not travel top-down; it often moves horizontally, across networks.

★ ★ ★

At the heart of any successful democracy, where the losers accept their loss to fight another day, is a sense of legitimacy about the process and the existence of a level playing field. Deep distortions in electoral finance can undermine that legitimacy and threaten democracy itself. In our view, there can hardly be a worthier, yet greatly underexplored, line of research for scholars of politics to pursue.

1 Political Finance in a Developing Democracy

The Case of India

Eswaran Sridharan and Milan Vaishnav

Indian elections are among the most contested polls in the world. In fact, they are so competitive that candidates speak not of 'contesting' elections, but of 'fighting' them. In 2014, the size of the electorate was a gargantuan 834 million, out of which 554 million (66.4 per cent) voters cast their ballots on election day in favour of one of 8,251 candidates representing 464 political parties.[1] While Indian elections have become increasingly free and fair over the past quarter century, the area of political finance remains decidedly murky; politicians spent an estimated \$5 billion on the costs of campaigning during the 2014 general election, the vast majority of which was not publicly disclosed. Not surprisingly, political finance is widely perceived to be one of the foremost drivers of corruption in the world's largest democracy.[2] In this chapter, we survey the legal and regulatory history of political finance in India, situating it in the context of India's political economy.

---

[1] Sruthi Gottipati and Rajesh Kumar Singh, 'India Set to Challenge U.S. for Election-Spending Record', *Reuters*, 9 March 2014.

[2] E. Sridharan and Milan Vaishnav, 'India', in *Checkbook Elections? Political Finance in Comparative Perspective*, eds, Pippa Norris and Andrea Abel van Es (New York: Oxford University Press, 2016), 64–83.

We devote special attention to recent developments, including new election finance initiatives implemented by the Bharatiya Janata Party (BJP) government of Prime Minister Narendra Modi in 2017. We also discuss possible areas of reform, including the regulation of political parties, which can lead to increased transparency and help the country break out of a corrupt equilibrium.[3]

THE POLITICAL AND ECONOMIC CONTEXT OF PARTY FINANCE IN INDIA

Before getting into the details of India's political finance regime, it is worth taking stock of India's broader political and economic evolution. This evolution, after all, has had a direct bearing on how money in politics has been regulated (or not).

Broadly speaking, the evolution of the Indian party system can be readily divided into three main phases.[4] The initial phase, which began with the first general election in 1952 and ended in 1967, was characterized by simultaneous Lok Sabha (lower house of Parliament) and state assembly elections—both of which were dominated by the hegemonic Congress party. Drawing on a deep well of popular support flowing from its role in the Independence movement, Congress

[3] In this chapter, we build on earlier work including Sridharan and Vaishnav, 'India'; E. Sridharan, 'Reforming Campaign Finance to Tackle Corruption in India: Possible Options from the International Experience', in *Fighting Corruption*, ed. Samuel Paul (New Delhi: Academic Foundation, 2013), 43–70; M.V. Rajeev Gowda and E. Sridharan, 'Reforming India's Party Financing and Election Expenditure Laws', *Election Law Journal* 11, no. 2 (2012): 226–40; E. Sridharan, 'Electoral Finance Reform: The Relevance of International Experience', in *Reinventing Public Service Delivery in India: Selected Case Studies*, ed. Vikram K. Chand (New Delhi: Sage, 2006), 363–88; E. Sridharan and Peter Ronald de Souza, 'Introduction: The Evolution of Political Parties in India', in *India's Political Parties*, eds. Peter Ronald de Souza and E. Sridharan (New Delhi: Sage, 2006), 15–36; E. Sridharan, 'Toward State Funding of Elections in India: A Comparative Perspective on Possible Options', *Journal of Policy Reform* 3, no. 3 (1999): 229–54.

[4] E. Sridharan, 'Why are Multi-Party Minority Governments Viable in India? Theory and Comparison', *Commonwealth and Comparative Politics* 50, no. 3 (2012): 314–43.

regularly won a majority, sometimes even a two-thirds majority, of parliamentary seats on the basis of a plurality of votes (typically ranging between 40–45 per cent).

This period of dominance came to an abrupt end in 1967, when the Congress lost assembly elections in half of India's then 16 major states. This widespread upheaval allowed opposition parties to consolidate, leading to a new phase in the party system that would last for more than two decades. Duvergerian—or two-party—dynamics played themselves out in both national and state assembly elections from 1967 to 1989, and this trend persisted even after 1989.[5] This pattern led to either a two-party (or two-coalition) system or a bipolar party system with the non-Congress opposition consolidating behind a particular party (with a few exceptions, such as the state of Uttar Pradesh).[6] However, the precise configuration of the bipolarities varied considerably across time and space; for example, the competition was between the Congress-Jana Sangh (the precursor of the present-day BJP) in some states; Congress-Left in others; and Congress versus a regional party in yet others.[7]

In the third phase, bookended by the elections of 1989 and 2014, the party system fragmented considerably, due to three major trends: the decline of Congress, the rise of the BJP, and the rise of regional parties. The net result of these dynamics was a fractured Lok Sabha in which no single party obtained a majority in the seven consecutive elections from 1989 to 2009, until the BJP's narrow majority in 2014. With the pan-Indian resurgence of the BJP following the 2014 general

---

[5] In the field of political science, Duverger's law holds that plurality-rule elections (such as India's first-past-the-post system) that are structured within single-member districts lead to the establishment of a two-party system. See Maurice Duverger, *Political Parties: Their Organization and Activity in the Modern State* (New York: Wiley, 1954).

[6] For detailed accounts, see Pradeep K. Chhibber and Geetha Murali, 'Duvergerian Dynamics in Indian States', *Party Politics* 12, no. 1 (2006): 5–34; E. Sridharan, 'The Fragmentation of the Indian Party System 1952–1999: Seven Competing Explanations', in *Parties and Party Politics in India*, ed. Zoya Hasan (New Delhi: Oxford University Press, 2002), 475–503.

[7] More accurately, these regional parties could be called state-based parties, as they were almost all based in a single state.

election results, it is possible that India has entered a new, fourth phase. However, it is too early to deliver a conclusive verdict on that score.[8]

These political transitions occurred against the economic backdrop of a heavily regulated economy. After gaining independence, India adopted an import-substitution industrialization strategy led by the public sector. Many industries were reserved for the public sector, nationalized, or forced to adhere to detailed state regulations concerning the setup, expansion, and import of inputs—such as coal, petroleum, steel, and power. The government wielded myriad instruments of control over the private sector, including a vast thicket of mandatory licenses and permissions, a monopoly over most of the banking system, and significant leverage as a consumer. Economic liberalization, beginning in the mid-1980s and picking up steam after 1991, has primarily taken the form of freer private sector entry into industries hitherto reserved for the public sector, combined with trade and foreign investment liberalization. But, there are still overarching state regulations in many areas, as well as an undesirably high level of state control over most of the banking system. Discretionary state regulation pervades environmental clearances, land use, and natural resources—both at the central (federal) and state levels—even as the old system of industrial licensing is no more.[9]

THE EVOLUTION OF INDIA'S POLITICAL FINANCE REGIME

India's political finance regime has also evolved in three broad phases, broadly tracking the country's overall political and economic history. The first phase began in 1947 and ended around 1990, which saw the emergence and consolidation of a corrupt, opaque equilibrium. The second phase, 1990–2003, witnessed the early beginnings of reform.

---

[8] Milan Vaishnav and Danielle Smogard, 'A New Era in Indian Politics', Carnegie Endowment for International Peace, 10 June 2014, accessed 17 October 2017, http://carnegieendowment.org/2014/06/10/new-era-in-indian-politics-pub-55883.

[9] Kanchan Chandra, 'The New Indian State: The Relocation of Patronage in the Post-Liberalisation Economy', *Economic and Political Weekly* 50, no. 41 (10 October 2015): 46–58.

The third phase, from 2003 to 2017, saw the emergence of greater transparency but very few—if any—structural changes. Given recent legislative changes introduced by the government of Prime Minister Narendra Modi in 2017, the overriding focus of reforms appears to be on curbing the use of cash at the expense of transparency. We elaborate below on the key developments of each of these phases.

The Emergence of a Corrupt Equilibrium: 1947–90

Internationally, we can identify four major features of political finance regulation: limits on expenditure, limits on contributions, public subsidy of elections and political parties, and reporting and disclosure requirements.[10] The evolution of political finance in India in these terms yields the following picture.

Under the 1951 Representation of the People Act (RPA), the foundational law that governs elections in India, there are strict limits on candidate spending. In terms of contributions, the then-dominant Congress party depended initially on membership dues, but rapidly shifted to private business as membership dues proved inadequate in keeping pace with the cost of increasingly competitive elections. This shift was encouraged by the fact that the government was heavily regulating businesses by licensing both capacity creation (and expansion) as well as imports. Businesses, therefore, gave money to parties and politicians in exchange for regulatory favours. This behaviour became rapidly institutionalized as part of the overarching, highly regulated, import-substituting industrialization strategy that characterized India's economic management. In this climate, businesses evaded taxes and 'donated' black money to political parties in exchange for policy or regulatory favours until engaging in such activities became an intrinsic part of running a business, rather than a choice.

During the decade of the 1960s, the first murmurs of political finance reform began to emerge as the broad contours of this new equilibrium became widely known. Indeed, the nexus between black money and political fundraising was mentioned as early as 1964, in the

[10] For a comprehensive survey of political finance across the world, see Reginald Austin and Maja Tjernstrom, eds., *Funding of Political Parties and Election Campaigns* (Stockholm: International IDEA, 2014).

reports of the Santhanam Committee on Prevention of Corruption, and again in 1971, in the Wanchoo Direct Taxes Enquiry Committee.

A key turning point in the history of political finance in India occurred in 1969, when the Indira Gandhi-led Congress government banned corporate donations to political parties. Gandhi pushed the move because a weakened Congress faced a credible challenge from conservative forces on its right flank, especially after it sustained heavy electoral losses in 1967. Congress feared that the pro-business Swatantra party, along with the Hindu nationalist Jana Sangh, would increasingly attract corporate donations, so banning the latter would deal a fierce blow to these rising challengers. However, Gandhi did not create any form of state funding or subsidy to political parties for elections to fill its place—a sharp contrast to the rise of public funding for parties in European democracies in the 1960s and 1970s.

The net result of this development was that, with company donations banned, there was no legal source of adequate finance for political parties. This inevitably meant a consolidation of the nexus between black money and politics. This tendency was reinforced by the policy shift from the late 1960s, engineered by Indira Gandhi, towards intensified government control of the economy. Beginning in 1969 and continuing through the first half of the 1970s, Gandhi tightened government control over the private sector, leading to a political economy of business financing ('donations') in exchange for regulatory and allocative favours. Newly imposed controls included the nationalization of 14 major private banks in 1969; the Monopolies and Restrictive Trade Practices (MRTP) Act of 1969, which intensi-fied regulation of big business; the Foreign Exchange Regulation Act (FERA) of 1973, which tightly controlled foreign investors; and the nationalization of coal mining, petroleum, and general insurance in the early 1970s. In hindsight, the banning of company donations in 1969—without adequately substituting for it with public funding—was a key moment in the path-dependent evolution of political finance because it strengthened ties between political parties and the black economy, while driving the funding of political campaigns further underground. The Congress, controlling most of the levers of power, stood to benefit in relative terms.

The next key development was the delinking of party and indepen-dent supporters' expenditure from candidate and candidate-authorized expenditure for the purpose of calculating a candidate's election spending. In other words, parties and independent supporters could spend unlimited funds on a political campaign without being subject to the strict limits on candidate expenditure. In 1974, the Supreme Court eliminated this loophole, ruling in *Kanwar Lal Gupta v. Amar Nath Chawla* that party spending on behalf of candidates would, in fact, be attributed to the candidate and, therefore, subject to the strict limits in place.[11] To circumvent this judgment, the government amended the RPA in 1975, introducing Explanation 1 to Section 77(1), which clearly stated that any spending by parties or independent supporters not authorized by the candidate would not count towards the spending limit. In effect, it removed any ceiling on party spending, rendering the candidate limit farcical. The end result was not surprising: the move touched off spending arms races in increasingly competitive elections.

The situation was altered slightly in 1979, when political parties were exempted from income and wealth taxes on the condition that they file annual tax returns.[12] Then, in 1985, Rajiv Gandhi's relatively liberalizing (delicensing) and pro-business government re-legalized company donations to political parties. Reversing Indira Gandhi's outright ban, the government amended the 1956 Companies Act to allow companies to donate up to 5 per cent of their average net profit over the prior three years, subject to board approval and declaration in their profit-and-loss accounts. However, there was no tax incentive for businesses to do so. In the end, the re-legalization after a gap of 16 years did not succeed in bringing donations above the table. Not only were there few incentives for shedding anonymity, there were actually positive *disincentives*. For instance, a company that openly supported a particular party, even the ruling Congress, would alienate opposition parties that might be ruling in states where the company had business interests. By the mid-1980s, there was simply too much water under the bridge; the system of opaque donations to parties and politicians in exchange for regulatory favours had become too deeply entrenched in a highly state-controlled business environment.

[11] *Kanwar Lal Gupta v. Amar Nath Chawla & Ors* decided on 3 October 1974. Citations 1975 AIR (308), 1975 SCR (2) 269.

[12] These annual tax returns, like most other income tax returns, were not subject to public disclosure.

The Beginnings of Reform, 1990–2003

The 1990s saw the beginning of a number of reform initiatives and proposals on political finance, emanating both from government and civil society. Minority governments, including minority coalitions and non-Congress parties, became more outspoken on the issue. Despite the increased chatter, many of the suggested changes never actually saw the light of day. And those that did operated at the margins, unable to fundamentally dislodge the corrupt equilibrium that prevailed.

The year 1996 saw two Supreme Court orders and one legislative change that had a bearing on the regulation of political finance. The first move occurred in January 1996, when the Supreme Court, in response to a public interest litigation (PIL) petition by the non-governmental organization (NGO) Common Cause, ordered political parties to file their annual income tax and wealth tax returns. Although parties were required to file annual returns since being granted tax-exempt status in 1979, no party had regularly done so. The ruling broke new ground, although it had serious limits. Thanks to the court ruling, parties were compelled to file returns, but they were often doctored and remained under wraps until 2008.

In April 1996, just prior to the general election, the Supreme Court again issued a landmark decision on political finance by ordering the second major legislative change of the period. The court ruled that party expenditures would once more count towards candidate spending ceilings if parties did not file audited accounts of income and expenditure. In effect, problematic Explanation 1 would no longer exempt party expenditures from the spending limit if such accounts were not filed. This reinforced the earlier court order and led to parties filing their tax returns and, thus, reporting their incomes and expenditures. However, the ruling did not mandate these returns be subject to independent audit and, hence, they remained the handiwork of crafty party-appointed auditors.[13]

In 1998, the government introduced the first significant state subsidy for elections: free airtime on state-owned television and radio.

---

[13] In addition, in July 1996, Parliament amended the RPA to shorten the campaign period from 21 days to 14 days, thus potentially reducing the scale of campaign spending.

The move built on the informal system in practice since the late 1970s, which had evolved with the consent of the ECI, parties, and government. The length of time each party had was based on a given time slab, with additional time based on past electoral performance for significant parties, which included seven national and 34 state parties. The same system was replicated at the state level for assembly elections.

In addition to these Supreme Court orders and legislative changes, there were a number of proposals for political party reforms in the 1990s. However, most of these reform blueprints went nowhere fast. We briefly mention them because they illustrate the fact that many prominent figures in Indian political life—from diverse quarters—recognized the knotty political finance predicament as far back as a quarter century ago.

In 1990, the Janata Dal-led National Front government of V.P. Singh set up the Dinesh Goswami Committee on Electoral Reforms. The committee's report recommended limited public subsidy in the form of vehicle fuel (the main campaign expenditure then), but left Explanation 1 intact and recommended a ban on company donations. But, much like in 1969, the committee did not propose to substitute the loss of corporate donations with a system of public funding.

Indian industry also became increasingly concerned about the issue of political funding during the 1990s. This concern was a result of the economic reforms of 1991—particularly trade and foreign direct investment (FDI) liberalization—which increased foreign competition and eroded profit margins, at a time of mounting political demands on Indian companies. In response to the concerns of its member companies, the Confederation of Indian Industry (CII) set up a task force which recommended state funding of elections.[14]

Although the CII proposal did not gain traction, the government continued to dabble in this area by setting up new reform commissions. The 1996–8 United Front government set up the Indrajit Gupta

---

[14] The funds were to be raised either by a cess (earmarked tax) on excise duty or through contributions by industry to a fund pool managed by the ECI. The money would then be distributed to parties by a transparent formula, creating, in effect, an election tax on industry. It also recommended that company donations to parties be made tax-deductible, and that shareholder approval be required for such board decisions.

Committee on State Funding of Elections. In its 1998 report, the Gupta committee recommended only partial state funding, including free television and radio broadcasts on state-owned channels, vehicle fuel, paper, and other campaign paraphernalia, up to certain limits.[15] It also said that parties that failed to maintain audited accounts for the ECI or submit income tax returns should be denied state funding. Parties would be required to receive all donations above Rs 10,000 by cheque/bank draft, so that all significant donations could be traceable.[16]

In 1999, Lok Satta, an NGO founded by activist-cum-politician Jayaprakash Narayan, proposed the introduction of tax-deductible political contributions, both for companies that were not government contractors and for individuals. That same year, the 170th report of the Law Commission of India recommended deleting Explanation 1 and imposing minimum standards of transparency and internal democracy in parties as conditions for state funding of parties. In 2002, the National Commission to Review the Working of the Constitution also recommended dropping Explanation 1. However, it did recommend providing state funding only after a comprehensive reform of political parties to ensure internal democracy and transparency, which would include requiring candidates to disclose their assets and liabilities. None of these proposals were implemented with the exception of free airtime on state-owned television and radio channels.

From 2003 to 2017: Greater but Limited Transparency

2003 marked the beginning of a series of significant, if still incomplete, steps forward in improving the transparency of political finance. The story of the first of these reforms dates back to November 2000, when the NGO Association for Democratic Reforms (ADR) filed a public interest petition demanding greater transparency on the backgrounds of aspirant candidates. The Delhi High Court responded by directing

---

[15] On state funding, the committee recommended a separate election fund pool to which the central and state governments would contribute together Rs 6,000 million annually (then $166 million) to enable partial state funding.

[16] The Gupta committee also left Explanation 1 standing and said nothing specific about company donations.

the ECI to collect and make public the criminal records, educational qualifications, and financial assets and liabilities of candidates (as well as their spouses and dependents). All parties resisted this move, but the judgment was reaffirmed, and the ECI issued an order making the above disclosures mandatory on 27 March 2003.

Arguably the most important legislative reform in campaign finance during this period was the Election and Other Related Laws (Amendment) Act passed in September 2003 by the BJP-led National Democratic Alliance (NDA) government. The law made corporate and individual donations to political parties 100 per cent tax-deductible under Sections 80 GGB and 80 GGC of the Income Tax Act respectively.[17] This created an incentive, for the first time, to contribute openly by cheque. The law also made it mandatory under Section 29C of the RPA for parties to list all donations received of Rs 20,000 and above to the ECI on an annual basis, with the names of the donors and amount received, thus introducing a limited degree of transparency.

The law also tried to close the loophole Explanation 1 opened up, by making it mandatory for candidates to report spending by parties and independent supporters towards their election, and stipulating that these expenditures would have to be counted for the purpose of the spending limit. However, the fine print undercut the larger stated objective. The law exempted the travel costs of the top leaders of recognized parties as well as party and independent supporters' spending on propagating the party's programme, as long as it does not favour any particular candidate. This last move, in particular, watered down the overall impact of the change.

The 2005 passage of the Right to Information Act (RTI), analogous to the Freedom of Information Act (FOIA) that operates in the United States, helped reshape the fight for greater transparency in India. Its impact on political funding, however, has been mixed. ADR used this new power to request that the Central Information Commission (CIC) make the income tax returns of political parties publicly available. Unsurprisingly, all parties resisted the demand, but in 2008 the

---

[17] Company contributions remained subject to the ceiling of five per cent of average net profit over the prior three years under Section 293A of the Companies Act.

CIC ruled in ADR's favour. This judgment forced political parties to publish their incomes and expenditures going back to 2004–5, thus providing a measure of transparency to party finances. This transparency is still incomplete, however, since the CIC did not insist on an independent or third-party audit, as recommended by the ECI.

The net effect of the candidate disclosure requirements introduced in 2003, the introduction of tax deductibility in the 2003 law, and the CIC's 2008 ruling under the RTI of 2005, is a modicum of transparency in party finance where there was virtually none before. However, these changes helped mainly on the margins. Parties still did not have to disclose the identities of donors if they were under the Rs 20,000 threshold. As it turns out, these anonymous donations constitute nearly 75 per cent of the income of six national parties.[18]

Despite the illusion of hyperactivity, the opaque political finance system, with roots in the 1969 decision to ban corporate donations without introducing an effective substitute, was still very much in place. Since 2013, there have been two noteworthy developments. First, in 2013, the Electoral Trusts Scheme allowed for the setting up of 100 per cent tax-exempt electoral trusts by companies, provided they disburse 95 per cent of their annual receipts (including surplus brought forward) to political parties. Also, under Section 182 of the Companies Act of 2013, the contribution limits for companies to parties was raised from 5 to 7.5 per cent of their average net profit over the prior three years.

The second notable development was the ECI's new transparency guidelines of August 2014, under which parties must identify all donors and amounts—with the exception of petty sums raised at rallies. However, these guidelines do not yet have the full force of law since, apart from the extraordinary step of derecognizing a party's symbol, the ECI has no power to fine or deregister a party that violates the new guidelines.[19]

[18] Only a relatively small fraction of national party donations comes from identified donors and in specified amounts, a pattern that also holds true for state parties.

[19] S.K. Mendiratta (legal adviser to the ECI), in conversation with one of the authors, 5 November 2014.

2017: A POSSIBLE INFLECTION POINT?

In 2017, Parliament legislated several changes to the country's political finance regime—the first time since 2003 that political finance appeared on the national policy agenda. This was likely a direct result of the public debate that ensued in the wake of the government's November 2016 decision to abruptly invalidate or 'demonetize' all high-value currency notes in circulation.

In the immediate aftermath of the dramatic demonetization announcement, many analysts pointed out that the manoeuvre alone was unlikely to have a sustained impact on India's black economy unless it was accompanied by complementary reforms in areas such as tax, administration, and regulation. For demonetization to have a lasting impact, overhauling the regulation of political finance is arguably one of the most critical areas for future reform. Indeed, the government came under criticism for stating, on the one hand, that demonetization would attack cronyism and corruption while, on the other hand, failing to articulate any new measures especially designed to address political corruption. The outcry was initially sparked by a statement made by the union revenue secretary (later reiterated by the finance secretary) that deposits of newly invalid currency notes into the bank accounts of political parties would not attract tax scrutiny. In narrow legal terms, this statement was innocuous; under Section 13A of the Income Tax Act, political parties have long been exempt from paying tax, provided that they adequately maintain their books.

But the outcry that followed forced ministry officials and subsequently even Union Finance Minister Arun Jaitley to address the issue, stating, 'The legal and taxation regime with regard to political parties remains absolutely what it has been in the last 15–20 years. There is not a single change that has been brought about nor is any change at the moment contemplated.'[20] The government's position was less than credible; arguing that one is constrained by decades-old law rang hollow when it had just implemented a draconian measure such as demonetization at a moment's notice.

---

[20] 'No Plan to Reprint Entire Demonetised Amount, Says Arun Jaitley', *Times of India*, 18 December 2016.

In an unusual New Year's Eve address to the nation, Prime Minister Modi noted that the public had spoken and the time had come for the country to consider how best to cleanse the financing of politics. 'Political parties, political leaders and electoral funding, figure prominently in any debate on corruption and black money. The time has now come that all political leaders and parties respect the feelings of the nation's honest citizens, and understand the anger of the people,' Modi said. While the prime minister stopped short of articulating a blueprint or roadmap for reform, he urged that all parties and leaders give up their 'holier than thou approach' to jointly discuss how to 'free politics of black money and corruption.'[21]

In principle, the government seemed to live up to its rhetoric and introduced several political finance reform measures in the 2017 Finance Bill. The core of the government's approach centred on three objectives—strengthening limits on cash giving, tightening income tax provisions, and introducing a new instrument known as 'electoral bonds'.[22] As with any new legislation, assessing their impact on political funding will depend on the quality of implementation and the details found in the fine print (which, in the case of electoral bonds, had yet to be issued at the time of writing). Nonetheless, we provide a preliminary analysis of the government's measures.[23]

Contributions

The first group of provisions strengthened limits on cash giving by changing the nature and limit of contributions to political parties. Under the status quo ante, no single anonymous contribution

[21] 'Full Text: PM Narendra Modi New Year's Eve Address to the Nation', *Indian Express*, 31 December 2016, accessed 6 June 2017, http://indianexpress.com/article/india/full-text-pm-narendra-modi-new-years-eve-address-to-the-nation-4453587/.

[22] Milan Vaishnav and Rebecca Brown, 'Crafty Indian Politicians Can Game the New Political Funding Rules Even in Their Sleep', *Quartz*, 1 February 2017, accessed 6 June 2017, https://qz.com/900922/budget-2017-why-arun-jaitleys-new-rules-to-clean-up-indias-political-funding-simply-wont-work/.

[23] For more, see Milan Vaishnav, 'Finance Bill Makes Funding for Political Parties More Opaque Than Ever', *Hindustan Times*, 29 March 2017.

to political parties could exceed Rs 20,000. Any donation over this threshold required the individual or entity making the donation to disclose their identity. The changes enacted in the bill modified this in several ways. For starters, the act instituted a new Rs 2,000 threshold for cash donations. Going forward, any donation above Rs 2,000 must be transferred via check or digital payment (interestingly, however, the act did not alter the Rs 20,000 limit for public disclosure). In addition, the act tied the new cash threshold to an individual rather than to any single contribution. This is an important detail because donors in the past regularly split their large contribution into many smaller donations (each below Rs 20,000) to avoid disclosure. This, of course, also allowed parties to obscure the identity of the vast majority of their donors.[24]

Under these new provisions in the Finance Act, anyone who donates more than Rs 2,000 *in aggregate* will have to disclose their identity. The final adjustment requires that corporations make all contributions via check or digital payment, rather than cash. Shortly before the bill was to come up for a vote on the floor of the Lok Sabha, the government attached two further amendments to the Finance Bill with little advance notice. The first eliminated the cap on corporate giving (which previously stood at 7.5 per cent of a corporation's average net profits over the previous three years) while the second dropped the requirement that firms must declare their political contributions on their profit and loss statements.

The government's proposals to limit cash in politics are notable and consistent with demonetization and the general move to curb the use of cash in the economy. Cash transactions, as many of the contributions in this book demonstrate, are rampant in electoral politics, difficult to observe and, therefore, hard to trace. Unfortunately, the government's measures do not provide adequate disincentives when it comes to cash. For instance, the government could have abolished cash contributions altogether, as opposed to simply placing a ceiling on cash donations at Rs 2,000. Whenever an arbitrary limit is imposed (whether it is 20,000 or 2,000), there is an incentive for those who want to game the system

---

[24] Interestingly, if donors choose the alternative route of electoral bonds that has been introduced (see section below), then disclosure of identities can be completely avoided.

to report amounts just below the threshold. While it is technically illegal for any one individual to donate more than Rs 2,000 without disclosure, it is not clear what will stop parties from claiming they have received multiple small donations from anonymous individuals since they do not have to keep records of those who give less than the limit in any case.[25]

Perhaps the most surprising omission was to require the simplest and most obvious form of identification be linked to any cash donation of any size: the contributor's *Aadhaar* number. For a government so committed on leveraging Aadhaar in an ever-increasing number of government programmes, this was clearly deliberate. And for many in civil society who have pressed for greater transparency in electoral finance, their opposition to Aadhaar meant they could not press for it in this case.

Tax Scrutiny

Beyond altering the fine print around donations, the legislation also aimed to tighten provisions of the Income Tax (IT) Act as they relate to political parties. While political parties in India are tax-exempt, under prevailing law, political parties are required to keep updated financial accounts, maintain records of the names and addresses attached to large contributions, submit their accounts for audit, and file their income tax returns on an annual basis (in exchange for receiving tax-exempt status).[26] The Finance Act stipulated that

---

[25] As one politician remarked to one of the authors, the biggest winner of this reform will be chartered accountants, who will be able to demand bigger pay cheques in return for their expanded financial jugglery. Indeed, as one journalist noted, 'Earlier, if a person had to give Rs 1 lakh in cash, they would make five receipts by breaking it up and keeping it under Rs 20,000. Now, they would have to make 50 receipts. It's a logistical nightmare but it still doesn't prevent the party from accepting cash donations.' Meghnad S., 'Why Jaitley's Political Funding Reforms Won't End Anonymous Donations', *The Wire*, 6 February 2017, accessed 6 June 2017, https://thewire.in/106262/jaitley-political-funding-reforms-budget-anonymous-donations/.

[26] In January 2017, the Supreme Court reconfirmed that the exception made to keep parties out of the tax net was one of executive determination, claiming that parties needed money to propagate their beliefs.

these tax returns should be submitted within the time prescribed. Previously, many parties did not submit their tax returns on an annual basis, while others failed to do so at all. This new provision ostensibly sought to close this loophole.

The lack of independent audit scrutiny and meaningful enforcement makes the new provision much better in theory than in practice. ADR has warned in the past that 'there is a lack of frequent and complete scrutiny of financial disclosures of political parties' by tax authorities.[27] If tax officials do not scrutinize party accounts, it will make little difference if the documents are submitted on time or with substantial delay. Equally, there is no categorical schedule of penalties if parties fail to file their accounts 'within the time prescribed'. Indeed, under the Companies Act, all private companies in India must file tax returns within 60 days of their last annual general meeting, and there is a clear escalating schedule of financial and penal penalties the longer the delay in filing returns.[28] Clearly, the ramifications for the public if a political party fails to file returns in time are substantially greater than if a private firm fails to do so. Yet the bite of the law is much stronger on the latter compared to the former.

Electoral Bonds

The third and final innovation in the Finance Act is the introduction of a new instrument, the 'electoral bond.' At the time of writing, the government has not fully elaborated the details of how this bond would operate, but a few basic principles seem clear based on government

---

[27] 'Additional Views of ADR/NEW on Political Finance and the 255th Report of the Law Commission of India', Association for Democratic Reforms and National Election Watch, April 2015, accessed 6 June 2017, http://adrindia.org/sites/default/files/Additional_views_ADR-NEW_political_finance_255th_Law_commission_ECI.pdf.

[28] Under Section 92 (5) of the Companies Act, 2013, if a company fails to file its annual return, 'the company shall be punishable with fine which shall not be less than fifty thousand rupees but which may extend to five lakh rupees *and every officer of the company who is in default shall be punishable with imprisonment for a term which may extend to six months* or with fine which shall not be less than fifty thousand rupees but which may extend to five lakh rupees, or with both.' (emphasis added)

documents and statements made by various finance ministry officials. Electoral bonds are time-limited bearer bonds that corporations can purchase from scheduled banks and subsequently transfer to a registered bank account of a political party. The fund flow would proceed entirely through the formal banking system, allowing for a step-by-step paper trail. However, the identity of the corporation purchasing the bond would not be publicly revealed (although, since the transaction is taking place via the banking system, regulators presumably would have access to this information). When the corporation deposits these bonds into a specially designated bank account of a registered party, the party would know who the donor is, but neither the party nor the corporation is required to disclose this information.

The upside to the new scheme is that corporations will now have a legitimate channel through which they can contribute funds to parties, as opposed to indulging in under-the-table transactions, while protecting their anonymity (which they greatly prize). But the upside is also the downside: transparency, as far as the public is concerned, is arguably the biggest victim; this is ironic considering the government explicitly framed the proposal under the heading of improving 'transparency in political funding'. Taking into account the elimination of the cap on corporate giving, the dropping of the requirement that firms disclose political giving on their financial statements, and the introduction of electoral bonds, 'corporations can now legally give unlimited sums to political parties who, in turn, can accept unlimited sums of money—all without having to disclose a single rupee'.[29] Advocates of the new changes rightly point out that there will be a digital paper trail (as there is with all banking transactions), but this trail will not be on public display, which means that electoral bonds will not change the opaque status quo for the better in the foreseeable future.[30]

---

[29] Vaishnav, 'Finance Bill Makes Funding for Political Parties More Opaque than Ever'.

[30] To be clear, corporations have good reason for wanting to donate anonymously: given the discretionary authorities that are vested with the state, any firm that publicly donates funds to one political party fears retribution if a competing party comes to power.

Net Assessment

The net effect of the recent changes in the rules could be an increased flow of funds to political parties by digital or cheque payments but absent disclosure of donor identities. Indeed, as the finance minister himself has said, part of the government's objective was to protect donor anonymity; the banks will know who bought electoral bonds but not to which party they were given. The question of who gave how much to which party will not be in public view. This is a far cry from transparency and disclosure of donor identities and amounts—standard in most developed democracies—but will boost (opaque) fund flow to parties over the next two years, something about which both parties and donors feel comfortable. We can expect an arms race in fundraising over the next two years before the 2019 election with the ruling party having an edge.

In the absence of public funding and/or increased tax deductibility, there is little incentive for donors to become more transparent. In fact, in a highly regulated political economy, there is no incentive to donate transparently to parties simply to support democracy without a *quid pro quo*. In a poor country with a regulated economy, there is a problem of donor self-interest that militates against the achievement of full transparency unless some system of adequate public funding is put in place. However, this system requires internal democracy and accountability in parties, something that most parties are loath to consider.

As of mid-2017, the push for further transparency of political parties and their finances remains stalled.[31] In June 2013, the CIC ruled that India's six national political parties (Congress, BJP, Communist Party of India [Marxist] [CPI(M)], Communist Party of India [CPI], Nationalist Congress Party [NCP], and Bahujan Samaj Party [BSP]) were 'public entities' that should be subject to disclosures under the RTI Act, and repeated this in March 2015. However, these parties have consistently failed to comply and the CIC, lacking any coercive or punitive powers, has thrown up its hands. In May 2015, the Supreme Court, in reaction to the non-compliance of political parties to the repeated orders of the CIC to make disclosures under RTI, asked the six national parties

---

[31] For the information in this paragraph, see Krishnadas Rajagopal, 'Can't Bring Political Parties Under RTI, Centre Tells Supreme Court', *Hindu*, 24 August 2015.

and the central government to respond as to why they could not be more transparent. The central government, for its part, stated that the CIC had erroneously concluded that parties are public authorities. To the contrary, it argued that parties are not established under the Constitution or any law made by parliament, and that there is already transparency of their finances under the reporting requirements of the 1951 Income Tax Act and the RPA.

★ ★ ★

Political finance reform is ultimately a collective action problem among political parties and between parties and donors that requires the right alignment of incentives. And there are some positive examples of such collective action in the past. The Model Code of Conduct, a mutually agreed upon code among parties, that governs election campaigns is an example. What are the incentives to break out of a corrupt and opaque equilibrium that is the long-run path-dependent outcome of banning company donations without substituting them with state funding?

Any viable reform of political finance not only has to be in the public interest, but it must also serve the interests of existing political parties. Until 1989, when the one-party dominant era came to an end, the conditions for collective action did not exist because the Congress party had no incentive to constrain its superior fundraising potential. The changes to the party system that began in 1989 and led to the emergence of a multi-party system have arguably created some of the enabling conditions for collective action on political finance reform, including full transparency and possibly state funding too. We do not discuss possible reforms here as they are discussed in detail in the concluding chapter by Kapur, Sridharan, and Vaishnav. However, we note that whether the solution is full transparency of donations and donor identities, or this combined with state funding of parties for elections or for general purposes, the key is some form of regulation of parties that requires internal democracy, transparency, and accountability; indeed, adoption of these principles should be made mandatory before any system of state funding is instituted. However, any such regulation of parties should also bear in mind that while they are performing public functions and overlap with the state when in power, they are ultimately private organizations representing citizen interests, and this character should not be destroyed by regulation.

From a broad comparative perspective, many aspects of India's political finance architecture are broadly shared. 40 per cent of countries (for which there is data) have limits on candidate spending.[32] 70 per cent of countries (including India) do not have any ceiling on spending by political parties. Likewise, another 40 per cent of countries have some form of limit on donations (although in 2017, India eliminated limits on corporate giving). Two-thirds of countries have direct public funding for parties and/or candidates. India and a collection of fragile democracies, including some Middle Eastern, African, and post-Soviet states, do not.

Taken as a whole, India's political finance system is heavily regulated on paper. In practice, however, loopholes and lax enforcement create a de facto laissez faire regime—especially when compared with developed democracies. India lacks any effective ceiling on party spending, effective limits on donations, public funding (except for limited time on state-owned electronic media), and a practical system of reporting and disclosure. Clearly, despite steps in the direction of transparency and curbing the deployment of cash in politics, India has a very long way to go.

---

[32] See Austin and Tjernstrom, *Funding of Political Parties*, for the data cited in this paragraph.

2 Money in Elections

The Role of Personal Wealth in Election Outcomes

Neelanjan Sircar

Even during the electoral campaign, it was apparent that the Congress party would not be able to hang on to power. In the 2015 Assam state election, after 15 years of Congress Party rule, strong anti-incumbency had set in and an ascendant Bharatiya Janata Party looked ready to take the reins. We were chatting in a small *kirana* shop (grocery and retail stall) in a remote village in the constituency of a minister in the incumbent Congress government. The kirana shop owners—Congress supporters themselves—admitted their party was in trouble, but they were certain the minister would win from here again. We interpreted their confidence as some sort of partisan bravado. Polling would take place the next day, and a few trucks and jeeps approached with young Congress party supporters waving party flags. But this was no ordinary campaign procession. As far as the eye could see, along the road cutting through miles of flat paddy fields, there was a line of trucks, jeeps, and cars waving flags. The kirana shop owners just smirked at us. We were stuck.

Forty-five minutes and hundreds of vehicles later, the procession mercifully passed, and we were finally able to leave the village. The vehicles had been rented, the supporters had been paid, and the party paraphernalia had been bought. The cost of this one procession alone was several times beyond the spending limit imposed on candidates for state elections; such was the comical disregard for the official spending rules. Needless to say, while the Congress was routed in the election, the minister held on to his seat. Candidate wealth matters to some degree in most electoral contexts, but such brazen displays of wealth in campaigning are rare in most democracies. However, this type of aggressive and visible use of personal wealth seems increasingly common in Indian elections. Is there something about the Indian electoral system that encourages such open use of personal wealth in campaigning?

This chapter investigates the role of personal wealth and self-financing candidates in Indian elections, namely why a candidate's financial capacity is an important feature of Indian electoral politics and how it structures the incentives of political parties.[1] One can analyse the role of money in elections from either a demand- or supply-side perspective. Demand-side analyses focus on how voters respond to various uses of money, whereas supply-side analyses focus on the sources of money in elections, as well as how these sources structure electoral competition. From a demand-side perspective, pure financial capacity matters for developing a good electoral organization and paying for campaign expenses. Apart from the usual costs of travel and advertising, financial capacity increases the ability of the candidate to pay for large events like rallies or feasts. Money can also be used to hire good 'polling agents' who mobilize voters at the level of the polling booth, and it might well be used for illicit purposes, like vote buying. But the role of money in attracting voters is a fairly widespread phenomenon, especially in the developing world, and has been studied extensively.[2]

On the other hand, Indian elections are unique from a supply-side perspective, especially in the extent to which candidates are expected

---

[1] In the 2014 national election, the spending limit was 70 lakh rupees (Rs 7,000,000), but candidates reported spending only 58 per cent of the limit. Even if, as it seems, candidates are lying about their expenditures, these limits do not appear to be particularly binding on financial expenditure. As such, it makes sense to think explicitly about the financial capacity of candidates.

[2] For an overview of the literature, see Susan C. Stokes, Thad Dunning, Marcelo Nazareno, and Valeria Brusco, *Brokers, Voters, and Clientelism: The Puzzle of Distributive Politics* (New York: Cambridge University Press, 2013). For a comprehensive volume on South Asia, see Anastasia Piliavsky, ed., *Patronage as Politics in South Asia* (Cambridge: Cambridge University Press, 2014).

to pay for campaigning costs themselves. Because the selection of candidates is essentially at the whim of a few elites in each party, there are disincentives for outside donations to any particular potential candidate. Furthermore, because individual legislators have a limited impact on policymaking in the Indian context, there is little benefit for special interests to devote resources to lobbying them. With few outside sources of funding, candidates must use personal wealth to self-finance increasingly expensive electoral campaigns. This study develops a theoretical framework to characterize the institutional and structural causes of self-financing candidates. This is an important topic of study because self-financing candidates may see running for office as an economic investment, and, thus, seek to recoup costs incurred during the campaign through corruption while in office. On the other hand, if the personal wealth of candidates does not have much impact on actual electoral outcomes, the study of money in Indian elections would be relegated to mere academic curiosity.

This chapter provides a systematic analysis of data on the personal assets of candidates for national legislature (Lok Sabha) over three elections between 2004 and 2014, and demonstrates that a candidate's personal wealth is strongly associated with his or her electoral fortunes. National elections provide a particularly good empirical basis for this study because they provide three waves of simultaneous elections across the highly differentiated and complex political terrain of India, unlike state elections which are non-simultaneous and thus confounded by the timing of election.

To preview the empirical results, this chapter demonstrates that a candidate's personal wealth, measured in terms of moveable assets, has a significant positive impact on the candidate's electoral fortunes. First, the chapter demonstrates that competitive parties (that is, those parties that can conceivably win in a constituency) select candidates that are approximately 20 times wealthier than other candidates. Thus, the wealthiest candidates—those with the greatest capacity to self-finance a campaign—are systematically selected by competitive parties. But even among these wealthy candidates from competitive parties, the wealthiest candidate has a greater probability of winning the constituency. In the median constituency in terms of wealth differential between the top two candidates, the wealthier candidate is about 3.8 times wealthier than his or her competitor. In such a scenario, the wealthier candidate is 10 percentage points more likely to win the constituency than his or her competitor, underscoring why wealthy candidates are so attractive to political parties. The empirical results strongly support the view that there are structural and institutional reasons for the outward display of wealth in Indian electoral campaigns.

WHY DOES SELF-FINANCING MATTER SO MUCH IN INDIA?

The personal wealth of candidates has received limited attention in the study of elections around the world. This is because personal financial capacity of candidates is less consequential in most electoral democracies.[3] Unlike in India, the financing of elections is heavily regulated by the state in the vast majority of democracies. In a study of 52 democracies, van Biezen and Kopecký report that only India, Switzerland, Latvia, Jamaica, Botswana, Mauritius, and Senegal neither provide state funding for parties nor explicitly regulate party finances.[4] Furthermore, outside sources of funding for candidates, such as corporations or other outside financiers, are more pronounced in most electoral contexts.[5] In fact, Jennifer Steen finds that spending personal money in elections is actually associated with a *lower* probability of winning in the election in the United States.[6] The logic of this result follows from the fact that the most electorally successful candidates are better at raising funds from outside sources, rather than spending their own money. In the United States, the marginal electoral impact of this outside money is significantly greater than the marginal impact of personal wealth because outside money financially bonds the candidate to a larger electoral coalition.

[3] A notable exception is the study of candidate position in party lists for European elections in Romania. See Sergiu Ghergina and Mihail Chiru, 'Practice and Payment: Determinants of Candidate List Position in European Parliament Elections', *European Union Politics* 11, no. 4 (2010): 533–52.

[4] Ingrid van Biezen and Petr Kopecký, 'The State and the Parties: Public Funding, Public Regulation and Rent-Seeking in Contemporary Democracies', *Party Politics* 13, no. 2 (2010): 235–54.

[5] Van Biezen and Kopecký, 'The State and the Parties', 235–54.

[6] Jennifer Steen, *Self-Financed Candidates in Congressional Elections* (Ann Arbor: Michigan University Press, 2006).

Yet, as explained in some detail in this chapter, there is reason to believe that the scale of funds raised explicitly for a particular candidate's campaign from outside sources is likely to be low in India.[7] With little adherence to spending limits imposed by the state, self-financing candidates emerge as potentially critical to successful political parties for two reasons: (a) they fill party coffers—money paid by candidates is often used to finance otherwise cash-strapped parties; and (b) money wins on the campaign trail—campaigns are expensive, and with little assistance from larger party funds or outside sources, candidates must use their own money to run a good campaign. There are reasons to be concerned by an increasing trend of dependence on self-financing candidates. First, if candidates must be personally wealthy in order to have some chance of winning an election, only a small percentage of the population can reasonably hold office, leading to a highly non-representative population of legislators. Second, if parties systematically select candidates primarily based on wealth, as opposed to other factors such as education or previous constituency service, then the population of legislators will be of lower quality in terms of constituency representation. Finally, and most importantly, if campaigns must be self-financed, then candidates may reasonably view contesting elections as an economic investment, leading to greater levels of corruption in office as legislators try to recoup the costs of contesting elections.

At the outset, it is important to note that parties in India display very little 'intra-party democracy'.[8] In other words, across parties in India, most candidates are selected by a small group of elite party functionaries rather than a process that explicitly incorporates the views of general party members or the population at large. While the method of candidate selection has been a major topic of study in European electoral politics,[9] little academic attention has been given to the

[7] This is corroborated by the numbers reported in Jennifer Bussell's chapter in this volume.

[8] E. Sridharan, 'Party System Fragmentation, Intra-party Democracy, and Opaque Political Finance', Center for the Advanced Study of India 'India in Transition' newsletter, 5 April 2009.

[9] Michael Gallagher and Michael Marsh, eds., *Candidate Selection in Comparative Perspective: The Secret Garden of Politics* (London: Sage 1988); Krister Lundell, 'The Determinants of Candidate Selection: The Degree of Centralization in Comparative Perspective', *Party Politics* 10, no. 1 (1988): 25–47.

subject in the Indian context.[10] Yet, the process of candidate selection in India has certainly garnered popular interest. In the run-up to any major election, Indian newspapers are rife with speculation about who will be given party tickets, the factions within parties, and the battles between potential candidates. Disaffected aspirants, who have been denied a ticket from their first party of choice, often quickly switch allegiances to another party or simply decide to contest the election as independent candidates. But most of these dynamics take place behind closed doors, and the public finally gets to know who will contest from which party and which constituency shortly before the election, often no more than a month before the election date.

Low levels of intra-party democracy and the costs of running an electoral campaign structure the incentives of potential outside campaign financiers, candidates, and political parties in important ways. Successful candidates for elective office are likely to be rewarded, both in social status and in monetary terms.[11] Thus, while electoral campaigns may be expensive, candidates may reasonably see fighting elections as an economic investment in the future; in this sense, contesting an election represents an entrepreneurial decision. At the same time, the highly centralized fashion in which most parties select candidates make outside support of candidates *a priori* a risky proposition, as there is little certainty as to which candidate will be given a party ticket and the constituency from which the candidate will contest the election. As such, it is likely that candidates will have to disproportionately rely on personal funds in financing their electoral campaign. Parties are likely to prefer candidates with significant personal wealth as well. If the costs of running a campaign are prohibitive, then the personal wealth of a candidate should also be associated with the winnability of a candidate. Simply put, political parties want to win elections, and selecting personally wealthy candidates may give them the best chance to do so, given the cost of campaigns.

[10] A notable exception is Ruchika Singh, 'Intra-party Democracy and Indian Political Parties' (Policy report no. 7, The Hindu Centre, 2015).

[11] Rikhil Bhavnani, 'Using Asset Disclosures to Study Politicians Rents: An Application to India' (working paper, University of Wisconsin-Madison, 2012); Raymond Fisman, Florian Schulz, and Vikrant Vig, 'Private Returns to Public Office', *Journal of Political Economy* 122, no. 4 (August 2014): 806–62.

A particular focus of this chapter is the behaviour of 'competitive parties,' that is, those parties that legitimately have some chance of winning the election in the constituency, and how they select candidates. This theoretically helps abstract away from the multiplicity of reasons a candidate might run for office towards the set of calculations and incentives in selecting candidates that are important for electoral outcomes. Candidates associated with competitive parties should be more focused on winning the election, and will tend to run the most expensive campaigns since they are directly contesting other candidates who may plausibly win in the constituency. The discussion below leads to a set of empirical hypotheses which are tested in subsequent sections of this chapter.

DISINCENTIVES FOR OUTSIDE FUNDING OF CANDIDATES

One can conceive of the returns to investing in a candidate along two dimensions. First, one is likely to invest in a candidate early on if funding will increase the candidate's chances of obtaining a party ticket, as in primary election systems. Thus, the method of candidate selection is likely to impact the willingness to donate to a candidate. Second, a donor will invest in a candidate if changing the candidate's opinion on an issue is likely to affect policy or distributional outcomes. Thus, the extent to which policy or distributional decisions are made in a centralized fashion within a party should impact the willingness to donate to a candidate.

In addition, a donor is more likely to fund a potential candidate if he or she believes that it will lead to benefits at the local level. For example, a building contractor may donate to a potential candidate if he or she believes it will lead to preferential local land access. But, as discussed earlier, the decisions about who will receive a party ticket and the constituency from which the candidate will contest are highly centralized decisions within the party. It, thus, makes little sense to donate to a potential candidate before party tickets have been announced, as there is a real chance that the donation will be wasted. This reality affects the willingness to donate to the candidate in two ways.

First, it limits the number of individuals likely to receive funds, and second, it reduces the amount of time available for a candidate to procure outside funds. After party tickets are announced, a donor is more likely to fund a candidate if he or she believes that the candidate has a genuine ability to impact policy or distributional outcomes in the constituency. But the candidates are hampered from doing so for at least two reasons. First, at the national level (the level at which data are analysed in this chapter), the 52nd Amendment to the Indian Constitution prohibits party members from 'defecting' against their own party by voting against the wishes of the party in the legislature. Failure to abide by this 'anti-defection' law entails expulsion from the party and legislature. This highly centralizes policymaking among the elites in a ruling party/coalition, with little ability for individual legislators to impact policy.

Second, incumbents gain no electoral advantage in future elections. In fact, for a long time, Indian elections exhibited a strong pattern of anti-incumbency,[12] although the pattern seems more mixed now. This implies that few legislators are able to acquire the reputation required to join the party elite with policy decision-making power. Taken together, there is little incentive for potential donors to donate to specific candidates, as opposed to party elites or the party at large. It should be noted, however, that legislators may still possess the power to award contracts in their own constituencies and may draw money from outright corruption instead of lobbying.

Because the institutional structure of the Indian electoral system provides disincentives for outside funding of individual candidates, it is likely that a significant portion of the campaign for individual candidates is self-financed, and thus only candidates with sufficient capacity to fund the campaign (through personal wealth) will run for elective office. Furthermore, campaigns are likely to be the most expensive for competitive parties, as these parties most aggressively compete for visibility. Accordingly, an empirical implication of this theory is that candidates from competitive parties should have greater capacity for self-financing, and thus greater personal wealth, than

[12] Leigh Linden, 'Are Incumbents Really Advantaged? The Preference for Non-Incumbents in India', (working paper, University of Texas–Austin, 2004); Yogesh Uppal, 'The Disadvantaged Incumbents: Estimating Incumbency Effects in Indian State Legislatures', *Public Choice* 138, no. 1 (2009): 9–27.

those candidates from non-competitive parties. The hypothesis is stated formally as follows.

Hypothesis 1: Competitiveness and Self-Financing. If incentives for outside financing are weak, then candidates contesting with competitive parties should have greater personal wealth than candidates for non-competitive parties due to a need for self-financing.

Party Incentives for Fielding Self-financing Candidates

Another implication of low intra-party democracy in Indian political parties is that the selection of candidates on the basis of their personal wealth likely follows from the core interests of the party elite. That is, if parties are systematically selecting wealthier candidates, then one must grapple with how candidate wealth serves the incentives of the party, given the centralized decision-making in the selection procedure. In perhaps the most systematic analysis thus far about the role of money in politics (especially in the context of criminality), Milan Vaishnav argues that the increasing costs of election campaigns has pushed parties towards self-financing candidates for two reasons. First, the actual cost of running a campaign implies that unless the candidate bears a significant portion of the cost, the party/candidate will have a difficult time winning the constituency. Second, with finite party coffers in an increasingly expensive electoral world, wealthy candidates are required to supply funds to the party.[13]

If candidates must bear a substantial portion of the campaigning cost, and the scale of the electoral campaign increases the chances of winning, then there should be a direct relationship between the personal wealth of the candidate and the 'winnability' of the candidate. This is especially the case when the candidate cannot turn to outside sources of funding, as discussed above. Winning is the lifeblood of political parties; without regularly winning elections, parties cannot survive. A major source of party funding is corruption in service delivery, something that can only be actualized when the party is in

---

[13] Milan Vaishnav, *When Crime Pays: Money and Muscle in Indian Politics* (New Haven: Yale University Press, 2017).

power.[14] Furthermore, it is likely that the economic benefits of corruption and rents while in office dwarf other sources of party financing.

In this scenario, the desire for parties to select the most winnable candidates implies that they will select candidates with great personal wealth. Unfortunately, a simple association between candidate wealth and the likelihood of winning a constituency is confounded by the fact that competitive parties are more likely to pick wealthier candidates simply because they have more expensive campaigns, as discussed above. If the relationship between personal wealth of a candidate and winnability is empirically accurate, the acid test is how candidate wealth impacts electoral outcomes between candidates that have some chance of winning the constituency. That is, even among competitive parties, the wealthiest candidate should have an advantage in winning elections at the constituency level. This leads to the following hypothesis.

Hypotheses 2: Self-Financing and Winnability. If parties care primarily about winning elections, and a capacity for self-financing makes a candidate more winnable, then among competitive parties, the wealthiest candidate should have the greatest chance of winning the constituency.

Self-financing candidates may also be useful for party finances as they can pay into increasingly strained party coffers. But this implies that parties face a tradeoff between demanding that candidates contribute to party coffers and letting the candidate spend on the campaign, which would increase winnability. Would parties really require a candidate to pay more to the party at the price of winnability? That seems unlikely. A more sophisticated version of the party financing thesis holds that the party selects candidates willing to pay a significant amount into party coffers in 'safe seats'. That is, the party places wealthy candidates in constituencies it is almost certain to win, and requires the candidates

[14] Robert Wade, 'The Market for Public Office: Why the Indian State is Not Better at Development', *World Development* 13, no. 4 (1985): 467–97; Jennifer Davis, 'Corruption in Public Service Delivery: Experience from South Asia's Water and Sanitation Sector', *World Development* 32, no. 1 (2004): 53–71; Jennifer Bussell, 'Why Get Technical? Corruption and the Politics of Public Service Reform in the Indian States', *Comparative Political Studies* 43, no. 10 (2010): 1230–57.

to pay a portion of their wealth to the party in lieu of spending on the campaign. In such a setting, parties can demand more from a candidate for their own party funds, both because the seat is nearly a sure thing and because campaign costs should be lower if the seat is not competitive. At the same time, because the candidate is nearly certain to win, aspirants are willing to pay more for these constituencies because this deal constitutes a safe bet. In short, the sophisticated version of the party financing thesis holds that the party effectively sells its safest seats to the highest bidder, drawing the wealthiest candidates who see the transaction as a low-risk investment.[15] As such, the wealthiest candidates in the party are placed in the seats that the party is most likely to win. This leads to the following hypothesis.

Hypothesis 3: Self-Financing and Party Financing. If the party relies on wealthy candidates as a significant source of funding, the wealthiest candidates in a party should be placed in constituencies in which the party's candidate has the highest chance of winning the election.

The second and third hypotheses may seem similar, but there is a key difference. The second hypothesis refers to a candidate's wealth in comparison to his or her competitor in the same constituency. The third hypothesis refers to the relative wealth of a candidate across all candidates contesting from the same party. These differences in how variables are operationalized to test the hypotheses, in addition to empirical challenges in estimation and causal attribution in assessing these hypotheses, are discussed later in the chapter.

DATA

In 2003, the Supreme Court of India mandated that any candidate for elective office at the state or national level must disclose certain pieces of information of public interest, such as pending criminal

---

[15] An alternate, but less likely, theory is that first-time wealthy candidates are asked to contest in harder-to-win seats in order to prove their allegiance to a party. This 'escalatory' model would suggest that candidates provide funds to parties as a down payment for future party tickets. As I show later, there is little evidence for any relationship between candidate wealth (vis-à-vis candidates in the rest of the party) and electoral outcomes that would suggest such a relationship.

cases, educational qualifications, and a detailed accounting of assets and liabilities. In practice, these public disclosures or 'affidavits', which are declared by the candidates themselves, are collected by the office of the chief electoral officer (CEO) within each state and made public over the Internet as a PDF document by the Election Commission of India (ECI). As such, the documents are not fully standardized across India in format or language. The civil society organization, Association for Democratic Reforms (ADR), which was involved in the court case described earlier, has undertaken the difficult task of parsing the original affidavits and putting the information contained therein into a comprehensible digital format on a single website, myneta.info. The data used in this chapter has been scraped from this website and provided to the author by one of the editors of this volume, Milan Vaishnav.

While one may reasonably be suspicious of data reported by candidates themselves, the results in this chapter will demonstrate that this self-reported data yields meaningful variation in characterizing personal assets and winning elections. It is important to note that there is some disincentive to lie because providing false information on affidavits is justiciable. Furthermore, there is weak evidence on the impact of the public dissemination of information contained in affidavits on electoral outcomes,[16] suggesting that it is not particularly costly to the candidate to reveal the truth in his or her affidavit. Nonetheless, one might expect that candidates either systematically underreport their wealth to avoid raising alarm or over-report their wealth to scare off competitors. However, if the numbers were dominated by faulty reporting that masked meaningful variation in the data, then one would expect to find self-reported asset data to largely be 'statistical noise' that is uncorrelated to electoral phenomena. Yet, as shown in detail here, the data exhibit an intuitive association between the self-reported asset data and election outcomes.

The analysis in this chapter focuses on the self-reported data on the combined personal assets of the candidate and his or her spouse. While it should be noted that personal wealth may be correlated to any number of factors that cannot be gleaned from the affidavit, such

---

[16] Rohini Pande, 'Can Informed Voters Enforce Better Governance? Experiments in Low-Income Democracies', *Annual Review of Economics* 3 (2011): 215–37.

as social status or fame, the wealth of the candidate is most directly
tied to his or her personal capacity to self-finance the electoral campaign. We do not have rigorous, standardized data across India on
campaign spending, especially because so much of the money used
during elections is from undocumented sources (as discussed elsewhere in the volume). For this reason, we must use the capacity for
self-financing as measured through personal wealth as a proxy for
actual self-financing.

Information on Assets

Each affidavit attested by a candidate provides a detailed breakdown
of the personal assets of the candidate and his or her spouse. Assets are
bifurcated into two large categories: immoveable and moveable assets.
Immoveable assets largely consist of land, property, and real estate.
In the affidavit, the current market value of immoveable assets is calculated as the sum of the current market value of assets owned in each
of the following categories: (a) agricultural land; (b) non-agricultural
land; (c) commercial buildings; (d) residential buildings; and (e) other
(usually partial interest from other properties). Moveable assets are
those assets that can be characterized as liquid resources (broadly
construed) available to the candidate. In the affidavit, the current
market value of moveable assets is calculated as the sum of the current
market value of assets owned in each of the following categories:
(a) cash; (b) deposits in banks and institutions; (c) securities; (d) pension
saving schemes; (e) life insurance schemes;[17] (f) loan advances;[18]
(g) motor vehicles; (h) jewellery; and (i) other (value of other claims
and interests). This chapter focuses on measures of total wealth and
moveable assets. Moveable assets are of particular interest because they
are more 'liquid' and can thus be quickly mobilized in the context of
an electoral campaign.

Affidavit data are available for the parliamentary elections of 2004,
2009, and 2014. Over these three elections, affidavits are available

---

[17] These data were also collected in 2004 and 2009 but were not added to
the value of moveable assets.

[18] The data on loan advances were not collected and were not a component of moveable assets in 2004 and 2009.

for 21,697 candidates. However, as with any such dataset with self-reported data, the quality of the data are uneven. Some data are not readable, and it is also worth noting that some errors in the data may emerge due to difficulties associated with web scraping. With these caveats in place, candidates had to report aggregate moveable assets/wealth of at least Rs 1,000 to be included in the analysis in this chapter (anything below this value would seem implausibly low).[19] These deletions from the data set removed 2,844 candidates for a new total of 18,853 observations across the three elections (4,336 in 2004; 6,510 in 2009; and 8,007 in 2014).[20] As with much financial data, measures of wealth are significantly right-skewed and are better viewed on a logarithmic scale, but this can be difficult to interpret for the lay reader. Thus, most of the descriptive data will be presented in terms of medians and not means of the wealth distribution.

Figure 2.1 describes the patterns of median candidate wealth for the entire sample over the national election from 2004 to 2014. There is a noticeable increase in the scale of funds, both in terms of moveable wealth and total wealth, over this entire period. Between 2004 and 2014, the median total wealth of candidates grew by approximately 330 per cent in nominal terms. If one adjusts for inflation, the median wealth rose 116 per cent in real terms. The median reported wealth of candidates in the 2014 national election of Rs 23.8 lakhs was approximately 27 times the nominal per capita income of India in 2014–15 of Rs 88,533, suggesting that candidates for elective office are significantly wealthier than the population at large. It should be noted, however, that 'stock' variables like wealth (of candidates) and 'flow' variables like income are not directly comparable—the comparison is merely illustrative. By the 2014 national election, moveable wealth constituted nearly a quarter of total wealth, demonstrating that the vast majority of candidate wealth still resides in real estate, agriculture, and other forms of immoveable wealth.

[19] Several plausible cutoffs were tried in this analysis and the results are not particularly sensitive to them.

[20] In 2004 and 2009, approximately 80 per cent of candidates are in the data set, whereas around 91 per cent of candidates are in the dataset in 2014.

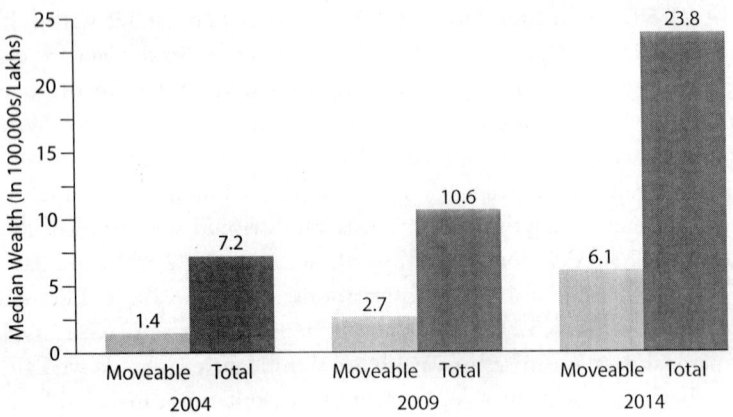

FIGURE 2.1   Median Moveable and Total Candidate Wealth 2004–14 (in Rs)
Source: Author's analyisis.

A Close Look at Asset Composition in 2014

A closer look at the 2014 election asset data provides a deeper under-standing of the composition of candidate assets. Figure 2.2 uses kernel density estimation to plot the distribution of moveable and total can-didate wealth in 2014 (note that the horizontal axis is on a logarithmic scale with 1 lakh = 100,000 and 1 crore = 10,000,000). Even on a logarithmic scale, moveable asset wealth is somewhat right-skewed, suggesting that a small subset of candidates have access to dispropor-tionately large liquidity. Moveable assets are of particular interest in this chapter, as these are the sorts of assets that can be quickly mobilized for the purposes of a political campaign. Accordingly, Figure 2.3 decom-poses the reported sources of moveable asset wealth in 2014.

   More than 80 per cent of the value of moveable wealth is nested in four types of assets: jewellery, cash, deposits, and vehicles. Those unacquainted with Indian social data and political campaigns may be surprised to see that the largest store of moveable wealth is jewellery. Jewellery is a convenient store of value for political purposes, as it allows for the movement of high asset value without much visibility. A small amount of jewellery may be worth crores of rupees and can be moved easily between individuals without being detected, whereas equivalent value in cash or property would be a much more visible form of exchange. Furthermore, almost 50 per cent of the value of

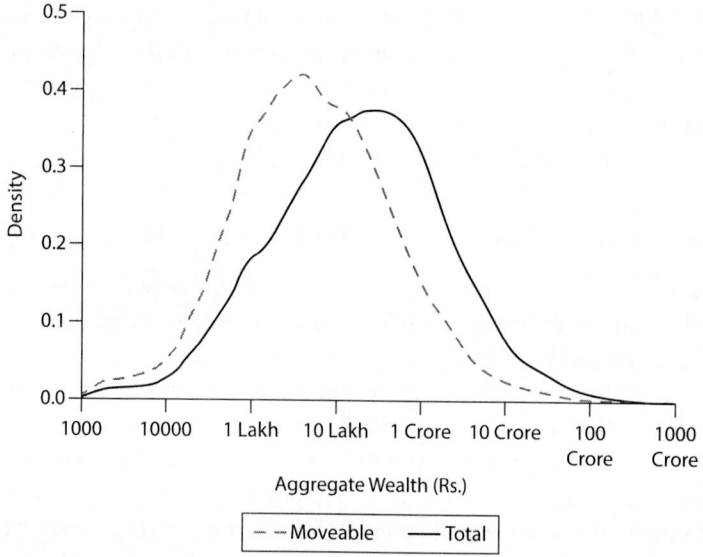

FIGURE 2.2 Density of Moveable and Total Wealth in 2014 on Log Scale (in Rs)
Source: Author's analysis.

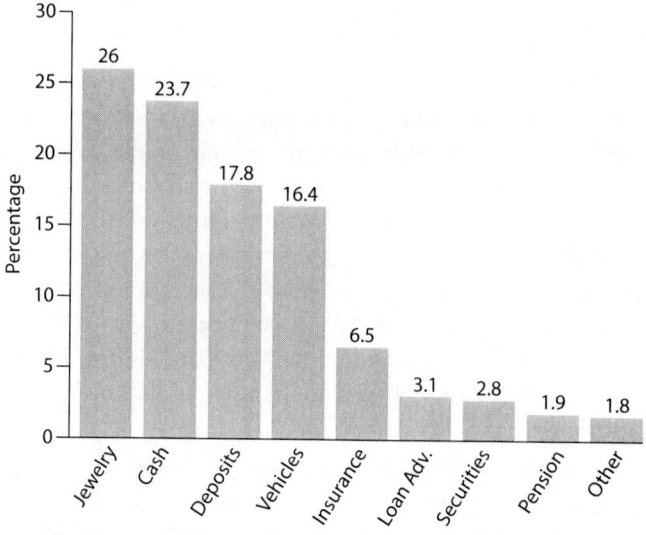

FIGURE 2.3 Decomposition of Sources of Moveable Asset Wealth in 2014 (in Rs)
Source: Author's analysis.

moveable wealth is either in cash or in jewellery, assets for which monitoring movement and exchange is extremely difficult. Thus, the decomposition of moveable assets of candidates provides some intuition as to why candidates can so easily flout any attempt to restrict campaign spending by the government.

SELF-FINANCING AND COMPETITIVE CANDIDATES

A particular focus of this study is the role of assets between candidates from 'competitive parties'. While there are a number of ways one can operationalize competitiveness of parties, the most natural way to do so is to isolate the top two finishers in each constituency, which is the approach taken in this analysis. While, in theory, one can consider conditions under which there are candidates from more than two parties that could conceivably win in a constituency, in practice, electoral outcomes at the constituency level in India are largely Duvergerian. That is, in the vast majority of constituencies, voters strategically coordinate on voting for one of two political parties, and therefore, there are only two parties that realistically have a chance of winning in the constituency.[21]

Data on Competitive Candidates and Assets

India has a total of 543 parliamentary constituencies (PCs). Given that this analysis takes place over three election cycles, there are 1,629 PCs that may be plausibly measured for this exercise. However, a number of competitive candidates failed to provide asset data that met our standard of at least Rs 1,000 in moveable and total wealth (or legibility of affidavits). This analysis requires a comparison of the assets of the two individuals receiving the most votes in each constituency, so PCs in which such data are not available have been dropped.[22] This yields a total of 1447 PCs (89 per cent of the plausible PCs) for the analysis, with 476 PCs in 2004, 443 PCs in 2009, and 524 PCs in 2014.

[21] Gary W. Cox, *Making Votes Count: Strategic Coordination in the World's Electoral Systems* (New York: Cambridge University Press, 1997).

[22] Practically, this means that all individuals reporting wealth less than or equal to Rs 1,000, and their respective constituencies (if such individuals were competitive), have been dropped.

The remainder of the analysis will primarily focus on moveable assets of competitive candidates because, as argued above, this is most crucial for conducting an electoral campaign. When one considers relative wealth between candidates, it is important to talk in multiplicative factors; such is the disparity in wealth between candidates even within a constituency. Over the sample, the median wealth ratio between the wealthier competitive candidate and the poorer competitive candidate, in terms of moveable assets, is 3.8. That is, if one calculates the ratio of moveable assets of the wealthier to the poorer candidates among the top two candidates across constituencies, the median case is that the wealthier candidate is nearly four times wealthier than the poorer candidate. Sometimes the wealth differentials are quite extreme; the maximum wealth ratio for competitive candidates in the sample is a little greater than 47,500. Furthermore, there is no discernible pattern in changes of wealth ratio across the three elections in the sample, suggesting these wealth disparities are fairly stable phenomena.

Hypothesis 1: Non–Competitive versus Competitive Candidates

The restriction of the analysis to competitive candidates would make little sense if there was nothing special about such candidates with respect to asset wealth. As argued in some detail in the section 'Why Does Self-Financing Matter So Much in India' candidates can typically expect little help from outside financial sources. Given the soaring costs of electoral campaigns, candidates are increasingly reliant on personal funds to run effective campaigns. Parties, understanding that candidates must shoulder a significant burden, strategically select wealthy candidates. The problem should be most acute for candidates in competitive parties, since there are increased pressures on such competitive candidates in terms of the visibility required to win an election, so the costs of such campaigns should be higher. Accordingly, section 2 hypothesized that competitive parties should field disproportionately wealthy candidates, that is, competitive candidates should be significantly wealthier than non-competitive candidates. Figure 2.4 provides a simple test of this hypothesis.

Figure 2.4 demonstrates that competitive candidates ('C') are several times wealthier than non-competitive candidates ('NC'), and

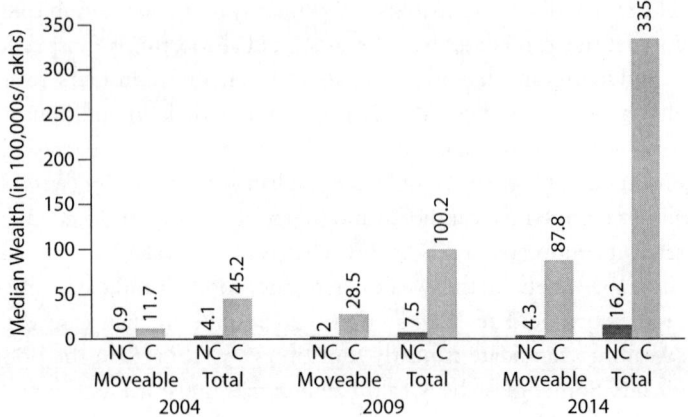

FIGURE 2.4 Comparison of Wealth of Competitive/Non-Competitive
Candidates across Elections
Source: Author's analysis.

the difference is growing. As shown above, the personal wealth of candidates has been increasing across the board, and the widening gap between competitive and non-competitive candidates is noticeable. While the median wealth—moveable or total—rose approximately fourfold for non-competitive candidates between 2004 and 2014, it rose approximately eightfold for competitive candidates. In 2004, the ratio of median wealth of non-competitive candidates to the median wealth of competitive candidates was 7.5–9 per cent (depending on whether one looks at moveable asset wealth or total asset wealth). But by 2014, the ratio had dropped below 5 per cent for both moveable and total asset wealth. This provides strong support for the first hypothesis that competitive parties systematically award party tickets to wealthier candidates. Furthermore, it demonstrates that increasing cost of election campaigns over time has only intensified the incentives of political parties to select wealthy candidates.

Political Parties and Self-financing Candidates

Figure 2.5 displays the reported median wealth for selected parties across the three election cycles among competitive candidates. A few points are worth noting. First, there is significant variation in median wealth across political parties in India. While the numbers are not

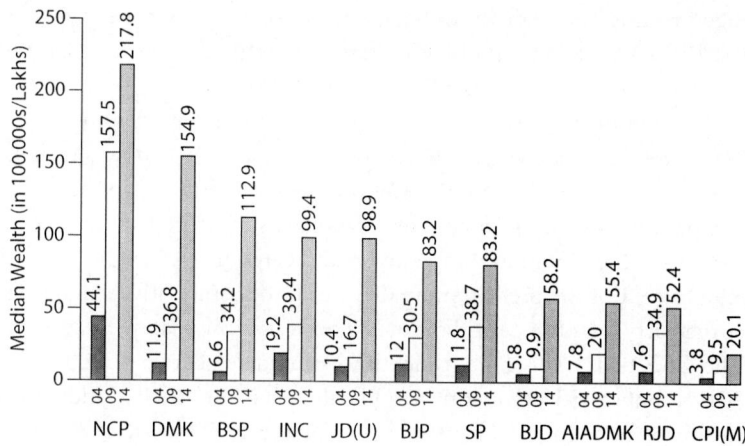

FIGURE 2.5 Median Candidate Moveable Wealth in 2004–14 for Selected Parties (in Rs)

Source: Author's analysis.

adjusted for inflation, it is clear that significantly more money was present across parties in 2014 as compared to 2004. Two increases in median wealth between 2004 and 2014 are particularly noteworthy, that of the Nationalist Congress Party (NCP), which already fielded wealthier candidates in 2004 but significantly more so (in 2014) than the other parties, and the BSP, a poorer party in 2004 that became one of the wealthiest by 2014. Also of note is the fact that the CPI(M) is consistently one of the poorest parties in India. This is probably due to a combination of leftist ideology and a strong party promotion structure that de-emphasizes self-financing as a criterion in the candidate selection process.

One criticism of the naive comparison of non-competitive and competitive candidates is that it is confounded by the branding of parties. Wealthier candidates may simply be drawn to well-known parties, whereas if they simply want to contest the election, they can run as an independent candidate or with a small, unknown party. A more nuanced analysis should see whether the wealth dynamics between non-competitive and competitive candidates is also observed within the same party. The geographic distribution of competitiveness of parties varies quite widely. Parties like the BSP and NCP have highly concentrated regional bases, creating clusters of competitiveness in certain areas. But these same parties often contest in places in which

they are not competitive. Other parties, like the Congress party or
the BJP, have national profiles and are competitive, or at least have a
discernible party base, over a larger swathe of the country.

The within-party analysis further confirms differences in grant-
ing tickets in areas where the party is competitive and where it is
non-competitive. The NCP demonstrates the largest gap between
competitive and non-competitive candidates; the median moveable
wealth of the 85 non-competitive candidates in the NCP is only
5.9 per cent of the median moveable wealth of competitive candidates
in the party over the period of study. This is not just a sample size issue.
The BSP had 1,284 non-competitive candidates between 2004 and
2014 (against 153 competitive candidates), but the median moveable
wealth of non-competitive candidates in the BSP was just 14.1 per
cent of median moveable wealth of competitive candidates in the party.
The national parties demonstrate less of a gap the median moveable
wealth of non-competitive candidates in BJP was 28.8 per cent of their
competitive candidates, and in the Congress, this number was 65.4 per
cent. Presumably, this points to a sharper gap between non-competitive
and competitive candidates within parties that have more regionalized
support bases. It is worth noting that, once again, the CPI(M) is an out-
lier in this analysis with median moveable wealth of non-competitive
candidates at 63.6 per cent of the median moveable wealth in competitive candidates, despite highly regionalized support.

This section conclusively demonstrates that there is a strong relationship between candidate wealth and obtaining a party ticket in a
constituency in which the party is competitive, confirming the first
hypothesis. While there is significant variation in candidate wealth by
party in the sample, the discussion above suggests that highly regionalized parties more strongly filter the wealthiest candidates into competitive constituencies. Of course, candidate wealth in and of itself may
make a candidate more competitive. A naive concern with the analysis
in this section would be that the relationship between candidate wealth
and competitiveness is driven by the fact that money makes winning
more likely at the constituency level. But such a criticism would ignore
the fact that most constituencies are stably Duvergerian in partisan
terms. That is, parties, for the most part, are well aware that they will
be among the top two finishers in the constituency before they select
candidates, and a candidate that does not contest from one of these

competitive parties typically has little chance of winning. In other words, it is not wealthy candidates that are making parties competitive but competitive parties that are selecting wealthy candidates. In fact, as the cost of election campaigns has grown over the past two decades, the number of first-time MPs has also grown, with 2014 recording the highest number since 1980 (315 out of 543 or 58 per cent).[23] Parties have been systematically selecting wealthier, inexperienced candidates, while those with political experience have little chance to win if they are not given a party ticket from a competitive party. Nonetheless, one expects that competitive parties select wealthy candidates precisely because they are expected to deliver better electoral outcomes. This is the subject of the analysis in the next section, which tests hypotheses about the impact of candidate wealth on electoral outcomes and party financing.

SELF–FINANCING CANDIDATES AND ELECTION OUTCOMES

This section investigates the relationship between candidate wealth and election outcomes. In order to demonstrate that there is a meaningful relationship between candidate wealth and winning elections, one must show that even if the analysis is restricted to competitive candidates at the constituency level, wealthier candidates are more likely to win the constituency. That is, wealth must have an effect on the probability of winning when restricted to candidates who have some positive probability of winning in the constituency. The naive relationship holds true. The wealthier competitive candidate wins the constituency 52.6 per cent of the time, suggesting that the wealthier competitive candidate is 5 percentage points more likely to win a constituency than the poorer competitive candidate. A simple chi-squared test shows this to be a statistically significant relationship ($p < 0.05$). Yet, as discussed in section 2, such a relationship can be evidence that wealthier candidates are simply better at winning elections (Hypothesis 2), or it may be that wealthier candidates, who are being used to fill party coffers, are being

[23] 'First-Time MPs in the 16th Lok Sabha,' PRS Legislative Research, http://www.prsindia.org/media/media-updates/first-time-mps-in-the-16th-lok-sabha-3277/, accessed 10 July 2017.

placed in safer seats (Hypothesis 3). Much of this chapter is dedicated
to demonstrating the robustness of the relationship between candidate
wealth and electoral outcomes, as well as disentangling the reasons for
this relationship.

Statistical Strategy

The dataset of competitive candidates requires the use of appropriate
statistical techniques to account for its unique data structure. There
are three major empirical challenges in modelling electoral outcomes
in this setting. First, the statistical technique must account for the fact
that if one competitive candidate in a constituency wins the election,
it necessarily implies that the other competitive candidate will lose
the election; this means that observations within a constituency are
not statistically independent. In order to rectify this problem, one has
to recognize that the average probability of winning across the two
competitive candidates is always 0.5 (under the natural assumption that
those finishing lower down have no probability of winning the election). If the explanatory variables for winning the election have no
predictive power, then the model should predict that each candidate
has a 50 per cent chance of winning the election. Thus, if a candidate
has an attribute for winning the election vis-à-vis the other competitive
candidate, the probability of the former winning the election should
increase by some amount, while that of the opposing candidate should
be decreased by the identical amount to ensure that the average probability of winning over the two competitive candidates is fixed at 0.5.

   This non-independence property across candidates in the same
constituency applies to the measurement of the impact of candidate
characteristics, since at all times, the model must account for the *relative
difference* in characteristics between the competitive candidates. For
instance, the probability of winning for candidates is not just a function
of how wealthy they happen to be, it is a function of the extent to which
they are wealthy compared to their opponents. This is something that
must be accounted for in the statistical model as well. Finally, the effect
of wealth may be dependent upon certain state-level or year-specific
factors, and especially the popularity of the political party. The political
party is coded uniquely for each state and year combination since the
popularity of each party fluctuates so greatly across geography and time.

The key observation to develop a useable statistical model is that mean probability of winning between the two competitive candidates is always identical, 0.5. This implies that if all the predictors are centred around their means in the constituency (considering only the measures from the top two candidates), the constant term in a logit-type regression is fixed at zero. In particular, let the variable win_{iv} be a binary variable denoting whether candidate i wins the election within constituency $v \in \{1,\dots,V\}$. Consider predictors $x_1,\dots x_J$. Denote the mean of predictor x_j in constituency v over the top two candidates as $\{\overline{x}_{jv}\}$. For clarity of exposition, we further denote the wealth indicator in our regression (the base 10 logarithm of moveable wealth of the candidate) in constituency v as $wealth_{iv}$ and the mean of the wealth of the two candidates as $\{\overline{wealth}_{iv}\}$. Using a logit regression model, since the dependent variable is binary, yields:

$$win_{iv} \sim logit(\pi_{iv}) \text{ where } \pi_{iv} = P(win_{iv} = 1)$$

$$logit(\pi_{iv}) = \log\left(\frac{\pi_{iv}}{1-\pi_{iv}}\right)$$

$$= \beta_0 + \beta_{wealth}(wealth_{iv} - \overline{wealth}_v) + \cdots + \beta_J(x_{Jiv} - \overline{x}_{Jv}) \quad (2.1)$$

Looking at the equation above, and given the previous arguments, it is apparent that β_0 is fixed at 0 (the odds are fixed at 1 and the log odds are fixed at 0), which effectively addresses the first concern of non-independence between candidates in a constituency. The concern about relative differences between candidates is addressed by mean-centring variables at the constituency level. However, the salience of candidate wealth may still vary across state, year, or party. In order to address this issue, a hierarchical regression model allowing the coefficients to vary by state and party is fit to the data. Note that because a party is coded separately for each state and year, such a regression also addresses variation across years. The complete regression model is then written as:

$$win_{iv} \sim logit(\pi_{iv}) \text{ where } \pi_{iv} \text{ denotes the probability } P(win_{iv} = 1)$$

$$logit(\pi_{iv}) = \log\left(\frac{\pi_{iv}}{1-\pi_{iv}}\right) = \beta_{wealth,sp}(wealth_{iv} - \overline{wealth}_v)$$

$$+\beta_2(x_{2iv} - \overline{x}_{2v}) + \cdots + \beta_J(x_{Jiv} - \overline{x}_{Jv})$$

$$\beta_{wealth,sp} = \beta_{wealth} + b_{wealth,s} + b_{wealth,p};$$
$$\text{for state } s \in \{1,\ldots,S\}, \text{ party } p \in \{1,\ldots,P\}$$
$$b_{wealth,s} \sim N(0,\sigma_s^2); \; b_{wealth,p} \sim N(0,\sigma_p^2) \tag{2.2}$$

where β and σ denote estimated parameters in the regression model, x_{jiv} denotes predictor j for candidate i in constituency v. All models were estimated using Markov chain Monte Carlo (MCMC) methods implemented through the statistical programme JAGS and called within the statistical framework R using the package R2jags with diffuse priors. The regression tables below summarize the estimated posterior distributions of the parameters of interest, most importantly the fixed coefficient (β_{wealth}) on the (base 10) logarithm of moveable wealth.

Hypotheses 2 and 3: Understanding the Relationship between Wealth and Electoral Outcomes

As shown in the beginning of this section, there is a discernible impact of wealth at the constituency level; that is, the wealthier candidate is more likely to win an election than a poorer candidate in a constituency. The regression framework described above allows for more careful examination of this phenomenon. First, the regression framework can model how the magnitude of the gap between the richer and the poorer candidate (instead of just who is richer and who is poorer) affects electoral outcomes. Second, using various predictors, the regression framework allows for an exploration of the different explanations for the relationship between candidate wealth and electoral outcomes. Finally, the regression framework allows the researcher to demonstrate the robustness of the relationship between candidate wealth and winning elections, as well as understand the estimated effects of a complicated model.

To develop some intuition of how the regression works, it is useful to think about the bivariate regression relating election outcomes to wealth, in a suitably transformed regression equation as described earlier. Consider some constituency where the wealthier competitive candidate, R, has one crore in moveable wealth (Rs 10,000,000) and the poorer candidate, P, has 10 lakhs (Rs 1,000,000). Above, we defined the wealth measure as the constituency mean–centred (base 10) logarithm of moveable wealth for each candidate. The base 10 logarithm of moveable wealth for R would be 7 and for P it would be 6, where the constituency-level mean between these two candidates would be 6.5. Thus, the transformed wealth measure for R is 0.5, and for P, it is −0.5. Notice that the difference between the measures for R and P is exactly 1. An easy interpretation of the regression coefficient is that it measures the relative difference in the probability of winning the election when the richer candidate is 10 times wealthier than the poorer candidate. The regression coefficient can be multiplied accordingly, depending on which wealth ratio the researcher wishes to consider. For instance, because the median wealth ratio is 3.8 and because the base 10 logarithm of 3.8 is approximately 0.58, a good approximation to relative difference in the probability of winning in the median case will be 0.58 times the regression coefficient.

It was argued that there are two major explanations for the relationship between candidate wealth and probability of winning a constituency. First, candidates with more wealth may be better at winning elections if they are able to spend more on the campaign. Second, parties may choose to sell their safest seats to wealthier candidates in order to extract wealth for party coffers. The first mechanism is directly tested using the statistical specification described above. In particular, the coefficient on the transformed predictor of candidate moveable wealth explicitly tests how the wealth gap between a candidate and his or her competitor in the same constituency affects the electoral outcome. In order to test the impact of strategic placement of the wealthier candidate in safe seats, one must look at the candidate's wealth vis-à-vis the average candidate wealth in the candidate's party. To develop some intuition of why this predictor makes sense, note that the regression in (3.2) is constructed so that when competitive candidates are identical in every way, the probability of winning the constituency is 50 per cent. If, however, the constituency is actually a safer seat for one of the parties, then the baseline probability of winning the constituency should be greater than 50 per cent for a candidate from that party. Given that the sophisticated party financing hypothesis holds that disproportionately wealthy candidates will be placed in these safer seats, the deviation of the candidate's wealth from the average candidate wealth in the party should predict a higher probability of winning the constituency.

To be precise, the quantity $\{\overline{wealth_p}\}$ measures the average of the wealth of all the candidates in the party (in the same state and year), where the average is again taken over the base 10 logarithm of moveable wealth of the candidate $(wealth_{iv})$. The regression is given by:

$$win_{iv} \sim logit(\pi_{iv}) \text{ where } \pi_{iv} \text{ denotes the probability } P(win_{iv} = 1)$$

$$logit(\pi_{iv}) = \log\left(\frac{\pi_{iv}}{1-\pi_{iv}}\right) = \beta_{wealth,sp}(wealth_{iv} - \overline{wealth_v})$$

$$+ \beta_{finance}(wealth_{iv} - \overline{wealth_p})$$

$$\beta_{wealth,sp} = \beta_{wealth} + b_{wealth,s} + b_{wealth,p};$$

$$\text{for state } s \in \{1,\ldots,S\}, \text{ party } p \in \{1,\ldots,P\}$$

$$b_{wealth,s} \sim N(0,\sigma_s^2); \; b_{wealth,p} \sim N(0,\sigma_p^2) \qquad (2.3)$$

The coefficients of interest in testing hypotheses 2 and 3 are β_{wealth} and $\beta_{finance}$. In particular, because β_{wealth} tests whether the wealthier candidate in a constituency has a higher probability of winning the election, it can be used to test whether self-financing candidates have a direct electoral impact (Hypothesis 2). Furthermore, as $\beta_{finance}$ tests whether wealthier candidates in the party have a higher probability of winning, controlling for relative wealth of the candidates, it can be used to test whether parties put disproportionately wealthy candidates in safer seats (Hypothesis 3). Table 2.1 displays a bivariate regression using

TABLE 2.1   Testing Electoral Impact and Party Financing Hypotheses

Dependent variable: Winning the Constituency (=1) [Logit]		
	(1)	(2)
Wealth	0.733***	0.736***
	(0.19)	(0.169)
Finance		0.077
		(0.108)

Source: Author.

Note: $^{\cdot}q < 0.10$; $^{*}q < 0.05$; $^{**}q < 0.01$; $^{***}q < 0.001$

Standard deviations of the posterior distributions for the coefficients are in parentheses. Note that q denotes the proportion of posterior distributions of the coefficient that has the opposite sign of the estimated coefficient (the mean of the posterior distribution for the parameter).

the within-constituency wealth gap measure between competitive candidates and the multivariate regression to test hypotheses 2 and 3. In principle, both β_{wealth} and $\beta_{finance}$ could be statistically significant in the multivariate regression, but as the result in Table 2.1 shows, there is little support for the sophisticated party financing hypothesis (Hypothesis 3), whereas there is robust evidence for self-financing candidates having direct electoral impact (Hypothesis 2).

At least as operationalized in this chapter, there seems to be little evidence that the selection of candidates is used to increase party finances as a general phenomenon. There are many news stories about parties selling party tickets to raise party funds, but perhaps these reports are exceptional phenomena. As argued above, parties that are regularly in power likely have far more lucrative options available for party financing than candidate selection, namely, corruption in service delivery and contracts. Furthermore, given that Indian elections are quite volatile,[24] it is unclear whether there are sufficient safe seats to support a party financing strategy. On the other hand, there is strong evidence from the regression analysis that those with greater capacity for self-financing, even among competitive candidates, have an edge when it comes to winning elections. If this is indeed the case, then it should be no surprise that the most competitive parties also angle for the wealthiest candidates.

The Robustness of the Impact of Candidate Wealth on Electoral Outcomes

The rest of this chapter is devoted to demonstrating the robustness of the relationship between a candidate's personal wealth and winning the election, as well as characterizing the results of the regression model. As Vaishnav has argued previously, a candidate's criminal background is a determinant of electoral success, and criminals that get selected for party tickets often have significant personal wealth, a phenomenon the author refers to as the benefits of 'money and muscle'.[25] In addition

---

[24] Pradeep Chibber and Irfan Nooruddin, 'Unstable Politics: Fiscal Space and Electoral Volatility in the Indian States', *Comparative Political Studies* 41, no. 8 (2007): 1069–81.

[25] Milan Vaishnav, *When Crime Pays*.

to an ability to intimidate non-supporters from turning out to vote, Vaishnav argues that those with criminal backgrounds can signal the capacity to deliver benefits to constituents using extra-legal means.[26] In a universe of weak state capacity, where the delivery of benefits is prone to leakage, this quality of candidates with criminal backgrounds may be attractive to voters. Another concern with the analysis above is that it ignores that wealthier people are otherwise high-status people who have, for instance, greater levels of education that make them more appealing to voters. The candidate affidavits also provide information on highest level of education completed and pending criminal cases, and it is important to demonstrate robustness of the impact of candidate wealth on electoral outcomes controlling for these two factors.

ADR, the civil society organization that makes affidavit information public, also publishes information on which candidates are 'facing major criminal cases'. Most people who run for elective office are high-profile individuals, and petty cases may be filed against such individuals for political reasons, such as some version of unlawful assembly. In order to avoid this problem, ADR provides an accounting of candidates that have been charged for more serious crimes like murder and rape (those that are serious allegations against the individual that are associated with violence and/or intimidation). Furthermore, these pending 'cases' are more than mere allegations, they are allegations a judge has determined have enough merit for the court to hear the case, much like an indictment. In the dataset, 16 per cent of competitive candidates are facing major criminal cases (note that those individuals convicted of such crimes are barred from running for office). There is clearly some electoral impact of this measure of criminality, as those with major pending criminal cases won their seat 56 per cent of the time and those without such cases won their seats 49 per cent of the time.

The affidavit data on the highest level of education completed may be categorized in a number of ways, as it provides a large number of categories. For the purposes of this analysis, three categories were created: (a) Below higher secondary (not graduating high school); (b) higher secondary or university graduate; and (c) post-graduate degree. The number of competitive candidates that are in these

---

[26] Milan Vaishnav, *When Crime Pays.*

categories are 518, 1,271, and 1,097, respectively. Once again, higher levels of education seem to have an impact on the probability of electoral victory. Among competitive candidates, those with a higher secondary/university graduate or post-graduate degree as the highest level of education each won about 51 per cent of the time, whereas those who had not passed the 12th standard won about 45 per cent of the time. Naturally, since both education level and criminality are correlated with probability of electoral success and economic wealth, it is important to check whether the relationship between candidate wealth and electoral victory is robust to controlling for these factors.

Table 2.2 estimates three regressions: (a) wealth ratio effects on electoral performance when controlling for whether the candidate faces major criminal cases; (b) wealth ratio effects controlling for criminality and whether the person has a higher secondary/university graduate or post-graduate degree as the highest level of education; and (c) wealth ratio effects controlling for criminality and whether the person has a higher secondary/university graduate or post-graduate degree as the highest level of education, with an interaction between wealth and criminality.[27] In this regression, the interaction cannot simply be evaluated as a coefficient on the product of the criminality and wealth variables because of the construction of comparing relative levels of wealth between competitive candidates in a constituency, rather than absolute levels of wealth of an individual candidate, and therefore two interaction terms (when the candidate is more/less criminal than the other competitive candidate) must be fit to make sense of the data.[28]

The coefficient remains of similar magnitude across the regressions in Tables 2.1 and 2.2 (without the interaction term), suggesting

[27] It is important to note that because the controls are not being varied by state and party, like the wealth measure, they will appear to have greater statistical significance.

[28] There are three distinct scenarios, vis-à-vis criminality: (a) someone with criminal cases running against someone without them; (b) someone without criminal cases running against someone with them; and (c) both candidates have the same level of criminality. The interaction term is constructed as interacting the first two cases with the wealth measure. This effectively varies the slope of the wealth coefficient by each scenario.

TABLE 2.2 Checking Robustness of Wealth Ratio Effects on Electoral
Performance

Dependent Variable: Winning the Constituency (=1) [Logit]		
(3)	(4)	(5)
Wealth		
0.739***	0.719***	0.856***
(0.155)	(0.177)	(0.177)
Criminality		
0.693***	0.722***	0.720***
(0.170)	(0.155)	(0.155)
HS/College		
	0.610***	0.617***
Graduate		
	(0.164)	(0.168)
Postgraduate		
	0.552**	0.554**
	(0.169)	(0.175)
Wealth x CvNC		
		−0.521'
		(0.309)
Wealth x NCvC		
		−0.585'
		(0.294)

Source: Author.

Note: 'q < 0.10; *q < 0.05; **q < 0.01; ***q < 0.001.

Standard deviations of the posterior distributions for the coefficients are in
parentheses. Note that q denotes the proportion of posterior distributions of
the coefficient that has the opposite sign of the estimated coefficient (the mean
of the posterior distribution for the parameter). Also note that CvNC denotes
a scenario in which the wealthier candidate is facing criminal cases while
the opponent is not, while NCvC denotes a scenario in which the wealthier
candidate is not facing criminal cases and the opponent is facing them.

a fairly robust result relating personal wealth of candidates to the
probability of winning an election. The median moveable wealth
ratio between the competitive candidates for the constituencies in
the sample is that the wealthier candidate is approximately 3.8 times
wealthier than the poorer candidate. In this median constituency,
the wealthier candidate is predicted to win 55 per cent of the time,
holding the level of criminality and education constant. That is, in
the median constituency, the probability of the wealthier candidate
winning is 10 percentage points higher, holding levels of criminality and education constant. The model also suggests that the average
citizen has little chance of winning against a criminal candidate, with
the criminal candidate winning 59 per cent of the time, holding

moveable wealth and education constant. At first blush, the criminality effects may seem stronger than the asset wealth effects, but it is important to remember that only 16 per cent of the sample is facing a major criminal case. If we consider candidates in the constituencies with the highest 16 per cent of wealth ratios (wealth ratios greater than 18), the wealthier candidate is predicted to win 65 per cent of the time. Thus, the asset effects are actually of somewhat greater magnitude than the criminality effects.

Model (5) evaluates the complicated relationship between criminality and asset wealth, showing a negative coefficient for each interaction. For the wealthier candidate, this means that the relative impact on winning of increasing the wealth ratio for a non-criminal facing a criminal is weaker than when both competitive candidates have the same criminality status. Moving from the median wealth ratio of 3.8 to the 75th percentile (wealth ratio of 10.56) for a non-criminal facing a criminal only increases the probability of winning from 43 to 44 per cent for the wealthier candidate according to the model. If there is no difference in criminality status between the candidates, for the same change in wealth ratio, the probability of winning increases from 56 to 61 per cent for the wealthier candidate. For the wealthier candidate, there is an impact in winning elections for a criminal facing a non-criminal when the wealth ratio is low, but this effect weakens at higher wealth ratios. Going from the median wealth ratio to the 75th percentile increases the probability of winning from 61 to 63 per cent for the wealthier candidate if the wealthier candidate is a criminal facing a non-criminal.

Figure 2.6 displays the probabilities of winning in the constituency of competitive candidates as a function of the wealth ratio between the richer and the poorer candidate (for both the richer and poorer candidate), holding levels of criminality and education constant. The bold curves are the predicted probabilities, and the intervals around the bold curves are the simulated 95 per cent confidence intervals for predicted values (from model (4)). While the ratios seem large, the graph only demonstrates up to the 70th percentile in wealth ratio (meaning that 30 per cent of the constituencies had a more extreme wealth ratio than what is portrayed in the graph). Even so, at the 70th percentile, the wealthier candidate is expected to win 58 per cent of time, 16 percentage points higher than the poorer candidate.

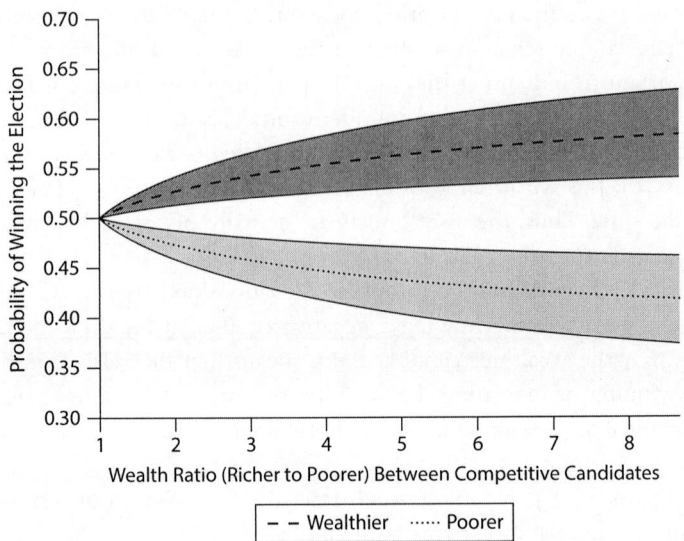

FIGURE 2.6   Probability of Winning as a Function of Constituency-Level
Wealth Ratio
Source: Author's analysis.

This section demonstrates the robustness of a phenomenon in
which the candidates with the greatest personal wealth have a discernible advantage in winning elections. These candidates are, therefore,
the most valuable to competitive parties, explaining why competitive
parties are likely to select the wealthiest candidates. Indian politicians,
and other potential legislators, are well known for their fickle party
loyalties. It is not uncommon to observe candidates jumping across
political parties from election to election. This stands to reason; a
wealthy candidate has a lot of bargaining power, as above all, parties
need to win elections. When coupled with low intra-party democracy that limits a legislator's impact on policymaking or affairs of the
party, individual politicians have strong incentives to re-negotiate their
party allegiances from election to election. Thus, much of what is taken
to be peculiar about the Indian electoral system can be traced to clear
structural and institutional explanations.

This chapter has provided a theoretical framework, in tandem with
quantitative evidence, to grapple with the role a candidate's personal
wealth plays in determining outcomes in Indian elections. While
the role of money is a common concern in the implementation and

regulation of elections all around the world, it should be readily apparent that the brazen display of wealth in Indian electoral campaigns is noteworthy. This chapter has argued that the outward display of money in Indian elections is not a function of political culture or economic development; rather, its causes are institutional and structural. By taking account of the incentives of potential outside donors, aspirants to electoral office, and competitive political parties, one can begin to understand the factors that lead to the phenomenon of wealthy candidates self-financing India's electoral campaigns.

High levels of uncertainty about which potential candidates will receive party tickets, as well as the constituencies from which they will contest, create disincentives for outside funding in election campaigns. Furthermore, the centralized structure of policymaking in Indian legislatures renders lobbying individual legislators less useful, although legislators may still draw funds from outright corruption in contracting. This creates strong pressures for self-financing, where wealthy candidates must foot the bill for increasingly expensive electoral campaigns from personal funds, as well as weak party loyalties. At the same time, the explicit display of wealth in campaigning increases the likelihood of winning, so competitive political parties are naturally drawn to wealthy candidates. This generates a unique electoral equilibrium in which candidates must self-finance campaigns to win an election, and competitive parties prefer to select the wealthiest candidates because they have the greatest capacity to self-finance campaigns.

In order to assess the theoretical framework, this chapter provides a detailed analysis of self-reported candidate affidavit data. Two empirical facts emerge to provide support for the above theory. First, candidates for competitive parties are about 20 times wealthier than candidates for non-competitive parties. Second, even controlling for other relevant factors, in the median constituency (in terms of wealth difference between candidates), the wealthier candidate is predicted to be about 10 percentage points more likely to win the constituency.

Of course, certain caveats are in order. Because the data is self-reported, one may question many of the claims in this chapter. But it is worth noting that even if candidates are systematically underreporting their wealth, the relationships between self-reported wealth and electoral outcomes and party competitiveness are still clearly discernible. It is also important to note that this chapter has only analysed the behaviour of candidates in national elections. But there are good reasons to believe the phenomena identified here are present at lower tiers, like state elections and even municipal or village elections, as the pressures for self-financing are even more acute at these levels. National elections are contested over large parliamentary constituencies and hold a lot of prestige, and given that this is the highest legislative office that can be held by a candidate from the party, there are at least some greater incentives for parties or outside players to finance such candidates. At lower levels of governance, it is hard to imagine a scenario in which there are greater incentives for party or outside funding of campaigns. In short, while this is an analysis of self-reported data for a small slice of those participating in Indian elections, it seems likely that patterns described here hold more generally. These ideas can be explicitly tested at the state level, as similar data exists for state-level elections across India.

Going Further

This chapter has argued that much of the disincentive for outside funding, and pressure for self-financing emanates from the low levels of intra-party democracy in Indian political parties. Given that party ticket selection is a highly non-transparent process, and that party elites control the levers of policymaking, there is little incentive for the larger population to get involved in any individual candidate's campaign. This state of affairs fundamentally shapes the incentives of political aspirants. The pressures to self-finance campaigns make running for office a costly investment for candidates, who may be looking to recoup their costs from corruption and other illegal activity when in office. Furthermore, the lack of say in policymaking for individual legislators, combined with little financial dependence on the party or partisan-committed funders, likely generates weaker party loyalties for politicians.

While the deepening of genuine intra-party democracy may be an ultimate goal, explicit state regulation of internal party affairs seems likely to cause more problems than it would solve. Nevertheless, certain ideas may be explored to change the current equilibrium in campaign financing. First and foremost, a process for state funding of parties or regulation of party finances,[29] like most of the long-standing democracies in the world, would likely address many of the issues raised in this chapter. If state intervention in campaign funding cannot be implemented, certain steps may make the selection of candidates a more predictable process (and thus make potential candidates more likely to receive outside funding). More stringent residential requirements for potential legislators, and a requirement to only contest from a single seat, would lessen the common practice of fielding incumbents from new constituencies that cannot be predicted ahead of time. A longer period between the final day to file for candidature and the polling date would also provide more time for candidates to procure such outside funds. As discussed earlier in this chapter, increasing the level of outside funding through a more participatory funding process should create broader and more engaged political coalitions supporting candidates, increasing the level of democratic accountability in the system and reducing the incentives for corruption for those elected.

The findings in this chapter have important implications for the study of democratic behaviour. In India, it shows that certain peculiarities in the system can be traced to structural and institutional factors. While it is easy to blame the ills of a system on a problematic political culture, focusing on institutional factors can offer practical approaches to bolstering the quality of democratic practice in India. As the costs of running an election campaign rise, incentives will only increase for parties to invest in self-financing candidates. Therefore, the problems associated with self-financing, such as increased criminality and corruption in politics, will likely persist without serious institutional reform. Furthermore, while the academic literature on political parties has taken an interest in intra-party democracy in and of itself, limited attention has been given to how it affects electoral finance and election

---

[29] It should be pointed out that recent policies have taken a step in the opposite direction, by creating a process under which money given to parties will be harder to trace. See Milan Vaishnav, 'Finance Bill Makes Funding for Political Parties More Opaque than Ever', *Hindustan Times*, 2 April 2017, accessed 10 July 2017, http://www.hindustantimes.com/analysis/finance-bill-makes-funding-for-political-parties-more-opaque-than-ever/story-5qKRhtDK5qnuzis8JiI9FO.html.

outcomes. This chapter provides an analysis of the structural conditions under which the self-financing phenomenon is likely to occur, drawing a crucial theoretical link between intra-party democracy and electoral campaigns and outcomes. The inability to properly regulate sources of money in elections—and structure incentives for a more participatory funding process—has led to an undesirable equilibrium in the Indian electoral system. While the pattern of campaign financing in India may be unique with respect to longstanding democracies, the Indian case can be instructive to many new democracies, which are likely struggling with very similar issues.

This chapter also represents a first cut at understanding the role of money in elections from a general quantitative lens, as it provides one of the first systematic analyses of candidate affidavit data that is collected on virtually each individual that contests the state or national election in India. But there is much that is not reported in these affidavits. Little is really known about other sources of funding in elections, beyond personal wealth, and how they impact overall election outcomes. This would require a similar systematic data collection effort from the Election Commission of India. Furthermore, there is little systematic evidence on the relationship between how much money is spent on the campaign and the wealth of the candidate, for example, the percentage of personal money actually spent on campaigns.

However, the candidate affidavits provide a significant amount of information, which when paired with other electoral data, can provide a deeper understanding of the role of money in politics in India. There is a remaining theoretical question about how parties evaluate the tradeoff between fielding inexperienced, wealthier candidates with experienced, less wealthy candidates. Empirically, one can characterize the wealth of first-time candidates vis-à-vis those who have run or held office before. Relatedly, one can explore the identity dimension by considering an analysis of constituencies reserved for Scheduled Caste or Scheduled Tribe candidates; these are also constituencies where candidates are likely to be less experienced.

A second theoretical question that remains to be explored is the extent to which parties strategically place their wealthiest candidates in constituencies that are known *a priori* to be competitive. For instance, one may characterize the average asset wealth of competitive candidates across constituencies with different levels of party alternation.

If underlying constituency competitiveness matters, then one should see a positive association between the amount of party alternation and the wealth of competitive candidates at the constituency level. Candidate affidavits constitute a rich, if underutilized, data source in the analysis of Indian politics. While much remains to be explored, this chapter shows how existing data can be leveraged to make nuanced claims about the role of money in Indian elections.

3   Builders, Politicians, and Election Finance[*]

Devesh Kapur and Milan Vaishnav

In many democracies, particularly in the developing world where accountability and regulatory institutions are weak, reported election expenditures are believed to be a fraction of actual spending.[1] This chapter investigates the claim that private firms can serve as one important source of so-called black, or undocumented, money in elections. Building on the literature on the 'regulation of entry', we theorize that the regulatory intensity of a sector is highly correlated with its rent extractive potential.[2] In other words, where firms are highly regulated by the state, politicians can exchange policy and

[*] We would like to thank Owen McCarthy and Reedy Swanson for excellent research assistance and Rebecca Brown for editorial help. We thank Conor Dowling, Matthew Levendusky, Maria Victoria Murillo, Philip Oldenburg, Neelanjan Sircar, Arvind Subramanian, Sandip Sukhtankar, and workshop participants at the University of Pennsylvania and the Center for Global Development for comments. Milan Vaishnav would like to thank the Smith Richardson Foundation and the Carnegie Corporation of New York for financial assistance. All errors are our own. Additional details can be found in an online appendix available on the authors' websites.

[1] Michael Pinto-Duschinsky, 'Financing Politics: A Global View', *Journal of Democracy* 13, no. 4 (October 2002): 69–86.

[2] Simeon Djankov et al., 'The Regulation of Entry', *Quarterly Journal of Economics* 117, no. 1 (February 2002): 1–37.

regulatory discretion for monetary transfers from firms that can finance election expenditures. One such sector is construction, which depends heavily on the availability of land, an input that is often tightly controlled by state authorities.

In this chapter, we examine the connection between builders, politicians, and election finance in India. In recent years, India has been beset by concerns over the illicit financing of elections—cited by some prominent observers as the country's biggest source of corruption.[3] Given the regulatory intensity of the state with respect to land and the construction sector's cash-dependence, builders have an incentive to pay for election expenses on behalf of politicians through unreported transactions in exchange for regulatory and policy favours.[4] Indeed, a survey of firms conducted by KPMG reports that businesses perceive construction/real estate to be the single most corrupt industry in India.[5] As the journalist Saritha Rai succinctly noted: 'Politics and real estate make for a cozy nexus—one a source of unaccounted cash and the other a conduit for expending the cash.'[6]

The overarching goals of this chapter are twofold. First, we seek to illustrate the cozy dynamics that exist between firms in the construction sector and politicians who regulate their activity but also

[3] Pratap Bhanu Mehta, 'Debating Election Finance', *Hindu*, 17 July 2002; Prem Shankar Jha, 'Overcome by a Sense of Betrayal', *Hindu*, 17 January 2013.

[4] Raghuram Rajan, 'What Happened to India?' *Project Syndicate*, 8 June 2012. The major sources of political corruption in India are widely thought to emanate from the sectors that are most heavily regulated, such as natural resources, land, spectrum allocation, and defence.

[5] 'Survey on Bribery and Corruption: Impact on Economy and Business Environment', *KPMG*, December 2011, accessed 16 May 2012, https://www.kpmg.com/Global/en/IssuesAndInsights/ArticlesPublications/Documents/bribery-corruption.pdf; Kerry Francis, Walt Brown, and Hema Hattangady, 'India and the Foreign Corrupt Practices Act', *Deloitte Forensic Center*, 2009. 32 per cent of firms surveyed by KPMG perceive construction and real estate to be the most corrupt sector—nearly double the figure for telecommunications, the next most corrupt. A report by consulting firm Deloitte states: 'Corruption in India appears to be more widespread in the construction industry, especially in large infrastructure projects.'

[6] Saritha Rai, 'His Humility My Work for the Richest Candidate', *Indian Express*, 3 May 2013.

seek campaign contributions from them. Second, we empirically test whether there is an electoral cycle in the activity of builders that is consistent with this alleged *quid pro quo*. Specifically, we hypothesize that, as elections approach, builders will have to direct some portion of their financial assets to fund political campaigns. As a result of this transfer, builders will face a short-term liquidity crunch at the time of elections. Construction activity will therefore temporarily decline as money exits the sector to finance elections. The empirical challenge we face as researchers is to measure this effect given the lack of reliable data.

Our novel approach is to use unique data on cement consumption, which we use as a proxy for construction activity. Cement is the indispensable ingredient of the modern construction sector, for which there is no material substitute. The construction sector is comprised of two principal components: real estate and infrastructure. We refer to 'builders' as shorthand for firms engaged in construction projects of either type. When construction activity increases, cement consumption rises and vice versa.[7] Empirically, we investigate whether the presence of elections is associated with an observable drop in cement consumption, consistent with shrinking liquidity in the construction sector around election time. To assess the relationship between elections and construction activity, we construct a panel dataset comprising information on the monthly consumption of cement and the timing of elections in India's 17 major states over the period 1995 to 2010. We exploit the staggering of state elections, which allows us to estimate a statistical model that controls for unobserved state and time-specific sources of variation.

We find that there is a statistically significant contraction in cement consumption during the month of state assembly elections. Furthermore, the contraction in cement consumption varies in accordance with the character of the elections and in line with our theoretical expectations. We conduct a range of tests (described in an online appendix available on https://milanvaishnav.com/ and https://casi.sas.upenn.edu/about/people/devesh) to assess the robustness of this result. Having built confidence in our core finding, we address several plausible challenges to our interpretation of the results.

---

[7] Senior executive of one of India's largest cement manufactures, in conversation with one of the authors, July 2011.

The chapter proceeds as follows. In the next section, we briefly summarize the literature on corruption and regulation. We then describe why the construction sector is particularly amenable to channelling black money for elections and present some stylized facts from the Indian case. In the third section, we summarize the logic of using cement consumption as a proxy for construction activity, present our hypotheses, and outline the data and methods we employ. Next, we present statistical evidence in support of our primary hypotheses on election timing and cement consumption and address the most plausible challenges to our interpretation of the findings. We conclude by summarizing the implications of our findings for the broader literature on democracy and elections.

CORRUPTION AND REGULATION

There is a large literature in economics on the regulation of entry, effectively summarized by Djankov.[8] This literature comprises numerous studies examining the relationship between government regulation of start-up business operations and several outcome variables—such as entrepreneurship, productivity, and economic growth. The subset of this literature that has received the most attention, however, is that which examines the relationship between regulation and corruption. Numerous cross-national studies have found that countries with heavier regulation of entry experience greater levels of corruption.[9]

As Djankov et al. and Djankov state, most of the studies in this area build on the theoretical foundations rooted in public choice theory, which views regulation as inefficient and harmful for social welfare.[10] The mechanism we test for in this chapter is consistent with what Djankov et al. call the 'tollbooth' view of regulation. According to this view, the prime beneficiaries of regulation are neither firms nor

---

[8] Simeon Djankov, 'The Regulation of Entry: A Survey', *World Bank Research Observer* 24, no. 2 (May 2009): 183–203.

[9] Djankov *et al.*, 'The Regulation of Entry'; Jakob Svensson, 'Eight Questions about Corruption', *Journal of Economic Perspectives* 19, no. 3 (Summer 2005): 19–42.

[10] Djankov et al., 'The Regulation of Entry'; Gordon Tullock, 'The Welfare Cost of Tariffs, Monopoly, and Theft', *Economic Inquiry* 5, no. 3 (June 1967): 224–32.

consumers, but politicians—or the individuals making the regulations.[11] Politicians can use their discretionary powers to exchange favourable regulatory dispensation in exchange for rents. As Shleifer and Vishny write, 'An important reason why many of these permits and regulations exist is probably to give officials the power to deny them to collect bribes in return for providing the permits.'[12] Covering campaign costs on behalf of politicians represents one specific manifestation of such rents. While firms do pay a cost when it comes to excessive regulation, politically connected firms can still reap benefits from the fact that regulation can be used to ward off potential competition.[13]

Builder–Politician Nexus

If regulatory intensity is correlated with corruption and rent-seeking, there is an *a priori* reason to expect that the construction sector will be a hotbed for such activity. Of course, this does not imply that construction is the *only* industry that acts as a conduit for black money that might be linked to elections. For instance, related work by Sukhtankar on India has shed light on the links between two other highly regulated sectors—sugar and telecommunications—and the illicit financing of politics.[14]

Nevertheless, the comparative literature is strewn with examples of a widespread affinity between the construction industry and politicians,

[11] Djankov et al., 'The Regulation of Entry.'

[12] Andrei Shleifer and Robert Vishny, 'Corruption', *Quarterly Journal of Economics* 108, no. 3 (1993): 599–617.

[13] George J. Stigler, 'The Theory of Economic Regulation', *Bell Journal of Economics and Management Science* 2, no. 1 (Spring 1971): 3–21. This is especially likely when the distinction between 'business' and 'politician' is blurred. As we elaborate below, self-dealing is often prevalent in intensely regulated sectors because politicians, their family members, and associates have an incentive to do business in these areas in order to exploit information asymmetries and privileged access.

[14] Sandip Sukhtankar, 'Sweetening the Deal? Political Connections and Sugar Mills in India', *American Economic Journal: Applied Economics* 4, no. 3 (July 2012): 43–63; Sandip Sukhtankar, 'The Impact of Corruption on Consumer Markets: Evidence from the Allocation of Second-Generation Wireless Spectrum in India', *Journal of Law and Economics* 58, no. 1 (February 2015): 75–109.

or what is often described as the 'builder–politician nexus'. For example, one study of 166 corporate bribery cases reveals that construction was the single most bribe-laden industry in the entire sample.[15] Chubb's classic study of Palermo, Sicily describes how local politicians seeking to rebuild the city following World War II used their regulatory leverage to provide preferred access to builders in exchange for campaign contributions.[16] Authors have described similar scenarios in settings as diverse as the Philippines, Spain, and machine-era America.[17]

The reasons behind this close association are straightforward. For starters, the construction sector requires access to adequate land, which is intensely politically and bureaucratically regulated in many countries.[18] Firms are under intense pressure to acquire land, obtain permissions to utilize the land for their intended purposes, and procure licenses for the actual execution of proposed projects. One of the key implications of this nexus is that builders have an incentive to serve as financiers of elections. Figure 3.1 presents the broad contours of this hypothesized *quid pro quo*, described as follows.

As a result of the regulatory intensity of land, politicians wield an enormous amount of discretion over business activity in sectors for which land is a primary input. They can intervene on behalf of favoured entities to expedite clearances and permits; grant waivers to existing regulations; or alter land use designations. Often, direct intervention by politicians on behalf of firms need not be necessary to ensure a favourable outcome for preferred firms. When the links

---

[15] Yan Leung Cheung, P. Raghavendra Rau, and Aris Stouraitis, 'How Much Do Firms Pay as Bribes and What Benefits Do They Get? Evidence from Corruption Cases Worldwide' (working paper 17981, National Bureau of Economic Research, April 2012).

[16] Judith Chubb, *Patronage, Power and Poverty in Southern Italy: A Tale of Two Cities* (New York: Cambridge University Press, 1982).

[17] John Sidel, *Capital, Coercion and Crime: Bossism in the Philippines* (Stanford: Stanford University Press, 1999); Elena Costas-Pérez, Albert Solé-Ollé, and Pilar Sorribas-Navarro, 'Corruption Scandals, Voter Information, and Accountability', *European Journal of Political Economy* 28, no. 4 (December 2012): 469–84; Steven Erie, *Rainbow's End: Irish-Americans and the Dilemmas of Urban Machine Politics, 1840–1985* (Berkeley: University of California Press, 1990).

[18] Sanjoy Chakravorty, *The Price of Land: Acquisition, Conflict, Consequence* (New Delhi: Oxford University Press, 2013).

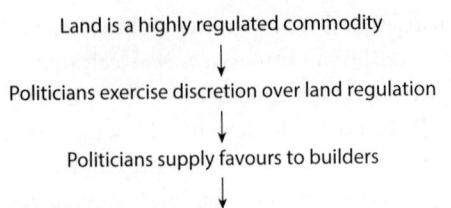

Land is a highly regulated commodity

↓

Politicians exercise discretion over land regulation

↓

Politicians supply favours to builders

↓

At election time, builders must provide politicians with money for elections

↓

Builders will face a short-term liquidity crunch at election time

FIGURE 3.1   Hypothesized Builder–Politician Nexus
Source: Authors.

between firms and politicians are publicly known, it sends a strong signal to regulators: enter at your own risk. The survival instincts of most government officials will ensure that acts of regulatory omission rather than commission will prevail.

Therefore, our hypothesis is that, as elections approach, builders will be compelled to finance some portion of politicians' campaign costs. Although this transaction imposes a short-term cost on builders, the transaction brings long-term benefits in terms of future goodwill.[19] The sector's regulatory intensity not only makes it a boon for filling campaign war chests but also provides politicians with a mechanism to enforce its 'contract' with builders. As a result of this exchange, we hypothesize that builders will face a short-term liquidity crunch around elections because they must redirect funds to cover campaign costs, money which otherwise could have been used towards business investments.

The India Context

The stylized facts of the Indian case track nicely with the generalized theory. In India, the primary piece of legislation governing land acquisition (until 2013) was the Land Acquisition Act, written in 1894 by British colonial authorities. Although the Congress-led government

[19] 'Donation to Political Parties Worries Builders', *IndianRealtyNews.com*, 14 March 2009, accessed 1 July 2013, http://www.indianrealtynews.com/real-estate-india/mumbai/donation-to-political-parties-worries-builders.html. A former Congress Member of the Legislative Assembly (MLA) is quoted as remarking: 'For builders, raising funds for candidates during elections is not a favour, but a transaction which can be encashed at a later date.'

revised the law in 2013, it did not materially diminish the role of the state in facilitating the acquisition of land. Indeed, the law governing land acquisition in conjunction with related laws, such as various land ceiling acts, have created a regulatory structure that empowers politicians and bureaucrats to manipulate control over land.[20] As a recent World Bank survey states, the management of India's land markets is replete with opportunities for rent-seeking due to the absence of four critical factors: a transparent system for land conversion; a clear definition of property rights; an effective system of land and property valuation; and a strong judicial system for addressing grievances. Furthermore, the Indian government is a major owner of prime real estate, which provides it with additional leverage.[21]

Since Independence, numerous attempts have been made to enact land reforms that would ostensibly reduce these discretionary powers. Yet, many of these efforts have been ridden with loopholes, since there is little incentive for politicians to alter the status quo given the benefits accrued under the current system.[22] The persistence of the bureaucratic morass dealing with land issues has served to consolidate entrenched methods of rent-seeking.[23] As one long-time scholar of

[20] Ballabh Prasad Acharya, 'The Indian Urban Land Ceiling Act: A Critique of the 1976 Legislation', *Habitat International* 11, no. 3 (1987): 39–51.

[21] World Bank, *Urbanization beyond Municipal Boundaries: Nurturing Metropolitan Economies and Connecting Peri-Urban Areas in India*, (Washington, D.C.: World Bank, 2013). The precise extent of the Government of India's land assets is unknown, and it is likely even the government itself does not know for sure. But, as one scholar argues, its holdings—especially those of the defence ministry, railways, military, and public-sector undertakings—are undoubtedly immense. See Bibek Debroy, 'All the Sarkar's Land', *Indian Express*, 13 November 2015.

[22] Sudha Pai, 'Our Land of Discontents', *Indian Express*, 20 May 2011.

[23] Lakshmi Srinivas, 'Land and Politics in India: Working of Urban Land Ceiling Act, 1976', *Economic and Political Weekly* 26, no. 43 (October 26): 2482–4. It is important to distinguish between sectors of the economy that are under the purview of the federal government and those that are state subjects. The liberalizing reforms that took place in India during the early 1990s focused on the former. The central government cannot mandate reform of sectors constitutionally under the states' purview. The source of this information is the authors' interview with a former general manager of one of India's largest urban transport projects, Washington, D.C., August 2012.

Indian politics has observed, 'The discretionary power the state has with respect to land is the single biggest source of corruption in this country'.[24]

According to the World Bank, out of 189 countries for which data are collected, India ranks 183 in terms of the ease of obtaining a construction permit.[25] A 2014 survey of transparency in 102 real estate markets around the globe places India in the middle of the pack (or 'semi-transparent'), at 40, 42, and 50 for Tier 1, 2, and 3 cities, respectively.[26] To provide a sense of how widespread the connection between politicians and builders is, Table 3.1 provides an illustrative list of four scandals that have made headlines in India in recent years. Each involves powerful politicians exercising the government's discretionary authority to favour selected firms looking to develop land.[27] We provide a more in-depth list of land-related political scandals in our online appendix available at https://milanvaishnav.com/and https://casi.sas.upenn.edu/about/people/devesh.

It is this regulatory intensity that accounts for the fact that many politicians are often key players in the construction industry. Indeed, numerous politicians have taken a direct financial stake in the construction industry.[28] Because land is a valuable commodity and India's construction industry is booming, many politicians are believed to deposit a portion of their own financial assets with builders involved

[24] Pratap Bhanu Mehta, 'It's Land, Stupid', *Indian Express*, 19 August 2010.

[25] World Bank, *Doing Business in 2016* (Washington, D.C.: World Bank, 2016).

[26] Jones Lang LaSalle, *Real Estate Transparency Index 2014*, accessed 18 May 2016, http://www.jll.com/greti/Pages/Rankings.aspx.

[27] To further elaborate the nature of the builder–politician nexus, Figure 1 in the online appendix summarizes the sequences of events using an example from the state of Andhra Pradesh.

[28] A builder in discussion with one of the authors, New Delhi, December 2012. A builder constructing a hotel in Mumbai told one of the authors that the government informed him it would only issue building permits if there were a *quid pro quo*. The *quid pro quo* sought was not cash but a five per cent equity stake in the hotel in the name of a firm connected to a local politician.

TABLE 3.1   Examples of Alleged Land 'Scams' in India

State	Time Period	Description
Maharashtra	2002–9	Four ex-chief ministers allegedly used defence land to build a posh apartment complex in downtown Mumbai for family members, political allies, and business cronies. The housing complex, known as the Adarsh Housing Society, was originally intended to house widows of army veterans.
Goa	2006–7	Town and Country Planning Minister Atansio Monserrate allegedly received over 260 million rupees from an ex-bureaucrat-turned-real estate developer to convert large tracts of agricultural land into settlement or commercial zones. As part of his portfolio, Monseratte oversaw the 2011 Regional Development Plan, which authorized the conversions.
Andhra Pradesh	2006–9	India's Comptroller and Auditor General (CAG) found that ex-Chief Minister Y.S. Reddy gave away nearly 90,000 acres of land to favoured private entities on an ad hoc, discretionary basis, resulting in an estimated loss of one trillion rupees to the state. The benefitting firms are alleged to have invested in YSR's son's businesses.
Karnataka	2006–10	A report of the state anti-corruption ombudsman found that ex-Chief Minister B.S. Yeddyurappa used his discretion to transfer government property to family members at a throwaway price. The family then sold the land to a mining company for a large profit.

Source: Various news reports compiled by the authors.

in construction.[29] One broker operating in the Delhi region revealed, 'It's commonplace for politicians to park funds in real estate companies, as it's a safe avenue and fetches the highest return.'[30] In addition to earning a decent return on their initial investment, politicians are also lured to the construction sector due to the sector's relative lack of transparency.[31] The recent history of the state of Maharashtra, for instance, contains numerous examples of powerful regional politicians with financial interests in construction.[32] Relatives of politicians often establish their own construction firms and reap the rewards from the value of their familial connections. A 2001 media investigation revealed that a quarter of ministers in the Gujarat state cabinet had familial or other close links with builders.[33] In other instances, politicians become covert backers of firms because they represent powerful entities whose support must be won and retained. As one MP asked rhetorically, 'Which builder will give you money during elections if his work is

[29] Rikhil Bhavnani, 'Using Asset Disclosures to Study Politicians' Rents: An Application to India' (working paper, Department of Political Science, University of Wisconsin-Madison, January 2012). It is also common for politicians to accumulate large tracts of land. An econometric analysis by Bhavnani of the changing composition of Indian politicians' assets revealed that extreme wealth increases between elections are driven by the growth of 'immovable' assets, which include land and buildings. According to the author, election winners 'with extreme asset increases also divest themselves of agricultural land and increase their holdings of nonagricultural land'. The process of land conversion is tightly controlled by politicians and bureaucrats and can result in large financial gains.

[30] Nivedita Mookerji, 'Realty a Safe Bet for Politicians to Park Black Money', *Business Standard*, 1 February 2013.

[31] The source for this statement is a senior executive of major infrastructure finance company in conversation with the authors, Mumbai, October 2012. As Rai artfully puts it, 'real estate is the asset class increasingly favoured by politicians as it sucks in as well as generates bagfuls of cash or "black money".' See Rai, 'His Humility My Work for the Richest Candidate.'

[32] Ashish Khetan, 'Land Grab. And How to Make Millions', *Tehelka*, 28 May 2012. One investigation into the builder-politician nexus in Mumbai, suggests 'almost every MLA and MP [Member of Parliament], both past and present, cutting across party lines, owns at least one real estate project, either directly or through family members or a proxy'.

[33] Ranjit Bhushan, 'Builders and Friends', *Outlook*, 19 February 2001.

not done?'[34] Of more recent vintage is the proliferation of builders who use their wealth, largely accumulated on the basis of political patronage, to contest elections directly.[35] It is nearly impossible to be a successful real estate player in modern India without possessing a certain baseline level of political connections.[36]

What helps grease the wheels of this *quid pro quo* is the industry's heavy reliance on cash and non-bank forms of finance. According to a Planning Commission (2011a) estimate, a mere 1.4 per cent of total gross bank non-food credit disbursed during the year 2010–11 went to the construction sector.[37] Yet, the sector, as a whole, accounts for over nine per cent of India's gross domestic product (GDP).[38] The industry's access to bank finance is limited for several reasons. First, the Reserve Bank of India (RBI) has imposed limits on the real estate exposure of a bank's lending portfolio due to concerns about speculative housing bubbles and the welfare of bank balance sheets.[39] Second, confusion over the role of state governments as facilitators in land acquisition has led to increasing litigation and bottlenecks, which add to the risk profile of builders.[40] Banks remain concerned about the lack of transparency in the construction sector, the legality of underlying

[34] Khetan, 'Land Grab. And How to Make Millions.'

[35] Sudipto Mondal, 'A Symbiotic Relationship', *Hindu*, 30 April 2013; Sreenivasan Jain, 'The Republic of Builders', *Business Standard*, 30 April 2013. For instance, the 2013 elections in the state of Karnataka saw at least a dozen major builder-turned-politicians contest from constituencies in or near the urban metropolis of Bangalore.

[36] Mehta makes the point on connected builders in starker terms, 'Several astonishing companies have arisen, on seemingly nothing but their ability to manipulate the political process.' See Mehta, 'It's Land, Stupid.'

[37] Planning Commission, Government of India, *Working Group Report on Construction for the Twelfth Five Year Plan (2012–2017)* (New Delhi: Government of India, 2011a); Ministry of Finance, Government of India, *Economic Survey of India, 2012–2013* (New Delhi: Government of India, 2013). Construction accounts for only three per cent of the total credit disbursed to the industrial sector in 2010–11. This compares to 63 per cent for manufacturing.

[38] Planning Commission, *Working Group Report on Construction.*

[39] Former Urban Development Secretary, Government of Karnataka in conversation with the authors, New Delhi, July 2012.

[40] Ministry of Finance, *Economic Survey of India, 2012–2013.*

land transactions, and inadequate safeguarding mechanisms to protect investments.[41] Third, there are few barriers to entry for builders seeking to join the marketplace; the industry lacks a unified regulator; and banks are reluctant to finance builders without established track records.[42] The Government of India estimates that small contractors execute over 90 per cent of all construction projects across India; out of 3 million existing business units, only 28,000 are officially registered.[43]

The availability of liquid forms of finance is further bolstered by the fact that the sector has enjoyed a massive boom era over the past two decades. Between 2000 and 2010, the construction industry has enjoyed a compound annual growth rate of 11 per cent.[44] According to government estimates, employment in the construction industry (which is largely unorganized) increased by 70 per cent between 2004 and 2009.[45] Builders, for their part, are quite content with the sector's reliance on cash—since the latter is necessary for side payments or 'speed money'.[46]

---

[41] According to the Planning Commission, *Working Group Report on Construction*, 'The construction sector is characterized by lots of project delays which are due to lack of adequate credit, harassment, problems in approvals, bad image of the contractors/builders, etc.'

[42] Joyita Ghose, 'The Real Estate (Regulation and Development) Bill, 2013', PRS Legislative Brief, 10 June 2014. A 2012 *Economist* analysis of the real estate sector states that the non-bank finance builders often rely on 'is not always kosher. One fraud expert reckons 80% of money-laundering in India uses property'. In 2016, Parliament passed The Real Estate (Regulation and Development) Bill, 2013, which will establish state-level regulatory authorities called real estate regulatory authorities (RERAs). It remains to be seen how effective or truly independent these new regulatory institutions will be.

[43] Planning Commission of India, Government of India, *Faster, Sustainable, and More Inclusive Growth: An Approach to the Twelfth Five Year Plan* (New Delhi: Government of India, 2011b). According to the Planning Commission, 95.5 per cent of contractors (or 29,600 companies) involved in construction have fewer than 200 employees.

[44] Planning Commission, *Sustainable, and More Inclusive Growth*.

[45] Ministry of Finance, *Economic Survey of India, 2012–2013*.

[46] Bhupesh Bhandari, 'An Industry Built on Black Money', *Business Standard*, 4 December 2014.

The affinity between builders and politicians is further compounded by the ineffectual regulation of election finance.[47] In recent years, the cost of elections has enlarged considerably, as a result of several, interconnected factors: growing electoral competition, the increasing size of constituencies, inflated voter expectations of handouts, and the growing complexity of elections (brought on by technological changes, such as the advent of social media). Formal limits on campaign expenditures do exist in India, but are widely seen as unrealistic. Political parties are neither able nor willing to regulate election spending internally and are not subject to serious independent scrutiny. Furthermore, political parties in India are organizationally weak and often unable to systematically raise significant funds on their own, limiting their ability to finance individual campaigns from their own coffers.[48] Second, efforts to regulate corporate contributions have not changed the under-the-table pattern of party funding because the potential costs of transparency outweigh any possible benefits.[49] Third, non-electoral mechanisms of accountability could help control the rising costs of elections, yet their unevenness has limited their effectiveness. For instance, India has a long tradition of a free media, yet the Press Council of India has warned that the practice of politicians paying journalists for favourable coverage was widespread.[50]

[47] M.V. Rajeev Gowda and E. Sridharan, 'Reforming India's Party Financing and Election Expenditure Laws', *Election Law Journal* 11, no. 2 (June 2012): 226–40; E. Sridharan and Milan Vaishnav, 'India', in *Checkbook Elections: Political Finance in Comparative Perspective*, eds. Pippa Norris and Andrea Abel van Es (New York: Oxford University Press, 2016).

[48] Milan Vaishnav, *When Crime Pays: Money and Muscle in Indian Politics* (New Haven: Yale University Press, 2017), Chapter Four. While all political parties collect membership dues, they are marginal to the cost of fighting elections.

[49] E. Sridharan and Milan Vaishnav, 'India'. From the perspective of politicians in India, there is great trepidation about being seen as openly taking money from private firms. In a country with a very high poverty rate, there is still widespread scepticism about profit-making by big business. See Rob Jenkins, *Democratic Politics and Economic Reform in India* (New York: Cambridge University Press, 2000).

[50] Press Council of India, 'Report on Paid News', 7 July 2010, accessed 15 March 2014, http://presscouncil.nic.in/oldwebsite/councilreport.pdf.

The realities of the Indian system point to incentives for private financing of elections, which open the door to methods of 'off-the-books' transactions. The overall magnitude of illicit election finance is difficult to determine. A 1999 independent election audit in 24 parliamentary constituencies found that the average winner spent Rs 8.3 million (when the limit ranged from 1 to 2.5 million).[51] One 2013 news report, citing the views of political money managers, estimated that a municipal councillor's election in a major metropolitan city will cost between Rs 3 and 5 million. The cost of a state election is far greater, ranging between Rs 10 and 50 million while contesting a parliamentary election will set candidates back between Rs 100 and 250 million.[52] Interdictions by the ECI prior to the 2016 state elections in Tamil Nadu have resulted in the seizure of over Rs 1 billion in illicit cash intended for election purposes.[53] This, of course, only represents what cash shipments authorities were able to intercept.

To quench the thirst for such 'off-the-books' financing, politicians often turn to private firms for assistance. It is important to note that firms typically do not provide direct cash transfers to politicians themselves. Rather, it is believed that they directly sponsor some portion of campaign costs; this means that no cash must directly change hands.[54] This is important because, in recent years, the ECI has stepped up enforcement on direct spending by candidates. Upon their formal nomination, candidates are required to furnish affidavits detailing their personal financial assets; and, upon the end of campaigning, must disclose their election expenditures. While the campaign is ongoing, the ECI uses a range of mechanisms, from hiring videographers to maintaining shadow election expenditure ledgers, to clamp down on

[51] E. Sridharan, 'Electoral Finance Reform: The Relevance of International Experience', in *Reinventing Public Service Delivery in India*, ed. Vikram K. Chand (New Delhi: Sage, 2006): 363–88.

[52] Bhavdeep Kang, 'Inside Story: How Political Parties Raise Money', *Yahoo! News*, 25 September 2013, accessed 17 May 2016, https://in.news.yahoo.com/inside-story--how-political-parties-raise-money-091455119.html.

[53] 'Unaccounted Cash Seized in Tamil Nadu Crosses Rs 100 Crore Mark', *Press Trust of India*, 15 May 2016.

[54] General counsel of a large infrastructure development company in conversation with one of the authors, Mumbai, July 2012.

off-the-books spending. Due to this increased scrutiny, candidates have incentives to encourage firms to directly cover invoices or incur spending on their own rather than provide direct monetary transfers.

Firms in the construction sector are not the only mechanism for funding elections. In India, there is anecdotal evidence of similar dynamics in other regulated sectors, ranging from liquor to mining.[55] Nevertheless, builders are an important piece of the puzzle. Scholars point out that the sector is ripe for circulating, or laundering, 'black money,' because the 'true' price of land (and, hence, whatever the land is eventually used for) is often not known; India, like many other developing countries, lacks an independent pricing mechanism for land.[56] The ability to undervalue land makes it an attractive investment for parking cash of questionable origin.[57] One estimate, derived by a real estate consultancy, surmised that as much as 30 per cent of all property transactions in India involved black money.[58]

In sum, builders require favours from politicians and politicians, in exchange, expect financial contributions during election season. However, because elections introduce some uncertainty about the precise future of the political landscape, it is not uncommon for politicians to deliver on some of their promises ahead of elections as a mechanism of securing funding. Conversations with current and former bureaucrats reveal two principal methods. The first is for politicians to grant builders sought-after 'change in land use' certificates, or CLUs, ahead of elections as a down payment.[59] Builders require CLU certificates

---

[55] M. Rajshekhar, 'How Corruption in Coal is Closely Linked to Political Funding', *Economic Times*, 7 August 2012; Mehboob Jeelani, 'Under the Influence', *Caravan*, 1 November 2013; Vaishnav, *When Crime Pays*. Political parties possess a diversity of mechanisms for funding elections, including the recruitment of wealthy individuals involved in criminal activity.

[56] World Bank, *Urbanization beyond Municipal Boundaries*.

[57] Arun Kumar, *Black Economy in India* (New Delhi: Penguin, 2002); Rai, 'His Humility My Work.'

[58] The estimate was attributed to the real estate consultancy, Liases Foras, and quoted in Bhandari, 'An Industry Built on Black Money.'

[59] Nagesh Prabhu, 'EC Spikes State's Plea Seeking Nod for Change of Land Use', *Hindu*, 30 March 2013. The ECI has, in a few instances, started cracking down on the pre-election issuance of CLUs when the Model Code of Conduct is in force. For example, the body refused to give the Government of Karnataka permission to issue several CLUs ahead of that state's 2013 state assembly election.

if they are to, say, convert designated agricultural land for commercial, industrial, or residential purposes.[60] The second mechanism, common in urban metropolitan areas, is for politicians to use their influence to green light increases in the 'floor space index' (FSI), or the ratio of a building's total floor area to the total size of the underlying parcel of land upon which it is built. One analysis of FSI increases in Mumbai revealed that decisions to allot more FSI to builders were more likely to be cleared ahead of elections.[61]

HYPOTHESES ON CEMENT CONSUMPTION

Analysing activity in India's construction sector presents difficulties for measurement because we lack reliable metrics. To overcome this, we use data on the amount of cement that is consumed in the major states of India on a monthly basis over a 15-year period. Cement consumption represents a suitable barometer of construction activity for two reasons. First, cement is the indispensable ingredient in virtually all construction; it has no obvious substitute as a binding agent for building materials. Industry research estimates that real estate accounts for roughly three quarters of India's domestic cement demand, with infrastructure accounting for the remainder.[62] Second, cement consumption closely tracks short-term trends in construction activity. Strictly speaking, our data are on cement purchases but industry insiders report that there is little lag time between purchases and consumption of cement due to high inventory costs, fear of

---

[60] Kang reports, 'The maximum CLU files are cleared before elections. The conversion of low cost agricultural land to high cost commercial land is well worth a substantial outlay in bribe money.' See Kang, 'Inside Story: How Political Parties Raise Money.'

[61] Shalini Nair, 'A Mumbai Pattern: Laxity for Real Estate before Election', *Indian Express*, 22 September 2014.

[62] 'Cement', India Brand Equity Foundation, August 2015, accessed 18 May 2016, http://www.ibef.org/download/Cement-August-2015.pdf. Land used for real estate is regulated by the government but the investments for building on that land are usually made by private interests. Infrastructure, such as dams and roads, consists of projects that are largely publicly financed on land that is publicly acquired and often executed through government contracts.

theft, and cement's unique chemical properties.[63] Hence, inventory is largely fixed since consumers do not build up large stocks of cement. Furthermore, large end-users purchase cement from the major cement companies directly rather than middlemen.[64]

Our core hypothesis is that cement consumption should exhibit a significant contraction during the month of the state election. Because builders are a leading source of election finance, one would expect activity in the sector to slow down during the month-long campaign period prior to election day. This is because existing liquidity in the sector is likely to dry up as resources otherwise slated for building must be channelled into electoral campaigns. Several commentators have noted this regularity, but only anecdotally and without firm empirical evidence. For instance, one account written ahead of the 2014 general election suggests 'many of India's real estate companies are now diverting funds from housing and other projects to election campaign contributions, which is why existing projects are being stalled while new ones are being halted completely'.[65]

To probe whether the mechanism underlying the link between cement consumption and elections is related to election finance, as opposed to some other factor, we propose a series of secondary hypotheses. Under India's federal constitution, the state governments—as opposed to the national government—have regulatory responsibility for land and associated activities such as construction. Hence, there are stronger incentives for builders to cultivate ties with state-level,

[63] An executive of a major cement manufacturer and CMA member firm in correspondence with the authors, January 2012. On its website, CMA also notes, 'Cement purchased in bulk and stored for long on-going construction needs proper care in preservation. Cement tends to readily absorb moisture from the surroundings ... and react with it chemically. Its binding property and strength depend upon its capacity for this chemical reaction, which is irreversible.'

[64] An executive of a major cement manufacturer and CMA member firm in correspondence with the authors, January 2012.

[65] Sunainaa Chadha, 'Delhi, Mumbai Realty Downswing Shows Nexus between Builders and Poll Funding', *Firstpost*, 12 April 2014, accessed 16 May 2016, http://www.firstpost.com/business/economy/delhi-mumbai-realty-downswing-shows-nexus-between-builders-and-poll-funding-1967243.html.

rather than national-level, politicians.[66] However, individual politicians in India derive their power largely by their proximity to party leaders. Given that all significant political parties at the state level also compete in national elections, there are secondary incentives for builders to assist parties in financing national election campaigns.[67] Therefore, we expect that the contraction in cement consumption will be significant in national elections, though of a smaller magnitude than in state-level elections.

However, elections in some states coincide with national elections; for instance, the last four state elections in Andhra Pradesh have coincided with national elections. In those instances, which we refer to as dual (or concurrent) elections, the need for election finance will be relatively greater. Therefore, we expect the magnitude of the contraction in cement consumption to be larger for dual elections than if only a state or national election is being held.

Fourth, we also expect to see variation according to the socioeconomic realities of the states. For instance, more urbanized states are comparatively richer; are more likely to possess well-developed real estate markets; and have higher demand for construction than their rural counterparts. As a result, linkages between politicians and builders are likely to be more intense in more urbanized states.[68] Thus, we expect that cement consumption should exhibit a larger contraction in urban versus rural states.

Our last hypothesis concerns political competition. There is substantial variation on this dimension in India, both across states as well as over time. The need for election finance is likely to be greatest for those elections where competition between parties is greatest and

---

[66] The opposite would be true, for instance, for the allocation of telecommunications spectrum or defence contracts, which are activities governed by the central government.

[67] Yogendra Yadav and Suhas Palshikar, 'Principal State Level Contests and Derivative National Choices: Electoral Trends in 2004–09', *Economic and Political Weekly* 44, no. 6 (February 7–13, 2009): 55–62.

[68] Chadha, 'Delhi, Mumbai Realty Downswing'. Indeed, one report on real estate trends states that the 'mutual dependence between builders and politicians is most acute in areas where land is in high demand, such as [the] fast-growing regions near New Delhi.'

uncertainty about the outcome is highest. Therefore, we hypothesize that the contraction in cement consumption should be comparatively larger in more competitive elections.

DATA AND METHODS

To test our hypotheses, we construct a data set of monthly data on cement purchases by state. The source of the data is the Cement Manufacturers' Association of India (CMA), an industry trade group whose members include the country's largest public- and private-sector cement manufacturers. One of CMA's primary roles is to serve as a comprehensive clearinghouse for information on the capacity, production, dispatch, and export of cement, using data collected on a monthly basis from its member companies.[69] CMA's data are proprietary but were provided to the authors by a member company. Monthly data on cement consumption (measured in metric tonnes) are available from April 1995 to March 2010, for a total of 180 calendar months per state. Our study emphasizes cement consumption, rather than production, because our hypotheses revolve around contractions in liquidity in the construction sector. We do not make any claims about linkages between electoral politics and the supply of cement (production), although we will address whether the contraction in cement consumption is a response to a corresponding contraction in production.

India is a federal parliamentary democracy comprised of 29 states and seven union territories. For our analysis on cement consumption, we focus on the 17 major states, which account for over 92 per cent of the country's population. We do not include data from three new states created in 2000 or most small microstates and union territories (Delhi is an exception). As of 2009–10, cement consumption in the 17 major states accounts for 90 per cent of the all-India total. Thus, we are confident that we are working with data that have considerable explanatory power.

Before proceeding, we address two concerns about the reliability of our data. First, one might question whether firms have an incentive to

---

[69] As a condition of their CMA membership, member firms are required to report data on their operations on a monthly basis.

report truthfully to the CMA, especially if data are shared with competitor firms. However, the CMA does not provide firm-specific data; it merely collects, aggregates, and reports data at the state level. Second, although CMA includes the biggest public- and private-sector cement manufacturers in India, not all cement firms are member companies. If, for instance, smaller cement manufacturers are underrepresented in the CMA, this could bias our results. To investigate, we compared government data on monthly cement production with the CMA data.[70] The government data include information from all cement manufacturers between April 1999 and March 2010. The two data sources are highly correlated (r = 0.98), providing additional confidence in our reliance on the CMA data.

To our dataset on cement consumption, we add information on elections from the ECI. Between April 1995 and March 2010, there were a total of 52 state elections across India's 17 major states as well as five national elections. Roughly one quarter of all state elections in our dataset coincide with national elections. State assembly elections take place every five years on a staggered schedule, although a state assembly can be dissolved before the conclusion of its full term and early elections can be called. Of the 52 state elections in our dataset, nine were unscheduled. Of the five national elections, two were unscheduled. In India's parliamentary system, the official campaign period prior to elections is very brief, lasting only a matter of weeks.

To test for electoral cycles in cement consumption, we adapt the model used by Akhmedov and Zhuravskaya in their study of opportunistic political business cycles.[71] Specifically, we estimate the following equation using regional monthly panel data:

$$\log \gamma_{it} = \sum_{j \in \{-6;6\}} \alpha_j m_{jit} + \beta_1 \log \gamma_{it-1} + \tau_t + f_{is} + \varepsilon_{it}, \qquad (1)$$

[70] We are only able to compare government and industry data on cement production because India's Ministry of Commerce and Industry does not collect data on cement consumption, as far as we are aware.

[71] Akhmed Akhmedov and Ekaterina Zhuravskaya, 'Opportunistic Political Cycles: Test in a Young Democracy Setting', *Quarterly Journal of Economics* 119, no. 4 (November 2004): 1301–38.

where i identifies states, t represents the month of the year, and y stands for the level of cement consumption (in log terms) in a given state-month (*Log Cement Consumption*). m_{jit} is an indicator variable that equals one, when t is j months away from the state election. Our model includes time fixed effects, τ_t, where there is an indicator for each month-year. This fixed-effects parameter controls for unobserved national-level trends as well as any general macroeconomic shocks. As in Akhmedov and Zhuravskaya, we also need to control for state-specific fixed effects as well as any state-specific seasonal or time shocks. Hence, we include the fixed effects term, f_{is}, for each of the 12 calendar months of the year (s) in each state, i.

Our primary variable of interest is m_{jit} when $j = 0$, which signifies the month of the state election (*Election*). In the base specification, we also include dummies for each of the six months preceding and following a state election (*Election-1*, *Election-2*, and so on). A negative coefficient on α_j when $j = 0$ would provide support for our hypothesis that the occurrence of a state election is associated with a drop in cement consumption. Finally, we include a lag of our dependent variable, log y_{it-1} in the model because we believe there are strong theoretical reasons for expecting that cement consumption exhibits temporal dependence.[72]

[72] Kyung So Im, M. Hashem Pesaran, and Yongcheol Shin, 'Testing for Unit Roots in Heterogeneous Panels', *Journal of Econometrics* 115, no. 1 (July 2003): 53–74; Nathaniel Beck and Jonathan N. Katz, 'What to Do (and Not to Do) With Time-Series Cross-Section Data,' *American Political Science Review* 89, no. 3 (September 1995): 634–47. Using the Akaike information criterion (AIC), we tested for optimal lag selection. In half of the diagnostic tests (run separately for each state), the results suggested we should include three lags of the dependent variable, while half of the tests indicated we should include four lags. The regressions below include three lags, but the results do not change if we include four lags. As an additional robustness test, we also run all our models without any lags of the dependent variable. The results do not change. In addition, we tested for unit roots using the test developed by Im, Pesaran, and Shin. Based on the mean of the individual Dickey-Fuller t-statistics of each unit in the panel, the Im-Pesaran-Shin test assumes that all series are non-stationary under the null hypothesis. Based on the test statistics, we can reject the null hypothesis of non-stationarity. We estimate all models using Ordinary Least Squares (OLS), using the correction for panel-corrected standard errors (PCSE) suggested by Beck and Katz to deal with non-spherical errors

We are also concerned about serial correlation in the data, so including a lag makes sense from a modelling perspective.[73] Summary statistics and details about our coding can be found in the Appendix to this chapter.

EMPIRICAL RESULTS

We begin with our baseline series of multivariate regressions in which we estimate the effect of state elections on (log) cement consumption. As seen in column 1 of Table 3.2, we first estimate our model without any fixed effects parameters, only including indicator variables for the election month and the six months before and after. The regression results indicate that state elections are associated with a significant decline in cement consumption, conditional on cement consumption in previous months. There is a slight increase in cement consumption immediately after the election, but otherwise the coefficient of the election lags and leads are insignificant. This basic specification does not control for time trends, so in column 2 we add time fixed effects—or indicator variables for every month-year combination. In column 3, we include only state-month fixed effects to account for state-specific seasonality in construction activity. Finally, in column 4, we include both time and seasonal fixed effects parameters (as in Equation 1 above). Across all models, our results show that state elections are associated with a consistent, statistically significant 12 per cent decline in cement consumption. Our point estimates for the election indicator are invariant to the inclusion of both time and seasonal fixed effects parameters; they are similar across models, both in terms of magnitude and statistical significance.

In the full specification (column 4), almost every other indicator variable marking the months before and after the election is insignificant (with the exception of the dummies for the six-month lag

---

(heteroskedasticity and contemporaneous correlation). All of these results are available in the online appendix.

[73] We tested for serial correlation using Wooldridge's test for linear panel data. The results indicate that we cannot reject the null hypothesis of no serial correlation in the data.

TABLE 3.2 Cement Consumption and State Elections

DV:	(1) Log Cement Consumption	(2) Log Cement Consumption	(3) Log Cement Consumption	(4) Log Cement Consumption
Election$_{t-6}$	0.02 [0.78]	0.02 [0.73]	0.04 [1.54]	0.06*** [2.69]
Election$_{t-5}$	−0.01 [−0.42]	−0.00 [−0.04]	−0.02 [−0.88]	−0.00 [−0.03]
Election$_{t-4}$	−0.00 [−0.12]	−0.01 [−0.38]	−0.02 [−0.84]	−0.02 [−0.69]
Election$_{t-3}$	−0.03 [−1.08]	−0.03 [−1.19]	−0.03 [−1.21]	−0.03 [−1.55]
Election$_{t-2}$	0.04 [1.27]	0.03 [1.24]	0.02 [0.83]	0.01 [0.55]
Election$_{t-1}$	0.04 [1.38]	0.02 [0.85]	−0.01 [−0.31]	0.00 [0.21]
Election	−0.12*** [−4.12]	−0.12*** [−4.71]	−0.12*** [−4.87]	−0.12*** [−5.44]
Election$_{t+1}$	0.09*** [2.95]	0.05** [1.97]	0.03 [1.33]	0.03 [1.29]
Election$_{t+2}$	0.02 [0.82]	0.04 [1.50]	0.03 [1.19]	0.03 [1.17]
Election$_{t+3}$	0.03 [0.89]	0.04 [1.40]	0.07*** [3.06]	0.04 [1.56]
Election$_{t+4}$	−0.01 [−0.28]	−0.01 [−0.57]	0.03 [1.16]	0.01 [0.63]
Election$_{t+5}$	−0.04 [−1.46]	−0.01 [−0.25]	0.02 [0.98]	0.04* [1.82]
Election$_{t+6}$	−0.03 [−1.05]	−0.04* [−1.65]	−0.01 [−0.51]	0.00 [0.20]
Fixed effects	–	Time	State-Month	Time & State-Month
Observations	2,856	2,856	2,856	2,856
R-squared	0.95	0.96	0.97	0.97
Number of states	17	17	17	17

Source: Authors.

Note: Z statistics in brackets. *significant at 10 per cent; **significant at 5 per cent; ***significant at 1 per cent. All models include three lags of the dependent variable. Model (2) includes time fixed effects; Model (3) includes fixed effects for each state-month combination; and Model (4) includes time and state-month fixed effects. Models are estimated using OLS with panel-corrected standard errors. Dependent variable is natural log of cement consumption.

and five-month lead). The results demonstrate a clear, election-related decline.[74]

National Elections

Next, we explore our hypothesis that the election-related contraction in cement consumption should be smaller for national (*Lok Sabha Election*), as opposed to state elections.

Recall, we expect that national elections will have a significant, negative effect on cement consumption due to the fact that construction firms have reason to curry favour with major political parties— all of whom straddle state and national politics. However, we expect that the election effect will be of a smaller magnitude than for state elections given that land use is primarily regulated by the states. To estimate the effect of national elections on cement consumption, we employ a slightly different model. Namely, we can no longer include a full set of month-year fixed effects to account for the time trend because the indicator for Lok Sabha (national) elections does not vary across states (for example, national elections are a common 'shock' simultaneously experienced by all states). Thus, for the regressions testing this hypothesis, we can only include fixed effects for years as well as for each state–month combination (for example, seasonal time effects). Column 1 of Table 3.3 reports the results of the baseline model (with no fixed effects). According to this basic specification, national elections are associated with a 10 per cent decline in cement consumption. In columns 2 and 3, we add year fixed effects and

---

[74] Figure 3 in the online appendix plots the coefficients, starkly demonstrating the decline in cement consumption during the month of elections. To ensure that our core result is not an artefact of the number of leading and lagging months that we decide to control for, we re-estimate the model including both sets of fixed effects, iteratively adding more dummies for the election lags and leads. The results (reported in the online appendix) indicate that the negative effect of elections is consistently robust as we increase the number of controls for lagging and leading months. The estimates are remarkably consistent when we control for up to 11 months of lags and leads. When we control for the 12 months lagging and leading the election, the size of the effect declines as does the significance.

TABLE 3.3 Cement Consumption and National Elections

DV:	(1) Log Cement Consumption	(2) Log Cement Consumption	(3) Log Cement Consumption	(4) Log Cement Consumption
Lok Sabha Election$_{t-6}$	0.03 [0.67]	0.04 [0.91]	−0.03 [−1.12]	−0.01 [−0.34]
Lok Sabha Election$_{t-5}$	0.02 [0.39]	0.03 [0.65]	0.00 [0.11]	0.01 [0.60]
Lok Sabha Election$_{t-4}$	0.07* [1.93]	0.09** [2.06]	0.04 [1.45]	0.05** [2.01]
Lok Sabha Election$_{t-3}$	0.05 [1.26]	0.05 [1.14]	0.02 [0.59]	0.02 [0.88]
Lok Sabha Election$_{t-2}$	−0.02 [−0.46]	−0.02 [−0.40]	0.00 [0.06]	0.01 [0.48]
Lok Sabha Election$_{t-1}$	0.04 [0.96]	0.03 [0.77]	−0.05** [−2.04]	−0.04 [−1.50]
Lok Sabha Election$_t$	−0.10*** [−2.58]	−0.10** [−2.37]	−0.06** [−2.26]	−0.05** [−2.01]
Lok Sabha Election$_{t+1}$	0.03 [0.81]	0.03 [0.63]	−0.04 [−1.51]	−0.04 [−1.48]
Lok Sabha Election$_{t+2}$	0.00 [0.03]	−0.00 [−0.06]	0.01 [0.51]	0.01 [0.26]
Lok Sabha Election$_{t+3}$	0.02 [0.64]	0.02 [0.48]	0.07*** [2.76]	0.06** [2.56]
Lok Sabha Election$_{t+4}$	−0.04 [−1.14]	−0.05 [−1.07]	0.02 [0.93]	0.03 [1.40]
Lok Sabha Election$_{t+5}$	−0.05 [−1.35]	−0.05 [−1.26]	−0.02 [−0.83]	−0.01 [−0.23]
Lok Sabha Election$_{t+6}$	0.02 [0.56]	0.02 [0.52]	−0.03 [−1.02]	−0.00 [−0.11]
Fixed effects	—	Year	State–Month	Year and State–Month
Observations	2,856	2,856	2,856	2,856
R-squared	0.95	0.95	0.97	0.97
Number of states	17	17	17	17

Source: Authors.

Note: Z statistics in brackets. *significant at 10 per cent; **significant at 5 per cent; ***significant at 1 per cent. All models include three lags of the dependent variable. Model (2) includes year fixed effects; Model (3) includes fixed effects for each state–month combination; and Model (4) includes year and state–month fixed effects. Models are estimated using OLS with panel-corrected standard errors. Dependent variable is natural log of cement consumption.

seasonal effects, respectively. The result holds although the coefficient is smaller once seasonal effects are included. In column 4, we include both sets of fixed effects and the results here indicate that national elections are associated with a per cent decline in the level of cement consumption.[75]

Dual Elections

Our next hypothesis posits that the magnitude of the contraction in cement consumption should be larger for 'dual' elections—those instances in which states are concurrently holding state and national elections—than if only a state or national election is being held. As column 1 of Table 3.4 attests, the negative effect of *Dual Election* on cement consumption is three times as strong as that of state elections. Dual elections are associated with a 38 per cent drop in the level of cement consumption. This result suggests the imperative for election finance is significantly larger when candidates for state and national elections need to raise funds for their respective campaigns simultaneously.

Urban–Rural States

We further hypothesized that the negative effect of elections of cement consumption should be larger in urban than in rural states. Columns 2 and 3 of Table 3.4 split the sample into urban and rural states. State elections are associated with a statistically significant decline in cement consumption across both urban and rural states. It appears at first glance that the effect is stronger for urban than rural states (15 per cent versus 11 per cent, respectively). Yet, regressions using an interaction term (not presented here) find that this difference is not statistically significant.

Political Competition

Our fifth and final hypothesis explores the effect of political competition on the relationship between state elections and cement consumption.

[75] We also experiment with adding additional dummies for the lags and leads of the election month dummy variable. The results can be found in the online appendix.

TABLE 3.4 Cement Consumption, Additional Hypotheses

	(1)	(2)	(3)	(4)
DV:	Log Cement Consumption	Log Cement Consumption	Log Cement Consumption	Log Cement Consumption
Sample:	All	Urban	Rural	All
Election$_{t-6}$	0.05** [2.06]	0.09*** [3.12]	0.06 [1.53]	0.06*** [2.79]
Election$_{t-5}$	−0.01 [−0.45]	−0.00 [−0.00]	0.01 [0.39]	0.00 [0.22]
Election$_{t-4}$	−0.01 [−0.46]	0.03 [0.85]	−0.06* [−1.69]	−0.01 [−0.51]
Election$_{t-3}$	−0.02 [−1.00]	−0.04 [−1.44]	−0.03 [−0.86]	−0.03 [−1.35]
Election$_{t-2}$	0.02 [0.96]	0.00 [0.04]	0.04 [1.03]	0.02 [0.75]
Election$_{t-1}$	−0.01 [−0.26]	0.00 [0.12]	−0.00 [−0.09]	0.01 [0.62]
Election	−0.02 [−1.05]	−0.15*** [−4.95]	−0.11*** [−3.04]	
Dual Election	−0.38*** [−5.86]			
Lok Sabha Election	0.00 [0.10]			
Election$_{t+1}$	0.02 [1.06]	0.06* [1.91]	−0.01 [−0.17]	0.04* [1.66]
Election$_{t+2}$	0.01 [0.56]	0.05* [1.77]	−0.00 [−0.10]	0.03 [1.33]
Election$_{t+3}$	0.06*** [2.61]	0.07** [2.21]	0.02 [0.50]	0.04* [1.67]
Election$_{t+4}$	0.03 [1.29]	0.01 [0.34]	0.03 [0.74]	0.02 [0.82]

(Cont'd)

TABLE 3.4 (Cont'd)

	(1)	(2)	(3)	(4)
DV:	Log Cement Consumption	Log Cement Consumption	Log Cement Consumption	Log Cement Consumption
Sample:	All	Urban	Rural	All
$Election_{t+5}$	0.03 [1.17]	0.06* [1.78]	0.01 [0.38]	0.05** [2.11]
$Election_{t+6}$	−0.00 [−0.17]	0.02 [0.66]	−0.01 [−0.20]	0.01 [0.37]
Low Margin				−0.02 [−1.29]
Med Margin				−0.01 [−1.53]
Fixed effects	Year and State-Month	Time and State-Month	Time and State-Month	Time and State-Month
Observations	2,856	1,512	1,344	2,856
R-squared	0.97	0.95	0.98	0.97
Number of states	17	9	8	17

Source: Authors.

Note: Z statistics in brackets. * significant at 10 per cent; ** significant at 5 per cent; *** significant at 1 per cent. All models include three lags of the dependent variable, time fixed effects, and fixed effects for each state-month combination. Model (1) uses year, rather than time, fixed effects. In Model (4), *High Margin* is the reference category. Models are estimated using OLS with panel-corrected standard errors. Dependent variable is natural log of cement consumption.

Specifically, we hypothesize that the contraction in cement consumption will be larger in more competitive elections. Our basic intuition is that more competitive elections are associated with greater uncertainty, increasing the returns to the marginal dollar of election finance raised. To capture the extent of political competition, we take the simple average of the margin of victory across constituencies in a given state (*Margin*). In the regressions, we then create dummy variables for each of three categories of competition. An election is classified as *Low Margin* if the margin of victory is in the 25th percentile or below (that is, where the margin of victory is 10 per cent or below). *Medium Margin* and *High Margin* elections are those between the 25th and 75th percentiles (between 10 and 14 per cent margin) and 75th percentile and above (greater than 14 per cent margin of victory), respectively.

Our results, from column 4 of Table 3.4, indicate that—relative to elections with high margins of victory—more competitive elections (or those where margins are classified as *Low Margin* or *Medium Margin*) are associated with greater declines in cement consumption, although the differences are not statistically significant. Since the cut-points chosen for classifying competitive elections are somewhat arbitrary, as an additional test, we also estimate a model using a dummy variable for whether the margin of victory is below the median margin of victory in our dataset. Here too, the results (available on request) demonstrate that elections where the margin is below the median are associated with greater declines in cement consumption, but once again the differences are not significant.

Alternative Explanations

Thus far, we have demonstrated that there is a robust, negative relationship between cement consumption and elections.[76] We believe this is indicative of the role builders play as financiers of elections. In this penultimate section, we address challenges to our interpretation of the results.

---

[76] We also conducted several other robustness checks, which we briefly describe in the online appendix.

Economic Uncertainty

One alternative explanation is that the decline in cement consumption is not symptomatic of the construction sector's role as a conduit for election finance, but instead the outcome of a decline in economic activity arising out of pre-election political uncertainty. For instance, Canes-Wrone and Park argue that, in advanced democracies, political uncertainty associated with elections induces private-sector actors to postpone investments with high costs of reversal.[77] Hence, elections are associated with a decline in economic activity, or a 'reverse business cycle'.

We do not believe that there is theoretical support for such a view in the context of India. For starters, the argument that general economic activity contracts on account of election-induced uncertainty stands in contrast to much of the literature on political business cycles in developing countries. Indeed, this literature suggests that policymakers in developing democracies induce short-term economic *expansions* (and increase deficits) before elections.[78] Studies of India have reached similar conclusions including work by Stuti Khemani, who finds support for an expansion in public works projects, such as road construction, in anticipation of elections.[79]

Furthermore, we can devise empirical tests to help us distinguish between the election finance explanation we favour and the alternative hypothesis regarding economic uncertainty. First, we exploit the fact that India's parliamentary system allows for both 'scheduled' and 'unscheduled' elections. The latter occur when a government fails a

---

[77] Brandice Canes-Wrone and Jee-Kwang Park, 'Electoral Business Cycles in OECD Countries', *American Political Science Review* 106, no. 1 (February 2012): 103–22.

[78] Adi Brender and Allan Drazen, 'Political Business Cycles in New Versus Established Democracies', *Journal of Monetary Economics* 52, no. 7 (October 2005): 1271–95; Min Shi and Jakob Svensson, 'Political Budget Cycles: Do They Differ Across Countries and Why?' *Journal of Public Economics* 90, no. 8–9 (September 2006): 1367–89.

[79] Shawn Cole, 'Fixing Market Failures or Fixing Elections? Elections, Banks, and Agricultural Lending in India', *American Economic Journals: Applied Economics* 1, no. 1 (January 2009): 219–50; Stuti Khemani, 'Political Cycles in a Developing Economy: Effect of Elections in the Indian States', *Journal of Development Economics* 73, no. 1 (February 2004): 125–54.

vote of no confidence or calls early elections. According to our election finance logic, we hypothesize that the contraction in cement consumption will be larger for scheduled elections (*Scheduled Election*) compared to unscheduled elections. When elections occur as scheduled, there is a degree of certainty that allows builders and politicians to coordinate activities and they have an ex ante schedule to guide their transactions. When unscheduled elections are held, it is likely to be more difficult for builders to adjust their activities accordingly. In addition, builders might be less certain about the political outlook for the state and the electoral fortunes of various parties.

The logic of economic uncertainty would suggest the exact opposite hypothesis: given the uncertainty attached to unscheduled elections (often sparked by political instability and/or unforeseen events), the pace of economic activity should slow down as firms grapple with a potential change in government. So, if uncertainty were driving the decline in cement consumption, this decline should be greater in unscheduled elections.[80]

To adjudicate between these two explanations, we re-estimate our baseline model, replacing our election dummy variable with a dummy variable for scheduled elections. Our results, for state and national elections, can be found in Table 3.5 (for ease of comparison, we also show our original results using the standard election dummy). The occurrence of scheduled state elections (column 2) has a significant negative effect on cement consumption. Cement consumption declines by 15 per cent during the month of scheduled elections. In line with our election finance logic, the coefficient on the scheduled state election variable is slightly larger than when we considered all state elections (column 1). As for scheduled national elections, we find that the negative impact is slightly more pronounced, comparing the result in column 4 to the baseline regression in column 3. Column 4 reports an 8 per cent decline in cement consumption for scheduled national

---

[80] There is another advantage to distinguishing between scheduled and unscheduled elections. Since elections in a parliamentary system can be considered endogenous, unscheduled elections might be related to economic factors that are correlated with changes in the construction sector. Hence, there is a concern that governments might call early elections for some reason that might also be correlated with changes in the economy that could impact the demand for cement.

TABLE 3.5 Cement Consumption and Scheduled Elections

DV:	(1) Log Cement Consumption	(2) Log Cement Consumption	(3) Log Cement Consumption	(4) Log Cement Consumption
Election Type:	State	State	National	National
Election$_{t-6}$	0.06*** [2.69]	0.06*** [2.76]	-0.01 [-0.34]	-0.01 [-0.30]
Election$_{t-5}$	-0.00 [-0.03]	-0.00 [-0.04]	0.01 [0.60]	0.01 [0.62]
Election$_{t-4}$	-0.02 [-0.69]	-0.01 [-0.67]	0.05** [2.01]	0.05** [2.07]
Election$_{t-3}$	-0.03 [-1.55]	-0.03 [-1.55]	0.02 [0.88]	0.02 [0.82]
Election$_{t-2}$	0.01 [0.55]	0.01 [0.54]	0.01 [0.48]	0.01 [0.54]
Election$_{t-1}$	0.00 [0.21]	0.00 [0.19]	-0.04 [-1.50]	-0.04 [-1.55]
Election	-0.12*** [-5.44]		-0.05** [-2.01]	
Scheduled Election		-0.15*** [-5.58]		-0.08** [-2.56]
Election$_{t+1}$	0.03 [1.29]	0.03 [1.27]	-0.04 [-1.48]	-0.04 [-1.52]
Election$_{t+2}$	0.03 [1.17]	0.03 [1.20]	0.01 [0.26]	0.00 [0.16]
Election$_{t+3}$	0.04 [1.56]	0.04 [1.56]	0.06** [2.56]	0.06*** [2.58]
Election$_{t+4}$	0.01 [0.63]	0.01 [0.63]	0.03 [1.40]	0.03 [1.34]

	(1)	(2)	(3)	(4)
Election$_{t+5}$	0.04* [1.82]	0.04* [1.87]	−0.01 [−0.23]	−0.00 [−0.15]
Election$_{t+6}$	0.00 [0.20]	0.00 [0.20]	−0.00 [−0.11]	−0.00 [−0.14]
Fixed effects	Time & State-Month	Time & State-Month	Year & State-Month	Year & State-Month
Observations	2,856	2,856	2,856	2,856
R-squared	0.97	0.97	0.97	0.97
Number of states	17	17	17	17

Source: Authors.

Note: Z statistics in brackets. *significant at 10 per cent; **significant at 5 per cent; ***significant at 1 per cent. All models include three lags of the dependent variable. Models (1) and (2) include time fixed effects and fixed effects for each state-month combination. Models (3) and (4) include year fixed effects and fixed effects for each state-month combination. Models are estimated using OLS with panel-corrected standard errors. Dependent variable is natural log of cement consumption.

parliamentary elections. Our results seem to favour an election finance logic over one of economic uncertainty.

Another possible objection, also related to the uncertainty argument, relates to regulations enacted by the ECI. From the time elections are announced to when the date results are made public, the ECI enforces a 'Model Code of Conduct', or a set of guidelines intended to create a level playing field so that the government does not exploit the benefits of incumbency for electoral purposes. When the code is in force, the government is unable to begin major new schemes or projects. It is plausible then that the model code contributes to a decline in infrastructure building. We do not believe this to be the case for two reasons. First, the model code only restricts the government from announcing new schemes and projects in advance of the elections.[81] It has no bearing on the government's implementation of existing projects. Second, given the time lag inherent in tenders, contracts, and so on, the code might delay announcements, but it most likely does not impact implementation. After all, according to data collected by the World Bank, it takes an average of 147 days (in Mumbai) for a firm to obtain a construction permit.[82]

As a final test of the economic uncertainty logic, we utilize monthly data on the level of industrial production to examine whether the decline in cement consumption is robust to controlling for the pace of general economic activity. We rely on the monthly index of industrial production (*IIP*), an aggregate statistic that represents the status of production in the industrial sector. Since the IIP is a national-level measure, we cannot use this data to analyse state elections. However, we can use it as a control in our regressions looking at national election cycles. The inclusion of the IIP variable does not alter our estimates of the negative effect of national elections on cement consumption (as seen in the online appendix).

Production Shortfalls

A second alternative hypothesis relates to output changes in the cement industry. For instance, it is plausible that cement producers will anticipate

---

[81] Ujjwal Kumar Singh, 'Between Moral Force and Supplementary Legality: A Model Code of Conduct in Indian Elections', *Election Law Journal* 11, no. 2 (June 2012): 149–69.

[82] World Bank, *Doing Business in 2016.*

a decline in consumption and cut production prior to elections. If production significantly declines before elections, one could contend that our results on consumption are a direct consequence of cutbacks in production. We do not expect that production will decline prior to elections because cement is a continuous processing industry with increasing returns to scale.[83] This means that producers incur high costs if they choose to reduce their overall rates of capacity utilization. Nevertheless, we re-estimate our empirical model using monthly data on cement *production*, rather than cement *consumption*, as our dependent variable. We find no evidence of an electoral cycle in cement production (Table 3.6). Across all models, state elections are not associated with a significant change in cement production. If anything, there is some support for a small increase in cement production in the month following elections. In any case, it does not appear that the observed decline in cement consumption around elections is a result of a corresponding decline in cement production.

Consumption Smoothing

Another possible objection to our findings relates to consumption smoothing. If, prior to elections, builders anticipate the need to redirect funds to election campaigns, wouldn't they take action to 'smooth' their consumption? After all, private firms are thought to prefer a stable consumption path over time. Thus, if businesses know that their consumption will likely decline in the future, they should anticipate this by gradually redirecting funds over time.

While an impulse to smooth consumption makes sense in theory, we argue that it does not happen in practice for at least two reasons. For instance, one could argue that builders might prefer to provide occasional payments to parties and candidates before elections. However, as argued above, builders typically do not transfer cash to campaigns; rather they directly cover campaign expenses because neither party

---

[83] Elwood S. Buffa and Rakesh K. Sarin, *Modern Production/Operations Management* (New York: John Wiley & Sons, 1987). 'Continuous' production industries such as oil refining and cement are characterized by a discontinuous production function, increasing returns to scale, inelastic factor substitutability, and high barriers to entry and exit.

TABLE 3.6 Cement Production and State Elections

DV:	(1) Log Cement Production	(2) Log Cement Production	(3) Log Cement Production	(4) Log Cement Production
Election$_{t-6}$	−0.01 [−0.15]	−0.02 [−0.43]	−0.02 [−0.50]	−0.02 [−0.58]
Election$_{t-5}$	−0.02 [−0.33]	−0.03 [−0.54]	−0.02 [−0.43]	−0.03 [−0.79]
Election$_{t-4}$	−0.01 [−0.16]	−0.02 [−0.31]	−0.05 [−1.30]	−0.04 [−1.00]
Election$_{t-3}$	−0.03 [−0.36]	−0.00 [−0.03]	−0.05 [−1.16]	−0.05 [−1.25]
Election$_{t-2}$	0.09 [1.27]	0.07 [1.05]	0.06 [1.48]	0.04 [0.96]
Election$_{t-1}$	0.01 [0.10]	−0.04 [−0.62]	−0.03 [−0.76]	−0.05 [−1.10]
Election	−0.03 [−0.38]	0.03 [0.48]	0.01 [0.20]	0.03 [0.74]
Election$_{t+1}$	0.21*** [2.86]	0.20*** [2.69]	0.05 [1.26]	0.07* [1.67]
Election$_{t+2}$	−0.04 [−0.98]	−0.05 [−0.96]	−0.02 [−0.40]	−0.03 [−0.78]
Election$_{t+3}$	−0.03 [−0.66]	−0.05 [−1.02]	0.01 [0.21]	−0.02 [−0.57]
Election$_{t+4}$	0.00 [0.08]	0.01 [0.15]	0.02 [0.59]	0.01 [0.20]
Election$_{t+5}$	−0.03 [−0.69]	−0.01 [−0.10]	0.01 [0.16]	0.00 [0.07]
Election$_{t+6}$	0.01 [0.13]	0.01 [0.12]	0.00 [0.03]	0.00 [0.10]
Fixed effects	–	Time	State-Month	Time & State-Month
Observations	2,579	2,579	2,579	2,579
R-squared	0.96	0.96	0.99	0.99
Number of states	17	17	17	17

Source: Authors.

Note: Z statistics in brackets. * significant at 10 per cent; ** significant at 5 per cent; *** significant at 1 per cent. All models include two lags of the dependent variable. Model (2) includes time fixed effects; Model (3) includes fixed effects for each state-month combination; and Model (4) includes time and state-month fixed effects. Models are estimated using OLS with panel-corrected standard errors. Dependent variable is natural log of cement production.

wants an official record of the transaction. This is particularly true for politicians, who do not want to have suspicious assets show up in their accounts (which they must publicly disclose under Indian law when filing their nomination papers). Thus, if builders, anticipating elections, redirected funds to politicians in instalments, it would defeat the purpose of keeping these transactions in the 'black'. Instead, politicians desire funds during election season because these funds can be directly routed into campaign expenditures, without keeping them on their own books—a 'cash in, cash out' system.

Second, because builders operate in a cash-intensive environment, there might also be constraints on their liquidity that hamper their ability to smooth consumption. First, as was mentioned earlier, banks are generally cautious about lending to the construction sector. RBI regulations mandate that banks' exposure to real estate lending be no more than 15 per cent of a bank's total deposits.[84] Second, banks are unlikely to provide builders with financing to address liquidity constraints in advance of elections when the underlying motivations are expressly political. Third, election-season borrowing is likely to be costly for builders because the cost of borrowing will increase if the general demand for credit is higher as elections approach.

Finally, builders are less concerned with production slowdowns than firms in comparable sectors because many customers in India's property market sign contracts with builders prior to construction (called 'bookings') and make substantial advance payments to builders up front (often with a corruption premium).[85] This is a consequence of the fact that there is a serious supply–demand imbalance in the marketplace, which tilts the balance of power in favour of builders rather than consumers.[86] Advance payments mean that builders in India are

[84] 'Master Circular on Exposure Norms and Statutory/Other Restrictions–UCBs', *Reserve Bank of India*, 1 July 2009; Ila Patnaik, Ajay Shah, and A. Suri, 'Managing Boom and Bust in Real Estate: What Lessons Can India Offer?' (working paper, National Institute of Public Finance and Policy, 2011). Patnaik, Shah, and Suri find that penetration of commercial finance in the real estate sector is very low in India.

[85] 'Property in Mumbai: The Minimum City', *Economist*, 9 June 2012.

[86] World Bank, *Urbanization beyond Municipal Boundaries*. This, in turn, is driven by artificial constraints on land use, which are kept in place in order to create 'scarcity rents' for vested interests.

far less concerned than they might otherwise be in other countries about the timely completion of projects.

It is also possible that builders accept the idea that providing election finance—and thus facing a short-term liquidity shortage—is part of the cost of doing business in a highly regulated economy. Builders may be willing to put up with a temporary slowdown in building activity if they are reaping benefits from the state in other ways.

Other Explanations

Before concluding, we briefly address several other possible alternative explanations. One alternative is that construction slows down during elections because labourers employed by builders are being used as temporary labour for campaigns. However, such a hypothesis assumes that only labour from the construction sector is used for elections and not from other sectors (we noted earlier our measure of industrial production does not decline during elections). There is no obvious reason why this might be the case.

A second alternative explanation involves migrant labour. Across India, the construction sector is thought to employ a significant number of migrant workers. If migrant workers return home to vote in elections, this might create a labour supply shortage in their state of residence—hence accounting for a slowdown in construction activity. However, this argument falls short because of India's system of staggered elections. A worker from the state of Bihar (a state with net out-migration) who is working on construction projects in Maharashtra (a state with net in-migration) might take leave to go home to Bihar to vote in its state elections. This could possibly have an impact on cement consumption in Maharashtra but it should not have any impact on cement consumption in Bihar. However, we find evidence of exactly the opposite effect: in this scenario, it is cement consumption in Bihar that declines.

A final alternative explanation relates to transportation. Construction activity could decline prior to elections if the transport of construction-related materials is constrained. Since trucks are in heavy demand around election time—for campaigning, transporting voters to rallies and to the polls, and ferrying election workers—there could be an election-induced shortage of transport vehicles, which might adversely impact construction activity. However, if this were the case, we would expect to see suggestive evidence of an election-related decline in economic activity. Yet, our regressions using cement production and those controlling for industrial production do not uncover any evidence of an economic slowdown around elections.

★ ★ ★

The presence of 'black' money is a well-known feature of elections in many developing democracies. Yet due to its opacity, much of what we know is based on anecdotal evidence or journalistic investigations. This chapter builds on the insights of a growing literature on regulation and corruption to empirically demonstrate—and quantify—illicit flows of election finance in India.

Due to the nature of state regulations governing land use, we focus on the role of the construction sector in providing off-the-books campaign contributions to politicians—a dynamic which the comparative record demonstrates is not uncommon. In particular, we use variation in the demand for cement to demonstrate the presence of an electoral cycle in building activity, using data from India. This effect is consistent with the belief that the sector serves as a key conduit of illicit election finance. Using a variety of models, we demonstrate that our key empirical finding is robust and address what we see are the leading objections to our interpretation of the underlying mechanism.

Our findings have broad relevance for the study of money politics in the developing world, where we are most likely to observe illicit election finance. There is a small, but growing literature in this area.[87] This chapter adds to this literature in two ways. First, it focuses on a specific sector—construction—that is widely thought to be linked with 'off-the-books' politics. Second, it contributes a novel measure for capturing election cycles in this sector that is consistent with its role as

---

[87] Daniel W. Gingerich, 'Dividing the Dirty Dollar: The Allocation and Impact of Illicit Campaign Funds in a Gubernatorial Contest in Brazil' (working paper, Department of Politics, University of Virginia, 2010); Maxim Mironov and Ekaterina Zhuravskaya, 'Corruption in Procurement and the Political Cycle in Tunneling: Evidence from Financial Transactions Data', *American Economic Review* 8, no. 2 (May 2016): 287–321.

a source of election finance. Our findings are also broadly related to the field of 'forensic' economics, which has developed innovative methods of estimating the private returns to political power. Work in this area attempts to estimate the extent to which firms benefit from possessing political connections.[88] A second strand of the literature attempts to identify the benefits politicians obtain on the basis of their political power.[89] In contrast to this larger literature, we place an emphasis on the role of election finance incentives rather than mere rent-seeking.[90] Given the centrality of the election cycle to our argument, this chapter is also linked to the literature on political business cycles.[91]

Looking ahead, we believe that this work has several implications for the field of political economy. Scholars need to pay greater attention to the role black money is playing across the developing world. If there are large sums of money moving through the political system independent of official expenditures, our estimates of election finance will be downward-biased if we do not take them into account. To date, much of the comparative literature focuses on licit flows, but such flows likely constitute but a fraction of total election spending in many developing countries.[92]

[88] Raymond Fisman, 'Estimating the Value of Political Connections', *American Economic Review* 91, no. 4 (September 2001): 1095–102; Asim Khwaja and Atif Mian, 'Do Lenders Favor Politically Connected Firms? Rent Provision in an Emerging Financial Market', *Quarterly Journal of Economics* 120, no. 4 (2005): 1371–411; Mara Faccio, 'Politically Connected Firms', *American Economic Review* 96, no. 1 (March 2006): 369–86; Seema Jayachandran, 'The Jeffords Effect', *Journal of Law and Economics* 49, no. 2 (2006): 397–425.

[89] Andrew Eggers and Jens Hainmueller, 'MPs for Sale? Returns to Office in Postwar British Politics', *American Political Science Review* 103, no. 4 (November 2009): 513–33; Raymond Fisman, Florian Schulz, and Vikrant Vig, 'The Private Returns to Public Office', *Journal of Political Economy* 122, no. 4 (August 2014): 806–62.

[90] Sukhtankar, 'Sweetening the Deal?' is a notable exception.

[91] Akhmed Akhmedov and Ekaterina Zhuravskaya, 'Opportunistic Political Cycles'; Shi and Svensson, 'Political Budget Cycles: Do They Differ Across Countries and Why?'; Brender and Drazen, 'Political Business Cycles in New Versus Established Democracies.'

[92] Susan E. Scarrow, 'Political Finance in Comparative Perspective', *Annual Review of Political Science* 10 (June 2007): 193–210.

Second, scholars should devote greater attention to understanding the drivers of election finance. For instance, greater political competition has often been perceived to be a positive development in democracies, as it provides voters with more choices and therefore better representation. However, more competition might also trigger greater electoral expenditure, as parties look to gain an advantage over their competitors. Similarly, more frequent elections have often been viewed as a means of delivering more accountability: after all, voters have more opportunities to follow Schumpeter's advice and 'throw the rascals out', if their expectations are not met. Yet, frequency can also have negative consequences: it can shorten representatives' time horizons and result in greater pressures to raise campaign funds. We need to develop a much better understanding of the determinants of the relative magnitudes of election finance.

Finally, as we argued at the outset of this chapter, the growing costs of elections—through legitimate or illegitimate channels—have serious implications for public policy as well as the status and functioning of democracy. In situations where public subsidies of elections are limited or non-existent, politicians are reliant on private sources of funding. Raising money from supporters raises at least the prospect of politicians shaping post-election public policies in ways that are beneficial to private interests.

Appendix

This appendix contains two items. The first is a table with summary statistics of the variables used in the quantitative analysis presented here. The second is a list of variables used, along with details of our coding strategy.

TABLE **3.A1** Summary Statistics

Variable	Obs	Mean	Standard Deviation	Minimum	Maximum
Election	3060	0.02	0.13	0	1
Scheduled Election	3060	0.01	0.12	0	1
Lok Sabha Election	3060	0.03	0.16	0	1
Scheduled Lok Sabha Election	3060	0.02	0.13	0	1
Dual Election	3060	0.00	0.06	0	1
Log Cement Consumption	3060	5.97	0.87	2.59	7.76
Log Cement Production	2802	5.38	1.76	1	8.07
Urban	3060	0.53	0.50	0	1
Margin	3060	0.03	0.05	0	0.26
Low Margin	3060	0.05	0.21	0	1
Med Margin	3060	0.12	0.32	0	1
High Margin	3060	0.05	0.22	0	1
IIP	2958	189.73	51.62	116.45	302.77

Source: Authors.

For those interested in more information regarding our statistical analysis, please refer to the online appendix, which can be found at http://milanvaishnav.com and https://casi.sas.upenn.edu/about/people/devesh.

CODING DETAILS

Election: Indicator variable that equals one during the month state elections are held. We use the following protocol for coding the month of elections. We use the date voters cast their ballots as the 'date of the election'. In those cases where elections occur in multiple phases (a common occurrence in larger states), we use the date on which voters in the first phase cast their ballots. If the election date occurs before the 15th of the month, we code the prior month as the election month. If the election date occurs after the 15th of the month, we code that month as the election month. Source: Election Commission of India.

Scheduled Election: Indicator variable that equals one during the month state elections are held according to schedule. Source: Election Commission of India.

Lok Sabha Election: Indicator variable that equals one during the month parliamentary elections are held. Source: Election Commission of India.

Scheduled Lok Sabha Election: Indicator variable that equals one during the month parliamentary elections are held according to schedule. Source: Election Commission of India.

Dual Election: Indicator variable that equals one during the month state and parliamentary elections are held concurrently. Source: Election Commission of India.

Log Cement Consumption: Natural log of cement purchases (measured in metric tonnes) recorded by CMA in a given state-month. Source: Cement Manufacturers' Association of India.

Log Cement Production: Natural log of cement produced (measured in metric tonnes) recorded by CMA in a given state-month. Source: Cement Manufacturers' Association of India.

Urban: Indicator variable that equals one if state is classified as urban. To classify states, we use population figures provided in the 1991 and 2001 census. We use the urban/rural population figures from the 1991 census to create an indicator for urban/rural states for the years 1995–2000. Using the 2001 census, we do the same for the years 2001–10. We code states as urban if their urban population is above the all-India median, and rural otherwise. Source: Census of India.

Margin: Simple average of the margin of victory across constituencies in a given state. Source: Election Commission of India.

High Margin: Indicator variable that equals one if the average margin of victory across constituencies in a given state is below the 25th percentile of elections in the data set. Source: Election Commission of India.

Medium Margin: Indicator variable that equals one if average margin of victory across constituencies in a given state is between the 25th and 75th percentiles of elections in the data set. Source: Election Commission of India.

Low Margin: Indicator variable that equals one if average margin of victory across constituencies in a given state is greater than, or equal to, the 75th percentile of elections in the dataset. Source: Election Commission of India.

IIP: Index of industrial production, an aggregate statistic that represents the status of production in the industrial sector for a given period of time compared to a previous reference period. Source: Ministry of Programme Statistics and Implementation, Government of India.

4   Navigating Fiscal Constraints

Dalit Parties and Electoral Politics in Tamil Nadu

Michael A. Collins

From the early 1990s, lower-caste voters have redrawn the contours of Indian democracy, inaugurating a period that pundits heralded as 'a new phase of democratic politics'.[1] 'Although overall turnout figures have not increased dramatically', as Yogendra Yadav has noted, 'the social composition of those who vote and take part in political activities has undergone a major change. There is a participatory upsurge among the socially underprivileged, whether seen in terms of caste hierarchy, economic class, gender distinction, or the rural-urban divide.'[2] In agreement, Zoya Hasan detected 'a dramatic upsurge in political participation', which she discerned particularly 'among the socially

---

[1] Yogendra Yadav, 'Reconfiguration in Indian Politics: State Assembly Elections 1993–1995', in *State and Politics in India*, ed. Partha Chatterjee (Delhi: Oxford University Press, 1997), 180.

[2] Yogendra Yadav, 'Reconfiguration in Indian Politics.' Also see Yogendra Yadav, 'Understanding the Second Democratic Upsurge: Trends of Bahujan Participation in Electoral Politics in the 1990s', in *Transforming India: Social and Political Dynamics of Democracy*, eds Francine R. Frankel, Zoya Hasan, Rajeev Bhargava, and Balveer Arora (Delhi: Oxford University Press, 2002), 120.

underprivileged in the caste and class hierarchy'.[3] Not only had social minorities begun to exercise their franchise in record numbers, but the period also witnessed the formation of autonomous parties advocating on their behalf.[4] In a study detailing how these developments altered the social composition of state legislative assemblies and the national parliament, Christophe Jaffrelot borrowed an expression from ex-prime minister V.P. Singh when he trumpeted a 'silent revolution,' referring to a mostly peaceful transition of political authority whereby 'plebeians' gradually began to dislodge an entrenched elite from elected office.[5] Taken together, these statements captured a critical transformation in Indian democracy, which they conveyed through a new, and ostensibly optimistic, lexicon.

While academic scholarship has surveyed the changing landscape of democratic politics in great detail, less attention has been paid to this 'silent revolution' vis-à-vis a parallel, disquieting growth in gross electoral expenditure. At a time when social minorities exercise their democratic franchise at an unprecedented rate, campaign spending has risen sharply from one election cycle to the next. Estimates provided by the Centre for Media Studies (CMS) project that aggregate spending in parliamentary elections more than doubled from 2004 to 2009, rising from Rs 4,500 to Rs 10,000 crore, before tripling to a staggering Rs 30,000 crore, or nearly US $5 billion, in 2014.[6] And, as M.V. Rajeev Gowda and E. Sridharan observe, political parties have acclimated to these heightened expectations with a clear penchant for fielding wealthy 'crorepati' candidates who are able to self-finance their

---

[3] Zoya Hasan, *Democracy and the Crisis of Inequality* (Delhi: Primus Books, 2014), 444.

[4] Pradeep Chhibber, *Democracy without Associations: Transformation of the Party System and Social Cleavages in India* (Ann Arbor: University of Michigan, 2001); Suhas Palshikar, K.C. Suri, Yogendra Yadav, eds, *Party Competition in Indian States: Electoral Politics in Post-Congress Polity* (New Delhi: Oxford University Press, 2014).

[5] Christophe Jaffrelot, *India's Silent Revolution: The Rise of the Low Castes in North Indian Politics* (New Delhi: Permanent Black, 2003); Christophe Jaffrelot and Sanjay Kumar, eds, *Rise of the Plebeians?: The Changing Face of Indian Legislative Assemblies* (London: Routledge, 2009).

[6] Anita Sharan, 'Campaign 2009 is Cool and Costly', *Hindustan Times*, 8 April 2009. 1 lakh equals 100,000; 1 crore is equivalent to 10,000,000.

campaigns and line party coffers.[7] Moreover, their study demonstrates a correlation between candidate expenditure and vote share, indicating that candidates who spend more tend to reap an electoral return on their investment.[8] Although expenditure does not in itself determine electoral outcomes, politicians recognize the influence of what is colloquially termed 'money power', professing that viable contenders must cross a minimum spending threshold to remain competitive. In effect, this often deters smaller, less affluent parties from facing elections independently and incentivizes a turn towards coalition politics.[9]

Placing this transformation of democratic practice in conversation with the accompanying uptick in campaign expenditure, this chapter raises a pair of questions regarding the electoral experience of social minorities in modern India. First, it queries how these new political actors—particularly Dalits (ex-untouchables), who continue to lag behind in development indicators and most often lack independent access to key sources of election finance—mobilize sufficient resources to fund their election campaigns. And, second, it considers how these fiscal constraints impact the democratic participation of Dalit political parties in India today, examining how the most prominent Dalit party in Tamil Nadu, the *Viduthalai Chiruthaigal Katchi* (VCK; Liberation Panthers Party), navigates challenges associated with election finance and electoral competition in a state widely reputed to host some of the country's costliest campaigns. This chapter presents an ethnographic study of electoral competition that considers how campaign finance norms affect the democratic participation of historically marginalized groups. Although financial constraints incentivize Dalit parties like the VCK to join electoral coalitions spearheaded by their more established counterparts, these arrangements do not strictly entail a *quid pro quo*

[7] M.V. Rajeev Gowda and E. Sridharan, 'Reforming India's Party Financing and Election Expenditure Laws', *Election Law Journal* 11, no. 2 (2012): 235.

[8] Gowda and Sridharan, 'Reforming India's Party Financing', 234. Also see Neelanjan Sircar's chapter in this volume.

[9] Hugo Gorringe, '"In the last elections we are so backward we didn't even get money to vote": Money and Elections in South India' (paper, annual conference of the British Association of South Asian Studies [BASAS], University of Nottingham and Nottingham Trent University, 20 April 2017).

exchange of vote banks for campaign resources and canvassing support. Rather, they entail complex negotiations that may undermine representative institutions, affect candidate selection, and structure the terms of electoral participation.

This chapter incorporates interviews taken with VCK politicians over an eight-year period (2008–16) and draws upon field research during the 2014 Lok Sabha Election (March–April) to consider how the VCK experiences an election campaign and navigates the challenges related to election finance and coalition politics. It opens with a brief historical snapshot of Tamil politics, introducing the state's Dravidian parties before proceeding to analyse how the formation of caste parties altered the electoral arithmetic (readers already acquainted with Tamil Nadu politics may prefer to proceed to the subsequent section). Next, it shifts our attention to electoral coalitions, assessing why smaller parties such as the VCK have relied foremost on financial and electoral support from their erstwhile Dravidian rivals. In return for these smaller parties mobilizing their constituents behind the alliance, the leading party finances and administers the campaigns of its coalition partners, lending critical vote-canvassing expertise and marshalling its extensive party infrastructure behind their candidates to bolster their electoral prospects. After outlining financial aspects of electoral coalitions, the chapter presents fieldwork from the 2014 Lok Sabha election, during which the author accompanied VCK General Secretary D. Ravikumar throughout his parliamentary bid, to examine tensions that surface on the campaign trail. Unpacking vignettes from the campaign period, the chapter provides an ethnographic study of electoral competition that explores how VCK candidates and party organizers navigate the fiscal constraints and social conflicts occasioned by democratic politics.

DECONSTRUCTING DRAVIDIANISM

Popular discourse often narrates the political history of Tamil Nadu as a hagiography of the Dravidian movement opening with the distinguished career of E.V. Ramasamy (EVR), a fiery iconoclast hailing from a wealthy merchant family in Erode. In 1925, EVR founded the Self-Respect Movement, an early precursor to the Dravida Kazhagam (DK), popularly known as the Dravidian Movement. Later rechristened *Periyar*, meaning the 'great sage', EVR professed principles of rationalism, self-respect, and caste eradication, while blaming societal ills on the disproportionate influence of Brahmins in the erstwhile Madras Presidency. In particular, he launched a vitriolic critique of Brahmin authority through inflammatory rhetoric that pitted a reified 'non-Brahmin' majority against a small Brahmin minority preponderant in government administration and educational institutions. The 'Brahmin' provided a malleable trope for the early Dravidian movement, signifying a foreign 'other' that was distinguished at times by religion (Hinduism), language (Hindi/Sanskrit), and apocryphal claims to ethnicity (Aryan); in effect, the 'Brahmin' provided the foil against which the 'Dravidian' was counterposed.[10] EVR's politics kindled an incipient ethno-nationalism that carefully glossed over caste divisions within Tamil society and crafted a social dichotomy that structured subsequent politics: 'Brahmin' and 'non-Brahmin'.

In 1949, acclaimed scriptwriter C.N. Annadurai, flanked by celebrated personalities in the Tamil film industry, steered a faction of young DK activists into party politics when he established the Dravida Munnetra Kazhagam (DMK), or Dravidian Progress Federation. Keen to seek their fortune in the newfound era of electoral democracy, DMK leaders harnessed the power of cinema and galvanized popular support through a politics of cultural nationalism that found a receptive audience in the early post-Independence period.[11] In 1956, the States Reorganization Act redrew territorial boundaries to establish more linguistically homogenous states in southern India; this, by implication, ensured a predominantly Tamil-speaking electorate in Tamil Nadu.[12] Language politics soon turned the tide in favour of the DMK. Although intermittent anti-Hindi agitations had gripped Tamil-speaking regions since the 1930s, tensions came to a head in 1965 when DMK politicians alleged that the central government intended

[10] M.S.S. Pandian, *Brahmin and Non-Brahmin: Genealogies of the Tamil Political Present* (New Delhi: Orient BlackSwan, 2008).

[11] Marguerite Ross Barnett, *The Politics of Cultural Nationalism in South India* (Princeton: Princeton University Press, 1976).

[12] Emma Mawdsley, 'Redrawing the Body Politic: Federalism, Regionalism and the Creation of New States in India', in *Decentring the Indian Nation*, eds Andrew Wyatt, John Zavos, and Vernon Hewitt (London: Frank Cass, 2003), 34–54.

to renew its earlier efforts to 'impose' Hindi as the national language. Speaking in a classical idiom evoking antiquity, DMK leaders stoked popular sentiments through an impassioned defense of an apotheosized 'Mother Tamil'.[13] As a testament to its broad appeal, the DMK featured among the first regional parties to wrest state power from the Indian National Congress in 1967.

Following his death on 3 February 1969, Annadurai was succeeded by M. Karunanidhi, a celebrated screenwriter known simply by his moniker: *Kalaignar* (the artist). Alarmed by the precipitous rise of cinema stars through party ranks, the DMK patriarch cast his eldest son, M.K. Muthu, in party-sponsored films as a shrewd endeavour to curb his rivals and consolidate his family's position within the party.[14] Whereas Muthu's acting career sputtered out of the gates, M.G. Ramachandran (MGR), an early DMK ally, converted his silver screen reputation as a patron of the poor into a real-life political persona.[15] Sensing a plot to arrest his ascendency in the party and convert his extensive fan base into Muthu supporters, MGR rattled sabres and raised allegations of rampant corruption against DMK leadership. Dismissed from the party in 1972, MGR converted his widespread network of cinema fan clubs into a grass-roots political infrastructure and, casting himself as the true heir to the principles of the late DMK founder, launched the Anna Dravida Munnetra Kazhagam (Anna's DMK or ADMK), to which he soon added the prefix 'All India' (AIADMK).[16] With MGR at its helm, the ADMK drubbed the DMK in the 1977 Tamil Nadu assembly polls, but health ailments cut short his tenure as chief minister. Following MGR's death on 24 December 1987, his former leading lady in the

---

[13] Bernard Bate, *Tamil Oratory and the Dravidian Aesthetic: Democratic Practice in South India* (New York: Columbia University Press, 2009); Sumathi Ramaswamy, *Passions of the Tongue: Language Devotion in Tamil India, 1891–1970* (Berkeley, University of California Press, 1997).

[14] Vaasanthi, *Cut-Outs, Caste and Cine Stars: The World of Tamil Politics* (New Delhi: Penguin, 2008), 56; Robert Hardgrave, 'Politics and the Film in Tamil Nadu: The Stars and the DMK', *Asian Survey* 13, no. 3 (1973): 288–305.

[15] M.S.S. Pandian, *The Image Trap: M.G. Ramachandran in Film and Politics* (New Delhi: Sage Publications, 1992).

[16] Sara Dickey, *Cinema and the Urban Poor in South India* (Cambridge: Cambridge University Press, 1993); Preminda Jacob. *Celluloid Deities: The Visual Culture of Cinema and Politics in South India* (Lanham: Lexington Books, 2009).

cinema field, J. Jayalalitha, consolidated her position in the party, which she led until her death in 2016.

From the late 1980s, however, Dravidian parties faced an insurgent challenge from 'below'. Whereas the DMK and AIADMK had peddled a monolithic vision of a 'casteless' Tamil society, the release of the Mandal Commission Report (1980), which endorsed a controversial extension of reservations (affirmative action benefits) to members of backwards caste groups, intensified the existing quota politics and undermined the Dravidian parties' capacity to gloss over caste-specific issues.[17] Appeals to 'Mother Tamil' failed to resonate as the vernacular of Tamil politics shifted from cultural nationalism to the politics of the backwards castes. First, in 1980, Dr S. Ramadoss founded the Vanniyar Sangam, a synthesis of 27 Vanniyar organizations representing Tamil Nadu's largest caste group under a single-point agenda: an exclusive reservation quota for Vanniyars in the state and central government and educational institutions.[18] After demonstrating the sheer depth of his political support through a 1987 road *roko* (blockage) protest that crippled transportation infrastructure and caused food shortages in the state capital, Ramadoss launched the Pattali Makkal Katchi (PMK), or Toiling People's Party, in 1989, which siphoned votes from Dravidian parties and often played spoiler in tight elections.[19]

---

[17] While Tamil Nadu had already established separate reservation quotas for backward castes (Backward Classes or BC in legal parlance), the Mandal Commission shifted the vernacular of Tamil politics from non-Brahmin to backward caste. In Tamil Nadu, this was led by the PMK, which demanded a separate reservations quota for Vanniyars, who subsequently gained formal recognition as a 'Most Backward Class' (MBC) group. In Tamil Nadu, most commenters use the term 'backward castes' to refer collectively to both BC and MBC communities; I follow this convention.

[18] Vanniyars, who are concentrated in Tamil Nadu's northern districts, constitute an estimated 12 per cent of the state population and comprise nearly one-third of the electorate in many constituencies. Across the 1980s, the Vanniyar Sangam mobilized Vanniyars though politics that underscored the relative deprivation of their community and demanded a separate reservation quota for their community.

[19] Historically, the DMK performed best in the state's northern districts. Because Vanniyars are concentrated in this region, the political growth of the PMK posed the greatest challenge to the DMK. See Andrew Wyatt

The following year, in 1990, national celebrations commemorat-
ing the birth centenary of Dr B.R. Ambedkar, a revered Dalit icon,
lawmaker, and chief architect of the Indian Constitution, spurred an
upwelling of Dalit mobilization. Across the 1990s, Dalit activists and
intellectuals launched virulent critiques against both Dravidian parties,
refuting their rhetoric of a 'casteless' Tamil society and raising allegations of endemic anti-Dalit bias. Pledging 'to turn the history of Tamil
Nadu politics on its head', Thol. Thirumaavalavan, among the most
prominent figures of this new generation of Dalit activists, mobilized
his community through impassioned rhetoric couched in a militant
idiom that envisioned political power as an asset (*sottu*) and beckoned
them to demand their due share. By the end of the decade, the largest
Dalit movements in the state, specifically Dr K. Krishnasamy's Pudhiya
Tamizhagam (New Tamil Society; PT) and Thirumaavalavan's Viduthalai
Chiruthaigal (Liberation Panthers), had gate-crashed the electoral arena
and entered party politics.[20] This transformation of non-electoral caste
organizations into political parties posed a sustained challenge to the
DMK and AIADMK, not only undermining their authority to speak
on the behalf of a 'unified' Tamil community, but charging their leaders
with shunting Dalit concerns while catering to a handful of affluent,
numerically preponderant backwards caste groups.[21]

Party System Change in South India: Political Entrepreneurs, Patterns and Processes
(New York: Routledge, 2010): 99, 102; S.V. Rajadurai and V. Geetha, 'A Response
to John Harriss' *Commonwealth & Comparative Politics* 40, no. 3 (2002): 120.

[20] Whereas Pudhiya Tamizhagam drew support primarily from Dalit-
Pallars in the state's southern districts, Viduthalai Chiruthaigal drew its core
support among Dalit-Paraiyars in the north, which are presumed to be the largest Dalit groups in the state. From 1992, Viduthalai Chiruthaigal was popularly
known as the Dalit Panther Iyakkam (DPI; movement). In 2006, Viduthalai
Chiruthaigal formally registered with the Election Commission of India
and thus became Viduthalai Chiruthaigal Katchi (VCK), or the Liberation
Panthers Party. Prior to 2006, VCK candidates contested under the election
symbol of allied parties. Hugo Gorringe, *Panthers in Parliament: Dalits, Caste,
and Political Power in South India* (Delhi: Oxford University Press, 2017); Hugo
Gorringe, *Untouchable Citizens: Dalits Movements and Democratisation in Tamil
Nadu* (Delhi: Sage, 2005); Andrew Wyatt, *Party System Change in South India.*

[21] The caste geography of Tamil Nadu enabled Dravidian parties to pit
locally powerful intermediate castes against Dalits in the electoral arena,

By the late 1990s, Dravidian parties had come to rely on political coalitions to face elections, wooing their erstwhile rivals with lucrative alliance pacts and, at times, allegedly sponsoring some parties to contest independently with an aim to split votes in their favour. Dravidian parties maintained their dominance, abetted by their influence over state institutions, extensive party infrastructures, and economic portfolios said to spread across construction, real estate, media, liquor, and private education, with additional revenue streams believed to flow from illicit mining and quarrying activity.[22] Further, both Dravidian parties dealt adroitly with successive national governments, leveraging their support at the centre to secure ministerial berths and procure the resources required to sustain state patronage networks.[23] Flush with financial means, the DMK and the AIADMK have not so much crowded out recent political contenders from the electoral arena as much as they have made use of party coffers to position themselves as the twin gateways into state politics, as chief custodians of the financial means and party machinery critical for election campaigns. Examining electoral coalitions in greater detail, the following section unpacks their associated financial aspects to investigate how money circulates during the campaign and its implications for allied parties.

---

exacerbating already contentious inter-caste rivalries. While Dalits are numerically preponderant across the state, comprising 20 per cent of the population, Tamil Nadu's largest Dalit castes are often less numerous than locally dominant intermediate castes (Dalit-Pallars and Thevars in southern districts, Dalit-Paraiyars and Vanniyars in northern districts, and Dalit-Arundhathiyars and Goundars in western districts). Scholarship lends credence to the close association of Dravidian parties with backward caste interests and has questioned the commitment of Dravidian parties to the most marginalized social segments. See John Harriss, 'Whatever Happened to Cultural Nationalism in Tamil Nadu? A Reading of Current Events and the Recent Literature on Tamil Politics', *Commonwealth & Comparative Politics* 40, no. 3 (2002): 97–117.

[22] John Harriss and Andrew Wyatt, *Business and Politics in Tamil Nadu* (Simons Papers on Security and Development, No. 50/2016, School for International Studies, Simon Fraser University, Vancouver, March 2016).

[23] 'Perfecting Patronage', *Economic and Political Weekly* 45, no. 50 (2010): 9.

COALITION POLITICS AND ELECTION FINANCE

'Our democracy is very expensive,' says VCK Propaganda Secretary
J. Gowthama Sannah as he leans forward across a wooden desk clut-
tered with legal cases.[24] Speaking just a few weeks before the 2014
Lok Sabha election from a shared law office at the Madras High Court,
Sannah continues, 'For a developing party like ours, money is a critical
factor when fighting elections and a shortage of funds requires that
we align with the more established parties,' referring to the DMK and
AIADMK. 'We have worked hard to consolidate our people,' he claims,
'but we lack sufficient resources to contest elections on our own and
this deficit poses a key dilemma.'[25] In response to financial constraints,
Sannah discloses, 'We have come to depend on the Dravidian parties.
They have been in power for so long and, therefore, possess ample
resources; they enjoy a wider financial network, and draw upon a
much broader economic base.' Although ruing this dependency, he
stresses that Dravidian parties provide necessary campaign resources,
monetary and otherwise, that bolster the prospects of VCK party
candidates. 'We hold clear principles,' Sannah asserts, 'but, frankly
speaking, principles do not always sell in an expensive electoral system.'
He continues: 'Electoral victory is critical for running a party. Once
you enter electoral politics, you must win elections. If you fail to do so,
you cannot survive.' While VCK organizers exude cautious optimism
for the future, they are wary of their present position, cognizant of their
party's less than stellar electoral record, having bagged three seats in the
state assembly and a solitary post in the national parliament since their
electoral turn in 1999.

Election campaigns in Tamil Nadu are extravagant affairs widely
reputed to be among the costliest in the country, but assessments of

---

[24] J. Gowthama Sannah, interview by author, 18 February 2014. Sannah
served as VCK propaganda secretary at the time of interview but has subsequently been appointed VCK deputy general secretary.

[25] This was particularly evident during the 2016 Tamil Nadu assembly
polls, which the VCK contested in a third front, the People's Welfare Alliance
(PWA), without the patronage of the DMK or AIADMK. PWA candidates,
who suffered a poll debacle, were portrayed in popular media as campaigning
while 'groping through holes in their pockets'. G. Jagannath, 'Third Front Facing Fund Crunch in Campaign', *Deccan Chronicle*, 7 May 2016.

gross expenditure are inherently imprecise as money flows into campaigns in staggered phases and from multiple sources. Electioneering kicks off well in advance of the notification period; that is, when the Election Commission of India (ECI) fixes polling dates and begins to monitor candidate expenditure. Prior to the notification period, Dravidian parties ink lucrative contracts with public relations firms and media consultants to gear up for the polls.[26] Nearly a full year ahead of the 2016 state assembly election, DMK Treasurer M.K. Stalin launched his *Namakku Naame* (We for Ourselves) yatra, a carefully choreographed journey designed to traverse all 234 assembly constituencies and address crores of voters. In local areas, Dravidian party leaders and candidates sponsor religious festivals and community fairs, organizing sporting matches alongside artistic and literary competitions where cash awards and prizes are dispensed among participants.[27] As the campaign machinery begins to hum, political organizers distribute party attire including banyans, saris, towels, dhotis, and mufflers among cadre, form booth-level planning committees, and cross-check voter lists to identify core and swing voters, a move said to facilitate cash distribution just prior to polling.

While the floodgates open well ahead of polling, spending intensifies once the ECI fixes polling dates and candidates file their nomination papers. In Tamil Nadu, Dravidian parties ply voters with cash, gifts, and alcohol during the campaign and woo public support with election manifestos laden with promises of 'freebies' to be financed by state tax revenue derived through liquor sales.[28] In recent years, these promises ranged from consumer electronics such as mobile phones and personal computers, to kitchenware, livestock, bicycles, and gold coins.[29] Further, the day-to-day expenses incurred by a campaign

---

[26] Sandhya Ravishankar, 'Old Wine, New Bottle: The Medium May Have Changed but the Message Remains the Same in Tamil Nadu', *Scroll.in*, 11 May 2016.

[27] R.K. Radhakrishnan, 'We Pay, You Vote', *Frontline*, 6 July 2016.

[28] Swaminathan S. Anklesaria Aiyar, 'Tamil Nadu Elections: Using Liquor Revenues for Freebies is not Economically Sustainable', *Economic Times*, 8 May 2016.

[29] Sreenivasan Jain, 'Almost Every Jayalalithaa Freebie, Including a Goat, Under One Tree', *NDTV*, 20 April 2016.

require considerable investment. Candidates traverse their constituencies in sprawling motorcades and host mega-rallies that may attract tens
of thousands of supporters, many of whom are paid to attend. Whereas
VCK candidates estimate that a budget assembly campaign requires a
minimum expenditure of Rs 50,000 per diem to meet basic expenses
and keep cadre on the ground, they project that Dravidian parties often
spend upwards of Rs 1 crore per week.[30] In fact, a leading VCK office-
bearer gauges that it is not uncommon for major parties and their
candidates to collectively spend Rs 5 crore in an assembly segment and
Rs 25–30 crore per parliamentary constituency to cover campaign costs
including food and wages (*batta*) for party cadre, rally expenses, vehicle
hire, petrol, salaries for booth agents, and what is sometimes referred to
as 'influence money' doled out to political rivals, neighbourhood and
caste associations, and even religious institutions.[31]

Then, there is the question of cash distribution, which is often
glossed over in media accounts as 'bribing' or 'vote buying.'[32] Although
the practice dates back to the early post-Independence period, the
salience of cash in state elections has surged from the early 2000s.[33]
First, during a 2003 by-election, AIADMK operatives reportedly
flooded rural pockets in Santhakulam assembly segment with cash and
gifts.[34] Then, in a survey of the 2006 Tamil Nadu Assembly Election,
CMS estimated that cash distribution had reached nearly 40 per cent
of the electorate. However, political insiders informed me that, in 2006,
Dravidian parties concentrated cash distribution among known party
supporters in an effort to retain existing vote banks and in select swing

[30] G. Jagannath, 'Third Front Facing Fund Crunch in Campaign.'

[31] V. Prem Shanker, 'Tamil Nadu Polls: How Money is Used as Instrument
to Woo Voters', *Economic Times*, 16 May 2016.

[32] For an excellent study of popular and academic discourses surrounding
'vote buying,' see Lisa Björkman, '"You can't buy a vote": Meanings of Money
in a Mumbai Election', *American Ethnologist* 41, no. 4 (2014): 617–34.

[33] In a 1962 speech at Kancheepuram, DMK founder C.N. Annadurai ap-
pealed that party supporters not allow cash payments from Congress to sway
their voting preferences. Sam from The Hindu Centre brought this video to
my attention.

[34] V. Prem Shanker, 'Tamil Nadu Polls'; Ilangovan Rajasekaran, 'The "M"
Factor', *Frontline*, 11 May 2016.

constituencies where they sought to tilt the scales in their favour.[35] But this all changed in 2009 when DMK operatives upped the ante during a state assembly by-election in Thirumangalam, where they reportedly covered the entire constituency with cash, distributing newspapers stuffed with Rs 5,000 per vote in what has since been dubbed the 'Thirumangalam Formula'.[36] Although this sum could not be replicated at a state-wide level, the DMK's inaugural attempt at blanket cash distribution signalled a new normal for Tamil politics. In recent years, Dravidian parties have fine-tuned their cadre-based cash distribution networks, which are said to reach a substantial majority of registered voters.[37]

Although media pundits and politicians alike readily concede that election campaigns are a costly affair, the sheer depth of their extravagance remains an open question. Not only does money flow into campaigns in staggered phases from multiple sources, but expenditure varies widely according to what my respondents refer to as 'candidate capacity' and, moreover, depends on the strategic value and competitiveness of a given constituency. Following the 2016 Tamil Nadu assembly election, one political commentator estimated that Dravidian parties collectively dispersed a bare minimum of Rs 1,000 crore in cash payouts directly to voters, whereas another pundit notched this figure between Rs 6,000 and Rs 9,000 crore.[38] Of course, both figures pertain solely to cash distribution and exclude costs incurred by campaign activity. When I raised the matter with a prominent VCK insider, he stated confidently that Dravidian parties may spend upwards of Rs 8 crore apiece in assembly segments and even as much as Rs 50–60

---

[35] CMS-India Corruption Study, *Lure of Money in Lieu of Votes in Lok Sabha and Assembly Elections—The Trend: 2007–2014* (New Delhi: CMS Research House, 2014).

[36] Sarah Hiddleston, 'Cash for Votes a Way of Political Life in South India', *Hindu*, 16 March 2011; A.S. Nazir Ahamed, 'Cash-for-vote: Genesis of the Thirumangalam formula', *Hindu*, 14 May 2016.

[37] R.K. Radhakrishnan, 'We Pay, You Vote'.

[38] See Sreenivasan Jain, 'Headline You Won't Read Post-poll …' *Business Standard*, 23 May 2016; 'Cash-for-vote May Result in Distribution of Rs 6,000–9,000 cr in TN', *Times of India*, 31 March 2016.

crore in parliamentary contests, all-inclusive figures that jive with those reported by media outlets.[39] Commenting on how the DMK and AIADMK are able to muster such profuse resources, he relates, 'Dravidian parties collect an election fund prior to elections. They first gather donations from their party members, which generates crores of rupees, and then amass far greater wealth upon soliciting contributions from corporates, media conglomerates, and industry.'[40] Moreover, both parties rely upon 'crorepati' candidates who finance the bulk of their own expenses.

Lacking political leaders of comparable means as well as independent access to key sources of election finance, the VCK has relied foremost on electoral coalitions with Dravidian parties to bankroll its campaigns. In exchange for support from allied parties such as the VCK, Dravidian financiers shoulder the lion's share of campaign expenditure, covering costs related to coalition propaganda, print and digital advertising, vehicle and equipment hire, political rallies, food, transportation, daily *batta* for party cadre, and additional day-to-day expenses incurred by campaign activity. Moreover, the Dravidian

[39] V. Prem Shanker, 'Tamil Nadu polls.' Although such a sum may appear outlandish, *CNN Money* cited one source that suggested upwards of $2 billion in 'black money' may have been spent to influence the 2012 assembly polls in Uttar Pradesh. Nick Thompson, 'International Campaign Finance: How Do Countries Compare?' *CNN Money*, 5 March 2012. Also, just prior to the 2016 assembly polls across India, as much as $9 billion entered the Indian economy, leading some to suspect that the upsurge in cash was related to the forthcoming assembly polls. See Charles Riley, 'Is Vote-buying Behind India's $9 Billion Dollar Cash Spike?' *CNN Money*, 11 April 2016. My respondents approximate that, in Tamil Nadu, half of electoral expenditure is allocated to cover electioneering expenses and the other half doled out to voters in the form of gifts and cash payments.

[40] In fact, such capital drives and party donations are well established. For example, The *Hindu* reported that three DMK districts secretaries representing Tiruvannamalai, Kancheepuram, and Tiruvallur together contributed more than Rs 20 crore to the general party fund over a five-year period beginning 2010–11. In total, the party declared Rs 158.52 crore in contributions and income, with far greater sums likely undeclared. See B. Kolappan, 'DMK Ahead in Receiving Donations, Ex-Ministers Top Contributions', *Hindu*, 25 March 2016.

patron administers allied campaigns, lending access to its extensive infrastructure and vote-canvassing expertise. Although Dravidian parties may earmark crores of rupees to finance allied campaigns, this cash circulates through its own party infrastructure, requiring that allied partners remunerate their own cadre and finance party-specific expenses. In effect, Dravidian benefactors commission their party apparatus to finance and administer allied campaigns, extending time-tested experience in vote-canvassing, marshalling their party infrastructure, and supplying cadre for electioneering work. Many of these expenses are remunerated in a closed feedback loop through lucrative contracts awarded to businesses associated with the party.[41]

In our conversations, former VCK candidates commented on coalition finance with marked candour, acknowledging the importance of external financial support while cognizant of the compromises that it entailed. A former assembly candidate recounted his failed 2011 bid, recalling:

> In 2001, the DMK supplied Rs 1 crore to support each of our assembly campaigns. In 2006, the AIADMK supported us during assembly elections and then, in 2011, we contested alongside the DMK. In 2011, the DMK allocated Rs 2 crore to finance my campaign, but this sum was managed strictly by DMK office-bearers under the category of my election expense. Every day, they may disburse some Rs 5,000 directly to me for my canvassing activities, fuel, posters, and related expenses, but they alone administer my election fund. On a daily basis, they may circulate Rs 10 lakh among their party cadre for vehicles, fuel, food, propaganda, *batta*, and other expenses.

Despite the coalition leading party allocating a handsome sum to finance their campaigns, VCK candidates nonetheless shoulder a share of the burden. They remunerate their cadre, purchase party-specific propaganda (that is, handbills, flags, posters, and the like), and cover

---

[41] Many election contracts do not run through party-affiliated businesses. For instance, the turn towards digital advertising has ushered PR and IT firms into electoral proceedings, although parties are nonetheless working to develop their own IT teams. The AIADMK reportedly amassed a team of nearly 82,000 'IT warriors' focused on digital canvassing during the 2016 Tamil Nadu State Assembly Election. See Staff Reporter, 'Poll Diary—May 15, 2016', *Hindu*, 15 May 2016.

miscellaneous expenses incurred by day-to-day activities not channelled through the leading party. Casting a wry grin, the candidate shrugs off the irony that despite strong financial backing he nonetheless accrued personal debts. He quips, 'Even though Rs 2 crore had been allocated to finance my campaign, I had to sell my personal vehicle to raise funds to cover my expenses!'[42]

Rather than an isolated case, this personal anecdote corroborates accounts shared by other party candidates. For instance, another former candidate recalls how the AIADMK allocated a generous sum to finance his 2006 assembly bid, but confirms that its office-bearers alone strictly managed the money, dispersing the funds through a combination of personal and party networks, with the AIADMK district secretary serving as the primary conduit. He recounts, 'In 2006, the AIADMK spent money through its own party structure; AIADMK office-bearers handled all the expenditure. Although their party provided substantial support to alliance partners including myself, AIADMK leaders managed the money themselves and, as alliance partners, we also bore many of our own expenses.' To supplement the AIADMK's financial support, the candidate mobilized an additional Rs 17 lakh through a combination of party funds, external contributions, and personal sources, yet he nonetheless recalls having been saddled with considerable post-poll debt. Pointing to the irony of campaign finance regulations, he grins when he confirms that even his personal spending, which amounted to a fraction of his AIADMK financier, exceeded the ceiling fixed by the ECI. Unfamiliar with the precise limit at that time, he fumbles for the figure, 'The expenditure limit may have been around Rs 8 lakhs. Actually, it was probably Rs 5 or 6 lakh; I don't recall.'[43]

Despite the financial support of allied parties, VCK organizers admit that monetary concerns factor among the 'important criteria' considered

[42] These personal expenses are frequently discussed as a wager: the pay-off is substantial if the candidate wins, often gained through rent-seeking in office, as evidenced by the considerable increase in personal assets that is often declared by elected representatives when seeking re-election.

[43] The ECI fixed a Rs 10 lakh ceiling for candidate expenditure in the 2006 Tamil Nadu assembly election.

when they select party candidates, even stating a preference for those deemed 'economically developed candidates'.[44] 'Can this person spend for their campaign?' one organizer asks rhetorically, before adding, 'If so, he will have an edge in a tight race.' 'When we select candidates,' another party organizer claims, 'we ideally seek individuals with their own financial means; those who own a car and can spend on their own without expecting party money.'[45] Yet, what some party leaders describe as a pragmatic accommodation of 'money power' has generated palpable resentment among much of the party's rank and file who, after decades of committed activism, feel shunted when party executive bypasses their candidacy applications in favour of wealthier aspirants. Long-time cadre contend that the party's *nouveau riche* joined after Thirumaavalavan dissolved the party structure in 2007 and conducted a fresh membership drive designed to court non-Dalits and religious minorities; a clear effort to broaden its social base, eschew the 'Dalit' label, and lend credence to its self-designation as a common party of 'democratic forces'.[46] But, friction between grass-roots activists hailing from lower-class backgrounds and the recent tier of middle- and upper-middle-class office-bearers has grown more pronounced in recent years.[47]

[44] This observation was made by multiple party organizers, yet candidate selection is widely left to the discretion of the party chairman, Thirumaavalavan, who did not comment on the role of personal wealth in candidate selection.

[45] In his analysis of VCK politics, Hugo Gorringe cites instances of VCK cadre criticizing the high fees that are now attached to applications for important party posts or to run on a party ticket. See Hugo Gorringe, *Panthers in Parliament: Dalits, Caste, and Political Power in South India*, 117.

[46] In September 2007, VCK leadership passed the Velachery Resolution, which dissolved the party structure and solicited fresh applications from previous office-bearers as well as new party members. The membership drive was designed, in part, to attract influential non-Dalits to join the party by offering plum posts. This, of course, riled many longitudinal VCK cadre. See Hugo Gorringe, 'Interview with Gowthama Sannah, Propaganda Secretary of the VCK', *The South Asianist* 2, no. 1 (2013): 76–7.

[47] Hugo Gorringe, 'From Untouchable to Dalit and Beyond: New Directions in South Indian Dalit Politics', *The South Asianist* 2, no. 1 (2013): 51.

The financial hurdle raised by elections offers a perennial challenge for the VCK, which has typically relied on political coalitions to
finance its campaigns. Commenting on this predicament faced by small
parties, a leading figure of the Congress party in Tamil Nadu stressed,
'Any small party that enters this electoral system, whether a caste-
oriented or regional outfit, must find their way through the Dravidian
parties simply to win a few seats in parliament or the state assembly.'[48]
As described above, Dravidian coalitions provide allied parties with the
financial means as well as organizational and technical support needed
to administer competitive election campaigns. Further, these arrangements enable smaller parties to 'piggyback' in other areas of expenditure
including print and televised media, state-wide political marketing, and
the more recent explosion in digital vote-canvassing efforts. Although
monetary concerns incentivize a turn to electoral coalitions, these
arrangements do not strictly involve a *quid pro quo* exchange of vote
banks for financial and organizational support because, as principal
financiers, the coalition leading party sets the terms of electoral participation. The following section explores inter-party negotiations to
offer ethnographic insights into how smaller parties such as the VCK
navigate tensions that arise on the campaign trail and investigate how
this impacts the electoral experience of autonomous Dalit parties and
their candidates.

LOK SABHA ELECTION OF 2014

Amidst the 2014 general election, VCK parliamentary candidate
D. Ravikumar stands atop an open-air jeep barrelling down rickety rural
roads connecting villages across Tiruvallur District in northern Tamil
Nadu. Today, an impressive entourage flanks his campaign vehicle,
including roughly 25 sports utility vehicles (SUVs) followed by a sea
of motorcycles with, of course, monitors from the ECI nipping at their
heels.[49] On this particular afternoon, the caravan loses its way and a

---

[48] S. Peter Alphonse, interview by author, 6 November 2013.

[49] For an account of the Election Commission of India and its expanding
role in the electoral process, see Alistair McMillan, 'The Election Commission
of India and the Regulation and Administration of Electoral Politics', *Election
Law Journal* 11, no. 2 (2012): 187–201.

wrong turn ushers the convoy into the neighbouring state of Andhra Pradesh. The mistake becomes evident when a polite bystander informs the candidate's driver that he is, in fact, no longer in Tamil Nadu. The navigator is cursed as engines roar to life and the caravan lurches back towards Tamil Nadu. A mounting anxiety is palpable among the organizers due to the sheer number of villages left to visit before ECI monitors, always lurking nearby, bring the activities to a screeching halt at 10:00 p.m., sharp. If a village is omitted, there is a prevalent concern that local leaders, waiting with shawls and firecrackers in hand, may interpret their absence as a political affront and reappraise their allegiance to the candidate.

Presently engulfed amidst a two-week blitz across Tiruvallur District, a motley caravan of rugged jeeps, SUVs, motorcycles, and autorickshaws (vehicles vary by day depending on local terrain) traverses half a legislative assembly constituency per day. As parliamentary districts often consist of six legislative constituencies, this entails 12 gruelling days of dawn-till-dusk electioneering during which the candidate greets voters across the district. Electioneering begins by 8 or 9 a.m. and concludes promptly at 10 p.m.; that is, when election monitors are visible. A festive atmosphere welcomes their arrival in remote villages and congested urban areas alike: crackers burst to announce the entourage's imminent arrival, and the caravan halts anywhere from 30 seconds to 15 minutes depending upon the size and electoral significance of the area, as the candidate and DMK leaders accept and bestow a reciprocal economy of silk shawls on local party organizers and address the crowd. Then, just as Ravikumar clasps his hands in a *vanakkam* gesture to implore the audience's support, the convoy abruptly sets off for the next destination. Impromptu delays impede its progress along the way: a key party figure faints in the midday heat; the PA system's battery dies and cannot be resuscitated despite a party engineer's most animated antics; and a residential annex catches fire when a cracker shoots awry, sending cadre scattering to fetch water to extinguish the blaze.

Across four weeks, I accompanied VCK General Secretary D. Ravikumar throughout his election bid in Tiruvallur District of northern Tamil Nadu. While the previous section unpacked how financial constraints incentivize smaller parties to join electoral coalitions spearheaded by their more established counterparts, the following section examines social frictions that surface on the campaign trail and investigates their implications for Dalit representation. These vignettes afford ethnographic insight into electoral competition, conveying how VCK candidates and party leaders experience an election as a smaller player in a major coalition and attending to tensions that arise during campaign execution. In what follows, I examine instances where direct electoral participation sometimes appears to silence the very voices often presumed to be 'surging' within India's expanding democratic arena, exploring inter-party negotiations and disputes occasioned by electoral politics. This section opens with an account of coalition formation, describing an instance when seat-sharing negotiations went awry and tensions spilled beyond the bargaining table into the vernacular press and public streets. Next, the chapter unpacks two vignettes from the campaign trail, leading with an account of a mass urban procession followed by a description of day-to-day vote-canvassing techniques.

Assembling the Cast

On 6 March 2014, the VCK inked a seat-sharing deal with the DMK for the forthcoming parliamentary contest.[50] In the prior 2009 Lok Sabha election, the DMK had allotted two seats to the VCK, Chidambaram and Villupuram constituencies, of which the party won the first handily by nearly one lakh votes while suffering a razor-thin defeat in the latter, coming up short by less than half of a percentage point.[51] In 2014, VCK organizers sought to increase their yield, requesting five parliamentary constituencies: four seats across their stronghold in the northern districts of Tamil Nadu along with Dharmapuri in the western districts, where recent anti-Dalit violence had effectively polarized the electorate and consolidated the Dalit vote bank.[52] While the VCK did not realistically expect to reap all five seats, it anticipated brokering a deal for three or, at the very least, retaining its previous allotment

---

[50] IANS, 'DMK Inks Seat Sharing Agreement with Dalit Party VCK', *Economic Times*, 6 March 2014.

[51] Thirumaavalavan won his bid by 99,083 votes whereas Swamidurai lost by 2,797 votes. Election Commission of India (ECI), 'Election Results—Full Statistical Reports,' http://eci.nic.in, accessed 10 December 2014.

[52] See R. Ilangovan, 'Caste Fury', *Frontline* 29, no. 24 (1–14 December 2012): 34–41.

of two 'winnable' seats. Instead, the DMK extended a solitary seat, Chidambaram, where VCK Chairman Thirumaavalavan served as the presiding MP.[53] After protracted albeit futile negotiations, VCK organizers begrudgingly accepted the DMK's offer. Why had they settled for less?

Days earlier, the AIADMK had expelled the beleaguered Communist parties—the CPI and CPI(M)—from its electoral coalition.[54] An act that many pundits speculated to be an ill-advised bout of hubris but later recognized as political genius, the AIADMK released an unprecedented declaration that it would contest elections in Tamil Nadu and Pondicherry independently without brokering seat-sharing arrangements with allied partners.[55] Wary that the DMK might embrace the exiled Communists as prodigal sons, perhaps prompting its own exclusion from the coalition, the VCK reluctantly accepted the DMK's proposal.[56] This, VCK organizers acknowledged, was less than ideal, but they nevertheless emphasized that a growing party such as theirs relies on the electoral support of an affluent, established party in order to conduct a competitive campaign.[57] Unsatisfied with the DMK's offer yet lacking viable alternatives, VCK leaders signed the seat-sharing deal, accepting the solitary seat.

Much to the chagrin of DMK party leaders, this pronouncement incensed a sizeable portion of VCK cadre who interpreted the paltry

---

[53] IANS, 'DMK Allots Chidambaram Constituency to VCK', *Business Standard*, 6 March 2014.

[54] S. Bridget Leena, 'AIADMK Parts Ways with Left Parties in Tamil Nadu', *Mint*, 6 March 2014.

[55] Syed Muthahar Saqaf, 'AIADMK Going it Alone for the First Time', *Hindu*, 10 March 2014. Although the AIADMK did face the election with allies, it did not allocate seats for their candidates to contest.

[56] VCK insiders who are familiar with the 2014 seat-sharing negotiations contend that the DMK misled them, stating that it could only offer one seat to the VCK in order to free up additional seats to bring the Communist parties into the alliance. According to party insiders, the DMK appears to have reneged on this promise and, upon finalizing the single-seat allotment to the VCK, made no more than an overture to the Communist parties.

[57] Gopinath 'Che Guevara', interview by author, 1 May 2014; Balasingam, interview by author, 19 April 2014; D. Ravikumar, personal communication, 18 April 2014; Gowtham Sannah, interview by author, 18 February 2014.

offer as an affront to the party's rising popularity, with some individuals even going so far as to dub the affair an instance of 'political untouchability'. In pockets across the state's northern districts, VCK activists, possibly at the behest of district leaders who harboured electoral ambitions, ripped DMK flags from flagpoles and effaced metal placards affixed to their pedestals.[58] At crowded intersections in Villupuram and Tindivanam, VCK supporters staged road *roko*s (blockages) and set ablaze effigies of DMK chairman M. Karunanidhi as well as his son M.K. Stalin, the DMK treasurer and presumed heir-in-waiting.[59] Ushering the protest into print media, a media-savvy VCK organizer facilitated an interview between party chairman Thirumaavalavan and *Dinamalar*, a popular Tamil daily, arranging for the article to run adjacent to a bolded caption proclaiming, 'We are ready to contest alone.' The DMK, whose Democratic Progressive Alliance touted strong support from social minorities, particularly Dalits and Muslims, mollified the situation by allotting a second seat in Tiruvallur District, situated just north of Chennai and bordering Andhra Pradesh.[60]

The DMK surrendered Tiruvallur District, in part, because party leadership forecast dim prospects in the constituency. Despite losing the previous Lok Sabha election in the district by a slim margin, recent intra-party squabbles had fractured the DMK's district administration into warring camps with little opportunity for pre-poll reconciliation.[61] Short on alternatives, the VCK, which altogether lacked a grass-roots presence in Tiruvallur, reportedly accepted the seat under the condition that the DMK pledge extensive support for both parliamentary campaigns.[62] With the coalition assembled, the VCK understood that

---

[58] 'DMK Offers One More Seat as a VCK Protest Snowballs', *Indian Express*, 9 March 2014.

[59] K. Ezhilarasan and Karal Marx L, 'VCK Fumes Over LS Raw Deal, Burns MK Effigy', *Indian Express*, 8 March 2014.

[60] B. Kolappan, 'DMK Mollifies VCK with One More Seat', *Hindu*, 9 March 2014.

[61] Some of these leaders were closely associated with DMK Chairman Karunanidhi's son M.K. Azhagiri who was expelled from the DMK a few months earlier.

[62] A VCK party insider recalled that DMK offered the Tiruvallur seat on condition that no further negotiations would take place. The DMK agreed to finance both campaigns and DMK Chairman M. Karunanidhi personally

it faced an uphill battle in Tiruvallur, where it hoped to stitch together a patchwork of Ambedkarite organizations strewn across the district, all the while relying on DMK office-bearers to mobilize their cadre and influence behind the candidate. Mindful that an unprecedented five-front electoral contest would soon engulf Tamil Nadu, a state that had long been regarded as a bipolar system led by the rival Dravidian parties, VCK leaders exuded cautious optimism on their prospects of winning both parliamentary seats and, thereby, securing recognition from the ECI. But, they remained cognizant that their party could just as easily draw a blank, as it eventually did.

In private conversations, VCK organizers acknowledge that their party relies upon financial support to face elections, pointing to the previous Lok Sabha contest as emblematic of how fiscal constraints impact election time decision-making. Upon reviewing internal nominations for the party's second seat in 2009, key decision makers expressed a concern that current office-bearers did not possess the financial clout necessary to finance a parliamentary campaign in Villupuram. After soliciting nominations from external candidates, the VCK first fielded S.P. Velayudham, a party outsider and real estate mogul who pledged to spend lavishly, but VCK leadership rescinded his candidacy following media reports that detailed an ongoing inquiry by the Central Bureau of Investigation (CBI) into an alleged land scam to the tune of Rs 171 crore.[63] Pressed for time, the VCK turned to K. Swamidurai, a retired justice in the Madras High Court and a known DMK sympathizer, on the final day of nominations.[64] Discussing his eleventh-hour nomination, party insiders profess that the retired judge was selected at the behest of DMK leaders in

---

requested that the VCK field its general secretary, D. Ravikumar, as the second candidate. Ravikumar has long acted as a conduit between DMK and VCK. Tiruvallur did not even factor among the initial list of five constituencies that the VCK presented to the DMK during seat-sharing negotiations.

[63] 'VCK Candidate in Land Cheating Case', *Indian Express*, 10 April 2009; 'Anticipatory Bail for VCK Functionary', *Hindu*, 1 May 2009, 8.

[64] 'VCK Changes its Villupuram Candidate', *Hindu*, 15 April 2009; 'Former Judge Files Nomination from Villupuram', *Hindu*, 25 April 2009; 'Total of 1298 Nominations Received for 39 Seats', *Hindu*, 25 April 2009.

exchange for, according to multiple sources, 'more generous campaign support'. One VCK leader, who forcefully expressed his dismay with the nomination, nonetheless underscored the pragmatic need to field a wealthy candidate, recalling, 'At the time, we felt that we could only win with money on our side.'

Viewed against this backdrop, the 2014 Lok Sabha election signalled improvement for some cadre as both candidates, Thirumaavalavan and Ravikumar, were respected party leaders rather than outside nominees. Still, the consequences of financial constraints on the party's electoral participation featured as a recurring motif in our personal conversations. Former party candidates acknowledge that their party, a relative newcomer in India's expanding democratic arena, relies heavily on financial support from an established party to bankroll its campaigns. Estimating a baseline expenditure, they project that, when supported by an affluent coalition partner, party candidates should however still spend between Rs 50 lakhs and Rs 1 crore to finance a parliamentary campaign. Despite underscoring the prominent role of what they refer to in English as 'money power', they nevertheless recognize that their challenges exceed economic constraints. Whereas campaign finance factors as the most frequently cited justification for Dravidian coalitions, VCK organizers acknowledge their limitations in vote-canvassing experience and party infrastructure, to which the chapter now turns.

Negotiating Allies

On the morning of 13 April 2014, I accompanied Ravikumar to the local office of the burly, congenial chairman of Avadi municipality, the largest urban centre in Tiruvallur District, whose smile radiates from beneath thin wire-rimmed spectacles as he boasts that this municipality, *his* municipality, is the largest in Asia—an apparent hyperbole. He hails from political pedigree, an established lineage of DMK office-bearers, and, on the side, commands an expanding share of Tiruvallur's lucrative garment exporting business, fulfilling contracts and dispatching brand-name merchandise across the globe. Furthermore, he recently diversified his business portfolio to include brick kilns, thereby joining an already sizeable list of DMK organizers with a firm foothold in the district's burgeoning construction industry. Considering the prime location of Tiruvallur District in northern Tamil Nadu, encompassing the industrialized outskirts of Chennai replete with defence manufacturing, special economic zones (SEZs), and industrial production, construction provides a constant stream of revenue, aside from when it reportedly stalls during election campaigns.[65]

Today, this DMK party heavyweight will parade his prestige through the crowded streets of urban Avadi, publicly conveying his support for Ravikumar's candidacy while concurrently displaying the sheer depth of his political clout, and, not to mention, keenly reminding those within earshot of his service to the constituency. That afternoon, he orchestrated a massive urban procession that clogged the municipality's dense arterial roads. Cars, motorcycles, autorickshaws, bicycles, and even a few horse-drawn carriages eked a path through the town centre at a snail's pace, waving colourful party flags and donning masks of DMK Chairman *Kalaignar* (the Artist) Karunanidhi and his son *Thalabathi* (the General) Stalin. The procession brought the city to a standstill for several hours as police cleared the pre-approved route and media personnel scurried across overpasses and scaled household rooftops to capture the best viewing angle, struggling to cram the entire spectacle within a single camera frame.

Ravikumar acknowledges that his campaign provides a prime opportunity for DMK office-bearers to demonstrate their influence and, moreover, 'grease' their cadre base. He also admits that the Avadi rally achieved little by way of bolstering the public standing of his party as it was DMK imagery that captured the limelight: red and black flags flutter in the breeze, cadre of both parties don paper masks in the likeness of DMK leaders, and loudspeakers broadcasted DMK party songs. As the day-to-day execution of his campaign is financed and managed by the DMK, the leading coalition partner, the candidates of smaller parties, Ravikumar quips, often feature as little more than 'mute spectators' of their own campaigns. Many VCK cadre were unreserved in their criticism of the day's procession, charging that the VCK was *present* yet not *represented* during the event, galled that DMK iconography subsumed their party's visual presence. But, while these cadre bemoaned that such spectacles merely serve to augment the stature of the DMK, they professed that such mega-rallies generate

---

[65] For a detailed discussion of the relationship between election finance and construction, see Devesh Kapur and Milan Vaishnav's Chapter 3 in this volume.

unparalleled public visibility and media exposure, which enables them to reach a mass audience and publicize their election symbol to the electorate. During our evening commute to the district office, Ravikumar confirms that such rallies, despite being 'a public nuisance,' generate the political visibility necessary to bolster his candidacy. This was particularly important in 2014, when the VCK was allotted its symbol more than a week into the campaign period and, therefore, had to rely upon media coverage to broadcast its 'ring' symbol across the electorate. Election symbols assist voters, especially those who are under-literate, in identifying their party on the ballot.[66]

Though the Avadi rally augmented Ravikumar's public visibility, it also generated financial tensions that surfaced as the campaign progressed. Many DMK leaders, including the chairman of the Avadi Municipality, use campaign rallies to bolster their personal stature, shore up support among their constituency, and maintain their vote bank. While candidates of small parties rely on Dravidian-style electioneering to ensure broad media exposure and instill confidence in the electorate regarding their electoral viability, such political spectacles accrue on the candidate's expenditure report, which the Election Commission fixed at Rs 70 lakh for the 2014 Lok Sabha Election. Although candidates routinely flout the Model Code of Conduct governing electoral proceedings and evade ECI-imposed spending limits, recent monitoring procedures including video surveillance constrict a candidate's ability to grossly under-declare costs associated with public canvassing activities.[67] The pinch of financial monitoring became evident towards the end of the campaign when Ravikumar,

---

[66] Small parties not yet 'recognized' by the ECI rely on broad media exposure to broadcast their election symbols, especially as their symbol may change from one election cycle to the next. In 2009 and 2014, the VCK lost court bids to be awarded the 'star' symbol, which is popularly associated with the party's flag, as the symbol had already been allocated to the Mizo National Front in Mizoram. A full week into the campaign, the VCK settled on the 'ring' symbol to contest the 2014 Lok Sabha Election. They had run under the 'two candles' symbol in 2009.

[67] For an account of how candidates capitalize upon loopholes in campaign finance regulations, see my piece titled 'Cash, Candidates, and Campaigns', Center for the Advanced Study of India 'India in Transition' newsletter, 24 July 2014.

caught between personal egos and campaign finance laws, implored local DMK leaders to send back fleets of SUVs, wary that their presence might attract ECI video teams and press his assessed expenditure beyond the prescribed limit, prompting fear of disqualification.

While some DMK office-bearers utilize the campaign period to service their vote banks and gauge the public pulse, treating it as a mid-term progress report ahead of assembly and local body elections, not all party leaders are keen to support what they call a 'non-party candidate'. Whereas DMK executives, who are intent to bolster their electoral prospects by tapping into additional vote banks, are the figures who finalize seat-sharing agreements with allied parties, district-level DMK organizers, those effectively tasked with administering the campaigns of allied candidates, may not share these incentives. Instead, local DMK leaders often regard allied candidates and cadre with suspicion, mindful to maintain their local backing and wary to cede ground to a newcomer and potential future rival. Upon arriving in Tiruvallur, Ravikumar's first order of business is to solicit support from district DMK leaders including current and former MLAs and MPs. Aware that many of these individuals vied for the seat he would soon contest, Ravikumar exercises a delicate finesse in these interactions, acting with deference towards DMK leaders and pledging to collaborate should he be elected. But VCK campaign organizers sense their reluctance to deliver votes and express concern that local DMK organizers may pocket funds allocated by the party executive. Should the VCK win the seat, its victory would only augment the party's leverage in future seat-sharing negotiations to retain Tiruvallur. Expressing scepticism over the commitment of local allies to his campaign, Ravikumar muses, 'Why would they want to create another power centre in the district? It's simply not in their interest.'

'You Canvass Your Votes, We'll Canvass Ours'

Ponnivalavan stands a hair above five feet tall, his modest stature belied by a bellowing voice that reverberates throughout the vehicle he deftly manoeuvres across rickety rural roads. Initially jovial, Ponni grows increasingly riled as the campaign progresses. Although he is Ravikumar's personal assistant, his vehicle is routinely pressed to the tail end of the campaign entourage. He curses the cavalier demeanour of DMK bigwigs whose freshly minted Toyota SUVs blaze past the candidate's aged Mahindra Scorpio and he chides their ability to wax poetically on Ravikumar's merits as the 'DMK coalition candidate' while also keeping a miserly finger on the purse strings. Despite his occasional rancour during our daily commute, Ponni nevertheless acknowledges the importance of his party's alliance with the DMK. In particular, he underscores that the DMK not only provides access to financial support and critical infrastructure but, moreover, mediates the contested physical and discursive terrain related to caste in an elec-toral campaign. This is critical because, despite the party's deliberate efforts to build inroads beyond the Dalit electorate, VCK infrastructure is concentrated in Dalit settlements with only limited penetration in non-Dalit areas across the countryside.

Throughout rural Tamil Nadu, Dalits most often reside in a sepa-rate colony, or *ceri*, spatially segregated from the upper-caste settle-ment, or *ur*; a caste geography that compartmentalizes the electorate and structures vote-canvassing practices. Ponnivalavan's observation materializes as we pass through a rural Vanniyar village, Tamil Nadu's single largest backward caste group that is widely perceived to be at loggerheads with Dalits. As we proceed through a settlement marked with Vanniyar-caste iconography such as caste movement flags and freshly painted wall murals, I ask Ponni, 'Would you canvass votes in this area in the absence of the DMK?' He emits an uncomfortable chuckle, 'No, no, we rely on the DMK to enter these areas. Without them, it would be difficult to canvass votes in OBC communi-ties across the countryside and, in particular', he concedes, 'among Vanniyar settlements'.[68] On multiple occasions, vehicles and motor-cycles bearing VCK flags and banners stall at the entrance of these settlements, waiting for the candidate to proceed through the village accompanied by DMK leaders before rejoining the entourage as it departs for the next destination.[69] When I inquired about this practice

[68] V. Ponnivalavan, interview by author, 3 April 2014.

[69] Some VCK cadre see improvement in the past 15 years of electoral par-ticipation, noting how in the party's inaugural campaign, the 1999 Lok Sabha Election, both VCK candidates Thol. Thirumaavalavan and D. Periyasamy were physically barred from entering non-Dalit settlements in the constituencies where they contested, Chidambaram and Perambalur, respectively.

with the candidate, he acknowledged that caste provides a basis for vote-canvassing techniques in many rural pockets and confirmed, 'the DMK doesn't care about caste, only winning,' intimating that DMK organizers perceive VCK cadre as an electoral liability outside of Dalit colonies.[70]

In private conversations, DMK organizers conveyed their nagging concern that the VCK's reputation as a Dalit party may forfeit coalition votes, especially among OBC communities. As Dalit voters never form a political majority, OBC votes are critical for their electoral prospects, even in a reserved constituency where only Dalits may seek election. By their calculation, DMK organizers regard the VCK more as a liability than an asset in attracting Tiruvallur's non-Dalit electorate, and, in light of this, they carefully stage-managed the VCK's physical presence on the campaign trail, a concerted effort rendered visible through a noticeable division in spatial and rhetorical aspects of electioneering. In varying registers, DMK organizers advised VCK party workers, 'you canvass your votes, we'll canvass ours', denoting a separation in vote-canvassing labour. Twice daily, in morning and evening sessions, party workers entered communities across the district to engage in door-to-door canvassing. Knocking on front doors or calling into open entryways, they distributed party flyers, interacted with voters, and requested the community's support. VCK cadre entered Dalit colonies extolling the merits of Ravikumar and the VCK, whereas DMK workers canvassed votes in the adjacent *ur*, or upper-caste settlement, soliciting votes for the 'DMK coalition candidate'.

Vote-canvassing practices rely heavily on local experts to navigate the caste geography. As our aged Mahindra Scorpio manoeuvres through ramshackle rural roads, it develops a revolving door through which local DMK figures file in and out. These individuals possess close familiarity of the local terrain, dictating which roads to navigate down and specifying those to be avoided. More importantly, these guides possess intimate knowledge of the caste and religious composition of local communities. A critical piece of information is ascertained prior to the caravan's arrival in each settlement, 'What is the main community residing in this area? This block? This colony?' The guides advise, 'Here is a Muslim enclave. Now we are approaching a

---

[70] D. Ravikumar, interview by author, 18 April 2014.

Dalit colony. Next is the caste settlement.' These notes are scrawled on a loose sheet of paper and delivered by hand to the open-air jeep where the candidate, flanked by DMK organizers, greets local party leaders and community members assembled in a public space. While caste provides a basis for a division of canvassing efforts, it also shapes the rhetorical content of stump speeches. Political speeches are tailored to the audience, foregrounding targeted welfare schemes and identity concerns before Dalits, pressing a sharp anti-Hindutva platform to religious minorities, and outlining an economic development programme for those referred to collectively as the 'non-Dalits' or 'caste Hindus'.

As the political entourage progresses through consecutive settlements, the master of ceremonies (MC) calibrates the candidate's introduction accordingly. The MC waxes poetically on the merits of Ravikumar as well as his prior accomplishments as an MLA, but his affiliation differs based on local demographics. As they advance through a backwards caste residential area, the MC rattles off: 'Ravikumar, the DMK coalition candidate selected by our most esteemed *Kalaingar*! Ravikumar is *Thalabathi* Stalin's candidate! Ravikumar is *Kavignar* (Poet) Kanimozhi's candidate! He is our DMK candidate! Ravikumar, the candidate who will achieve victory!' All the while, the MC elides mention of Ravikumar's party and its chairman, Thol. Thirumaavalavan. When entering a Dalit colony, the MC flips the script: 'Ravikumar, he is the candidate of *Ezhuccitamilar* (the 'Surging Tamilian') Thirumaavalavan! He is *Puratciyalar* ('Revolutionary') Ambedkar's candidate! *Viduthalai Chiruthaigal Katchi* candidate, Ravikumar; the candidate who will attain victory!' In effect, the candidate's affiliation with the VCK is carefully tailored in response to local caste and religious demographics. Whereas the VCK brand reverberates throughout the Dalit *ceri*, it remains conspicuously absent outside of these settlements.

When I discussed vote-canvassing techniques with the candidate, he affirmed, 'Despite being in the DMK coalition, VCK cadre still do not canvass votes in some areas', asserting that DMK organizers 'assume full control of the campaign and take charge of vote-canvassing procedures outside of the [Dalit] *ceri*.'[71] Likewise, Nilavanathu Nilavan,

---

[71] D. Ravikumar, interview by author, 18 April 2014.

the VCK campaign manager in Tiruvallur, stated that in many areas, and particularly in rural pockets, Dalits focus on canvassing ceri votes while DMK cadre concentrate their activities in non-Dalit colonies. Declaring that this division is less pronounced in cities and towns, he says, 'Depending on the local context, VCK cadre may work alongside DMK cadre who canvass non-Dalit votes in those areas.'[72] In a separate conversation, VCK Headquarters Secretary Balasingam reports that, on some occasions, VCK cadre may canvass votes in non-Dalit settlements, but only when they are accompanied by the DMK, intimating that they typically limit their canvassing efforts to Dalit colonies. After a pause, he adds, 'Otherwise, problems may arise', implying that their presence may aggravate already existing communal tensions and jeopardize their electoral prospects.[73] Ironically, a prime opportunity to represent Dalit interests features among the party's most constrictive moments.

★ ★ ★

In the Model Code of Conduct governing electoral procedures, the ECI stipulates that 'there should be no appeal to caste or communal feelings for securing votes'.[74] While explicit reference is generally avoided, caste maintains a near ubiquitous presence on the campaign trail. Stated candidly in private conversations, DMK organizers regard the VCK more as a liability than asset in constituencies where its candidates contest, concerned that the VCK's popular reputation as a Dalit outfit may forfeit coalition votes among critical caste constituencies. In response, the DMK carefully stage-managed the VCK's physical and visual presence throughout the campaign, adhering to an established formula for political rhetoric and a carefully scripted division of vote-canvassing labour. This view from the campaign trail illustrates that democratic politics does not inherently suspend existing social

---

[72] Nilavanathu Nilavan, interview by author, 21 April 2014.

[73] Further, Balasingam suggests that these tensions were much more pronounced in the VCK's campaign in Chidambaram District, where the Vanniyar-oriented PMK has a stronger presence. Balasingam, interview by the author, 19 April 2014.

[74] Election Commission of India, 'Model Code of Conduct for the Guidance of Political Parties and Candidates'. www.eci.nic.in, accessed 11 August 2015.

prejudices or supersede entrenched institutions of inequality, but may, in fact, be premised on their persistence. While popular conversations sometimes reduce democratic politics to its quantitative dimension, the aggregation of vote banks in tireless pursuit of an electoral majority, it encompasses complex negotiations for the VCK, which must tread a difficult path that manages the exorbitant costs of electoral competition while maintaining its popular reputation for Dalit advocacy.

In 1943, Dr B.R. Ambedkar offered a prescient critique of money in politics that continues to resonate today. Referring to the distinguished careers of his contemporaries, M.K. Gandhi and M.A. Jinnah, Ambedkar declared, 'In establishing their supremacy they have taken the aid of "big business" and money magnates. For the first time in our country, money is taking the field as an organized player.'[75] Yet, in recent decades, this distinction between business and politics has only become further obscured. In contemporary Tamil Nadu, the leading political parties not only enjoy reciprocity with key corporate and industrial houses, but manage diverse portfolios whose profits, presumed to be acquired through a combination of legal and illicit means, provide a steady stream of revenue that finances election campaigns and bankrolls notorious cash-for-vote schemes. 'The DMK and the AIADMK have made the election campaign a costly affair,' VCK Chairman Thol. Thirumaavalavan recently charged, adding, 'A fledging party like us will not be able to match their money power.'[76] Indeed, the financial hurdle erected by electoral competition provides a perennial challenge for Tamil Nadu's most prominent Dalit party.

In the past decade, the salience of money in elections has only intensified. Commenting on this, N. Gopalaswami, a former chief election commissioner (2006–9), reckons that election spending has risen most sharply in states that performed particularly well in the post-liberalized economy and, specifically, in the southern states of Tamil Nadu, Andhra Pradesh, and Karnataka where 'a boost in economic activity has increased opportunities for rent-seeking.'[77]

---

[75] B.R. Ambedkar, 'Ranade, Gandhi and Jinnah', in Dr. Babasaheb Ambedkar, *Writings and Speeches*, Vol. 1 (Bombay: Government of Maharashtra, 1979 [2014]), 227.

[76] G. Jagannath, 'Third Front Facing Fund Crunch in Campaign.'

[77] N. Gopalaswami, interview by author, 24 July 2016.

Recounting his first-hand experience in the electoral field, Thirumaavalavan observes that campaign spending has increased markedly beginning with the 2006 Tamil Nadu Assembly Election. Corroborating Gopalaswami's conjecture, Thirumaavalavan avers that greater profits garnered through political corruption factor as a prime catalyst for rising campaign expenditure. Further, he attributes this growth in campaign spending to a fragmentation of the state's once bipolar party system and the reliance of the Dravidian parties on 'crorepati' candidates. Anticipating a change in the political field, he predicts, 'The Dravidian parties are losing their base because parties such as ours are splintering their votes. They have been forced to alter their strategy to preserve their vote share and have grown more reliant on money power over the past decade.'[78]

As discussed in this chapter, Dalit parties in Tamil Nadu have relied foremost on Dravidian parties to finance and administer their campaigns. Most politicians with whom the author spoke described this dependence as par for the course. Flush with financial means and equipped with extensive party infrastructure, the DMK and AIADMK have established themselves as the twin gateways into state politics. In exchange for the support of allied partners, Dravidian parties finance the lion's share of their expenditure and administer their campaigns, extending monetary, organizational, and technical assistance to bolster their electoral prospects. Although Dravidian patrons may earmark crores of rupees to finance their election campaigns, VCK candidates are nevertheless responsible for satisfying a share of these costs, including remunerating their own party cadre and covering party-specific expenses. From the experience of VCK party organizers, coalition politics is not simply a *quid pro quo* exchange of electoral support for financial assistance and vote-canvassing support, but it also includes complex negotiations that, in the recent past, have directly affected candidate selection, structured electioneering practices, and set the terms of electoral competition. Although the VCK undoubtedly contributed to a social revolution that ratcheted up Dalit expectations, after nearly two decades of electoral competition the party's future prospects remain muddled

---

[78] Thol. Thirumaavalavan, interview by author, 30 July 2016.

in the democratic arena. Yet, VCK leaders aspire to play more than a bit role in state politics and are constantly honing their political acumen. Reflecting on the parliamentary campaign, Gopinath, the VCK headquarters secretary generally called by his alias 'Che Guevara,' mulls, 'Today, we are watching and we are learning,' adding after a brief pause, 'Our time will come.'[79]

[79] Gopinath 'Che Guevara', interview by author, 1 May 2014.

5 Money and Votes

Following Flows through Mumbai and Bihar

Lisa Björkman and Jeffrey Witsoe

Drawing on ethnographic accounts and survey data from two extremely different (in some ways even 'most different') sites in India—the first from the city of Mumbai and the second from rural Bihar—this chapter brings anthropology's longstanding tradition of debate and theorization of money—that is of the work of transaction, exchange, and gifting in the contestation and reproduction of social trust and of relational hierarchies—to bear on four issues related to how we might understand the role of cash in Indian elections.

First, reframing theoretical debates about the role of money in elections allows us to push past conventional concerns on how transactional dimensions of monetary exchange might impact the workings of democratic accountability, and to instead explore the work that monetary exchange accomplishes in the producing, performing, and (re)configuring of social networks and hierarchies. Conventional theories of cash exchange (that is, contract theory) hinge upon the overly simplistic presumption that increased flows of election-season cash are a sign and substance of a decline in democratic accountability. We demonstrate instead that money is a medium and a methodological entryway for exploring how political contestation actually happens in practice. That is, rather than asking whether money is 'good or bad for democracy', we argue that the anthropology of money helps us understand just what it electoral democracy actually is and does.

Second, building on this theoretical reframing, the chapter asks *between and among whom* money is being exchanged. In contrast with the common presumption that candidates and voters are the primary parties to cash exchange, the empirical accounts from Mumbai and Bihar reveal the dense and diverse fields of social relation and political mediation that election-season cash exchange both produces and inhabits.

Third, the chapter investigates conventional presumptions concerning the *directional flow* of monetary exchange (that is, the presumption that money flows from above from party to voter, in an exchange for votes which flow in an upward direction) by turning attention to the origins of exchanged money. We show how the money that changes hands during the election flows laterally and multidirectionally from a wide variety of sources, speculation upon the origins of which comprises a key dimension of the 'work' that election-season monetary exchange accomplishes. These ethnographies challenge accounts that would describe sociopolitical mediation (or 'brokerage') as a 'conduit' for a purchase-like transaction between voters and candidates. Instead, building on a Latourian distinction between *intermediary* and *mediation* (where the former is a passive conduit that does not act on or alter the resource it conveys, while the latter is enlisted in the production and transformation of that resource), the chapter demonstrates that the relationship of democratic representation cannot be understood as a social contract, but rather as a dense web of socio-material relations in which money plays just one part.

What we find is that election-time cash both originates in, and is distributed through, translocal networks that are increasingly important in everyday political life. The flows of cash index candidates' access to these networks. Mapping the social and spatial geographies through which election cash flows reveals the ways in which economic change is transforming electoral politics, and also the ways in which political relations are transforming regional economic activities.

VOTE BUYING AND VOTE BANKING: UNPACKING CONCEPTS

In order to unpack the conceptual interventions suggested by our ethnographic accounts, it is helpful to first lay out the analytical frameworks and theoretical debates over 'vote buying' and 'vote banking'. The idea of 'vote buying'—which suggests an unholy marriage of modern institutions and universalist imaginary of liberal democracy with particularistic and short-sighted impulses of marketized exchange—demonstrates both continuity with as well as divergence from the concept of 'patronage politics', often known in the Indian context as 'vote banking'. It is thus worth spending a moment to elaborate on the 'vote banking' idea, and to situate it within the broader historical framework of scholarship on Indian political development. In his classic 1955 essay on 'The Social Structure of a Mysore Village,' written during the first decade of independence, M.N. Srinivas famously introduced the term 'vote bank' into discussions of India's post-Independence electoral politics:

> The coming of elections gives fresh opportunities for the crystallization of parties around patrons. Each patron may be said to have a 'vote bank' which he can place at the disposal of a provincial or national party for a consideration which is not mentioned but implied. The secret ballot helps to preserve the marginal affiliation of the marginal clients.[1]

In Srinivas's formulation, 'vote banking' describes a process involving three different categories of actor: voters, parties, and 'middlemen'. The interconnections among these actors are characterized as vertical in structure, involving two separate spheres of caste-inflected patron–client interface: first, between the voter and the broker, and then between the broker and the party. Each domain of interaction is mediated by a different set of social obligations. Relations of patronage between voters and brokers, Srinivas explains, are mediated at the local (village) level by caste and class: brokers are higher-caste landowners and money lenders, with whom poorer and lower-caste masses have longstanding ties of social, ritual, and economic obligation. At election time, these social ties are activated in order to deliver votes to a preferred party. For Srinivas, transfers of material goods (the 'consideration which is not mentioned but implied') were not simple market exchanges or purchases, but rather productive of 'bonds' between the masses and the party, mediated by relations of social trust already existent between

---

[1] Mysore Narasimhachar Srinivas, *The Social Structure of a Mysore Village* (New York: Bobbs-Merrill, 1960).

voters and their local 'leaders'. By providing gifts via 'brokers' to the voters, Breeding argues that parties 'demonstrated to citizens that the party would look after citizens' interests'.[2] In the second sphere of interface—between the brokers and the party—the patronage goods placed at the disposal of local leaders serve to shore up the power and authority of village-level caste elites in the face of social churning, tamping down any potential or actual challenge to privilege posed by post-Independence lower-caste movements.[3]

Srinivas's account of 'vote banking' in Mysore, published so soon after Indian Independence, provided a disappointing account of the extent to which the universalist ideals of universal suffrage upon which the Congress-led nationalist movement was based had been internalized by the electorate. As political historian David Gilmartin explains, Indian election law framed in the constitution 'celebrates the legal status of the individual not as the bearer of a particularistic culture, but as a universal vessel of free will and legal rights. That an official, legally recognized "voter" is a rational, autonomous actor is the conceit that justifies government by consent—and defines the people.'[4] Indeed, India's 1951 Representation of the People Act had as a central aim the safeguarding of the individually reasoning voter from 'undue influences' emanating from society, banning 'the systematic appeal to vote or refrain from voting on grounds of caste, race, community or religion or the use of, or appeal to, religious and national symbols, such as the National Flag and the National Emblem, for the furtherance of the prospects of a candidate's election'.[5]

The phenomenon of 'vote banking' gestures at the tensions between an ideal of an individual voter articulating personal, autonomously generated opinions and the reality that 'voters are not simply individuals

[2] Mary Breeding, 'The Micro-Politics of Vote Banks in Karnataka', *Economic and Political Weekly* 46, no. 14 (2–8 April 2011): 76.

[3] Breeding, 'The Micro-Politics of Vote Banks in Karnataka', 76.

[4] David Gilmartin, 'Election Law and the "People" in Colonial and Postcolonial India', in *From the Colonial to the Postcolonial: India and Pakistan in Transition*, eds Dipesh Chakrabarty, Rochona Majumdar, and Andrew Sartori (New York: Oxford University Press, 2007), 56.

[5] Cited in Gilmartin, 'Election Law and the "People" in Colonial and Postcolonial India', 75.

defined by the universalistic claims of law, but cultural beings, defined by fluid, particularistic, and often highly affective bonds and prejudices'.[6]

Srinivas's description of vote-bank politics is echoed in scholarly accounts[7] of post-Independence Indian politics more broadly: until the general election of 1967, Indian elections were dominated by the highly centralized Indian National Congress party, with electoral mobilization strategies and party authority hinging on what Rajni Kothari describes as 'intermediate networks which take on the form of autonomous sub-systems'.[8] Similarly, Kohli describes how the 'Congress system' operated through a 'chain of important individuals stretching from village to state, and eventually to the national capital, welded by bonds of patronage'.[9]

The dramatic reconfigurations in India's socio-economic, demographic, cultural, and institutional landscapes since the 1970s,[10] scholars have argued, altered patterns of political patronage. Jaffrelot notes the breakneck speed at which the Indian electorate expanded during these decades (increasing from 173 million in 1952 to 400 million in 1984), with increased rates of voter participation among non-elites (and non-literates), and a proliferation of regional-level opposition

[6] Gilmartin, 'Election Law and the "People" in Colonial and Postcolonial India,' 56. This tension, Gilmartin notes, must not be interpreted as a clash between Western ideals and Indian society, but rather, as inherent in liberal democratic theory itself.

[7] See, for example, Yogendra Yadav, 'Electoral Politics in the Time of Change: India's Third Electoral System, 1989–99', *Economic and Political Weekly* 34, no. 34/35 (21 August–3 September 1999): 2393–9; Rajni Kothari, *Politics in India* (New York: Little, Brown and Company, 1970); Atul Kohli, *Democracy and Discontent: India's Growing Crisis of Governability* (Cambridge: Cambridge University Press, 1990); and Joop de Wit, *Poverty, Policy and Politics in Madras Slums: Dynamics of Survival, Gender and Leadership* (London: Sage, 1997).

[8] Kothari, *Politics in India*, 91. Kothari uses the term 'system' to describe Congress-dominated politics of the early Republic.

[9] Kohli, *Democracy and Discontent*, 186.

[10] Yadav (1999) has described this as the 'democratic upsurge' of India's 'second electoral system'.

parties.[11] When, in 1989, the head of the newly elected National Front coalition, V.P. Singh, announced that 27 per cent of all government jobs would be reserved for India's Other Backward Classes (OBCs),[12] caste identity gained a new kind of political salience in Indian electoral politics. While Singh's decision to implement the Mandal Commission Report's recommendations for OBC reservations contributed to the National Front government's electoral failures the following year, as Corbridge and Hariss point out, the new laws about OBC reservation had significance insofar as they altered 'the terms of political debate'.[13] For the first time, caste identities were conceptualized and politicized as a way to access the power of the state, and lower-caste Indians began to participate in electoral politics at unprecedented rates.[14] While caste identity had always been politically important (mobilized at the local level via the vote-banking processes characteristic of the Congress system, and later by regional opposition parties in the 1970s and 1980s), what we see in the 1990s, Yadav argues, is the emergence of caste as part of a 'politics of presence', in which it became 'respectable' to 'talk about caste in the public-political domain'.[15]

As regional, linguistic, and caste-based identities gained new political salience in Indian electoral politics, historians have shown, state-level party organization became more significant, with state and local elections consistently seeing higher voter turnout levels than general elections. Reflecting the growing significance of identity politics, general elections saw a proliferation of regional, linguistic, and caste-based parties, as well as an explosion in the number of candidates contesting elections. It was in this context of a dramatically increased and largely illiterate electorate that the Election Commission

[11] Christophe Jaffrelot, 'Voting in India: Electoral Symbols, the Party System and the Collective Citizen', in *Cultures of Voting: The Hidden History of the Secret Ballot*, eds Romain Bertrand, Jean-Louis Briquet, and Peter Pels (London: Hurst, 2007), 78.

[12] 22.5 per cent were already reserved for so-called 'Scheduled Castes' and 'Scheduled Tribes'.

[13] Stuart Corbridge and John Hariss, *Reinventing India: Liberalization, Hindu Nationalism and Popular Democracy* (Cambridge: Polity Press, 2000), 220.

[14] Stuart Corbridge and John Hariss, *Reinventing India: Liberalization, Hindu Nationalism and Popular Democracy*, 220.

[15] Yadav, 'Electoral Politics in the Time of Change', 2397–8.

introduced new procedures designed, as Jaffrelot puts it, to 'create the conditions for rational and independent voting'—that is, in order to thereby curb the kinds of clientelist dynamics described by Srinivas as 'vote banking'. For instance, the use of electoral symbols aimed to empower illiterate voters; more stringent enforcement of the secret ballot sought to allow the voting of individual preferences without fear of retribution; and the introduction of electronic voting machines promised to curb electoral fraud.[16] Yet Jaffrelot finds that voting technologies designed to 'free' the voter from social dependencies and traditional solidarities in order to produce a modern, independently reasoning electorate of 'citizen-individuals' have been put to work for quite different ends by low-caste groups who have used electoral processes to pursue 'community' goals.[17]

Indeed, while accounts of 'vote banking' have continued to dog both scholarly and popular accounts of Indian politics, contemporary observers have noted the changing nature of such practices in light of the dramatic institutional, cultural, and socio-economic and demographic transformations just described. Breeding, for instance, has argued that increasingly stringent enforcement of the secret ballot has not done away with, but rather has transformed dynamics of patron–client obligation in specific ways.[18] In Srinivas's account, Breeding notes that exchanges of material goods for electoral support take on something of the character of a *contract*, with gifts functioning (in a Maussian sense) as productive of enduring social obligations that, if not reciprocated, carry prohibitive social, ethical, and economic sanctions. With institutional reforms shoring up secrecy of the ballot, Breeding points out, 'citizens can accept gifts from all parties and still vote however they desire'. In this post-reform context, patronage gifts should be understood as

[16] Jaffrelot, 'Voting in India', 79.

[17] Bertrand, Briquet, and Pels demonstrate that the ideology of the secret ballot attributes the technology with 'an intrinsic persuasive force, such that its implementation is a necessary and almost sufficient condition to create an inexorable movement towards the democracy of the citizen-individual'. See Romain Betrand, Jean Louis Briquet, and Peter Pels, 'Introduction: Towards a Historical Ethnography of Voting', in *Cultures of Voting: The Hidden History of the Secret Ballot*, eds Romain Bertrand, Jean-Louis Briquet, and Peter Pels (London: Hurst, 2007), 5.

[18] Breeding, 'The Micro-Politics of Vote Banks in Karnataka'.

largely symbolic: 'Parties supply benefits as gestures,' Breeding argues, 'often to their already loyal supporters'.[19]

In a similar vein, citing the increased political competition resulting from the proliferation of parties, Guha has suggested that the notion of 'vote banking,' while still relevant, has taken on a new meaning:

> We still use the term coined by Srinivas; however, we mostly mean it now to capture a solidarity that is horizontal rather than vertical. 'Vote bank' is not what a single patron commands; rather it denotes a collective political preference exercised by a particular interest group. In India, this interest is defined principally by primordial identity—of caste or religion or language. But one can also think of 'vote banks' being constituted by shared material or moral interests.[20]

For Guha then, it is not the *form* but the *direction* of influence characterizing vote-bank politics that has changed: while stricter enforcement of the secret ballot means that vote buying has lost much of its coercive character, institutional reforms have not produced an electorate of autonomously reasoning voters, freed from the 'undue influences' of community and society. On the contrary, liberation from the vertical ties of patronage has shored up horizontal social identities, ultimately deepening the tendency of the Indian electorate to vote as ascriptively delineated social groups—to market themselves, that is, to various parties as 'vote banks'.[21] By obscuring the extent to which a social grouping reciprocate gifts with votes, Guha argues, the electoral reforms have helped to reverse the direction of vote-bank influence, transferring the moral hazard from voter to party, which is left with little assurance that material inducements will actually secure the sought-after votes of a particular group.

In a slightly different vein, Partha Chatterjee critiques the notion articulated by Guha that the 'interests' of vote banks are given by ascriptive identities like caste or religion, pointing to the fundamentally

---

[19] Breeding, 'The Micro-Politics of Vote Banks in Karnataka', 73.

[20] Ramachandra Guha, 'The Career of a Concept', *Hindu*, 1 January 2008.

[21] This shift from vertical patronage ties to horizontal networks of authority in Mumbai is characterized by Hansen as the supplanting of '*ma-baapism*' by '*dadaism*'. Thomas Blom Hansen, *Wages of Violence: Naming and Identity in Postcolonial Bombay* (Princeton: Princeton University Press, 2001), 72.

modern spheres of politics in and through which such groups and their claims are articulated.[22] Community groupings offering votes in exchange for material benefits, Chatterjee suggests, should be understood as part of a broader 'strategic politics' through which the urban poor in modern India make claims on the state.[23] The imperatives of democratic legitimation, Chatterjee argues, produce 'political obligations' for state actors to 'deliver civic services and welfare benefits' to the urban poor, who are excluded from formal spheres of rights and citizenship by virtue of the fact that their 'habitation or livelihood lies on the other side of legality'.[24] The extent to which the poor are able to make such claims—to 'effectively make its claim in political society'—Chatterjee suggests, effectively hinges upon the 'moral rhetoric of community' through which a 'population group' articulates itself as a proper and deserving recipient of governmental beneficence. Chatterjee argues that although the relations produced in political society may appear to 'resemble the supposedly traditional forms of patronage and clientelism', the sphere of political practice taking place in political society is a more recent phenomenon, inextricably intertwined with the 'governmental practices' of the modern state in the past few decades. Groups constituted in political society, Chatterjee maintains, 'make instrumental use of the fact that they can vote in elections' in order to forge useful connections with powerful actors. 'Communities,' Chatterjee contends, are 'some of the most active agents of political practice' in contemporary India, for whom the vote is a strategically used tool for extracting material benefits from the bourgeois capitalist state.[25]

While accounts such as those of Chatterjee, Guha, Breeding, and Jaffrelot—for all their differences—gesture towards the redistributive,

---

[22] Partha Chatterjee, 'Community in the East', *Economic and Political Weekly* 33, no. 6 (7–13 February 1998), 277–82.

[23] Chatterjee suggests that the sphere of political society is a modern phenomenon, 'enmeshed in an entirely new set of governmental practices that are the functions only of the modern state in the late 20th century'. See Chatterjee, 'Community in the East,' 282.

[24] Partha Chatterjee, *The Politics of the Governed: Reflections on Popular Politics in Most of the World* (New York: Columbia University Press, 2006), 56.

[25] Chatterjee, 'Community in the East', 281–2.

if not quite emancipatory, potential of contemporary forms of vote-bank political practice, other theorists, particularly those of the liberal tradition, have been more sceptical. In his work on Tamil Nadu, for instance, de Wit has argued that the political developments of recent decades have supplanted what he characterizes as the genuinely redistributive system of Congress-era clientelism (in which 'very considerable patronage' resulted in significant infrastructural, educational, and industrial investments) with a more pernicious form of 'machine-style' politics characterizing contemporary Tamil Nadu.[26] De Wit's discussion of the machine politics draws on Scott's classic formulation:

> The machine politicians could be viewed as brokers who, in return for financial assistance from business elites, promoted their policy interests when in office, while passing on a portion of the gain to a particularistic electorate from which they 'rented' their authority.[27]

Indeed, de Wit describes how, beginning in the 1970s, Tamil Nadu politics has become more 'machine-like,' with parties courting the political support of 'banks' of ascriptively defined groups of voters ('specific castes, poor women, Dalits and public sector workers') with 'schemes and subsidies designed to benefit specific groups of voters'.[28] By 'appeasing' target groups with material benefits and short-sighted welfare schemes—that is, by prioritizing 'short-run particularistic gains at the expense of long-run transformations'—machine-style politics, de Wit argues, has had overwhelmingly negative effects on both social welfare as well as socio-economic prospects, not only for the targeted groups, but in the state as a whole.[29] With election-time exchanges theorized as 'machine-like,' socially identified banks of voters are cast not as agentive collectivities possessed, as other theorists suggest, of real bargaining power, but rather as manipulated and exploited subalterns, victimized by what de Wit calls a 'politics of illusion' wherein 'the Tamil Nadu poor are tied to the political system by (promises of) material benefit and by almost personal, emotional ties to the

---

[26] de Wit, *Poverty, Policy and Politics in Madras Slums*.

[27] James C. Scott, 'Corruption, Machine Politics, and Political Change', *American Political Science Review* 63, no. 4, 1142.

[28] de Wit, *Poverty, Policy and Politics in Madras Slums*, 72.

[29] de Wit, *Poverty, Policy and Politics in Madras Slums*, 72.

highest authority'.[30] By de Wit's account, poor voters are not modern political subjects (Pel's independently reasoning citizens) but rather are inextricably entangled in 'emotionally' inflected traditional solidarities and social relations that prevent them from acting (or perhaps even perceiving) their own as well as society's 'real' interests.

De Wit's account of the difference between Congress-era clientelism and contemporary 'machine-style' politics in Tamil Nadu mirrors a theoretical distinction drawn by Schaffer between 'patronage' and 'vote buying' as one based largely on the different temporalities character-izing each modality of exchange.

> Vote buying is a last-minute effort to influence electoral outcomes, typically taking place days or hours before an election, or on election day itself. The benefits derived from patronage, in contrast, tend to be less episodic and election-centred, since they are distributed within the context of enduring relationships between patrons and their clients.[31]

Whereas 'patronage politics' produces and shores up 'enduring relationships' between particular groups of voters and political lead-ers, Schaffer suggests, the immediacy of election-season 'vote-buying' transactions—in which cash is given as a direct payment for votes at an election—lends such exchanges the character of market purchase.[32]

---

[30] de Wit, *Poverty, Policy and Politics in Madras Slums*, 72.

[31] Frederic Charles Schaffer, *Elections for Sale: The Causes and Consequences of Vote Buying* (Boulder, Co: Lynne Rienner Publishers, 2007): 6.

[32] Schaffer places 'vote buying' at the far end of a theoretical continuum of electoral campaign practices through which material benefits are directed at voters: from 'programmatic' to 'clientelistic'. In 'programmatic' offers, Schaffer writes, 'candidates package material benefits into policy programmes that are available to everyone, supporters and opponents alike'; clientelistic induce-ments, by contrast, direct benefits only to a candidate's supporters, and only at election time. On the 'programmatic' end of the spectrum are 'allocational' policies directed at categories of beneficiaries across the entire electorate ('the unemployed' or 'the elderly'). Next, 'pork barrel' promises offer policies and public works projects specifically to the geographic districts of a particular candidate. Patronage politics involves 'material support' to 'individuals, families or communities within the context of enduring asymmetric, but reciprocal, relationships'. Finally, at the far 'clientelistic' end of the spectrum, 'vote buy-ing' offers 'particularistic material rewards to individuals or families'. Schaffer's

Vote buying, Schaffer suggests, is more harmful to democracy than is patronage, having negative implications for democratic accountability:

> If politicians get elected on the basis of short-term contracts—money for votes—they have little reason to care about the formulation of policies, the construction of programmatic parties, and practices of accountability. In the best cases, vote buying establishes a continuous obligation to provide clientelist services to constituencies. In the worst cases, it cuts the nexus of representation between voters and politicians. Once votes are paid for, politicians may feel free of any debt to their voters. In this case, purchased delegation is unconstrained delegation.[33]

Cash transfers, Schaffer thus argues, suggest a situation wherein politically immature voters simply auction their votes off to the highest bidder, forfeiting any claim to substantive representation as well as any hope that politicians might act in the 'public good'. Indeed, an additional democratic deficit suggested by Schaffer's formulation is that vote buying 'subverts the meaning of elections as instruments of collective decision making, since it tends to replace deliberation over public issues with narrow calculations of individual interest'.[34] The voting poor have assumed the modern mantle of individual rationality in matters of short-term benefit and market exchange, but without becoming mature, autonomous political subjects with programmatic political preferences vis-à-vis questions of the broader public good. Yet the idea that votes have been commoditized—as the 'vote buying' idea suggests—exists in theoretical tension with the concept of 'vote banking': if votes are freely exchangeable by individual voters according to a single measure of value (money), what are we to make of the continued political salience of groups of voters— 'vote banks'—to whom money is ostensibly distributed as a marketized exchange for votes? That is, if material benefits are distributed to voters through the mediation of traditional forms of authority and identity,

---

programmatic-clientelistic spectrum thus involves variation along two axes: the recipient of the benefit (general or specific) and the time frame of the exchange (long-term or immediate).

[33] Schaffer, *Elections for Sale*, 11.
[34] Schaffer, *Elections for Sale*, 9.

then what sense does it make to speak of these transfers in the language of individual rationality and market purchase?

To summarize, scholars of Indian politics generally agree that the decades since the 1970s have seen the decline of the kinds of hierarchical patronage patterns that Srinivas describes as 'vote bank' politics, and the emergence of new forms of 'banking' wherein material goods and particularistic benefits are directed towards horizontal, caste-based, and community-based social groupings in exchange for a block vote. Debates have hinged largely on whether this new form of vote bank politics represents exploitative, machine-style politics in which the poor are excluded from true democratic participation and debate on questions of governance and social policy, pacified and purchased with short-term particularistic welfarism, or whether vote banking might be possessed of redistributive possibility and even emancipatory potential. The distinction is adjudicated by the question of temporality.[35] If material benefits are productive or demonstrative of enduring commitments to particular groups of voters, they are less pernicious, perhaps even democratic. If instead the transaction begins and ends with the act of voting, then it suggests the forfeiture on behalf of voters of any claim to longer-term programmatic benefits.[36]

---

[35] Schaffer categorizes material benefits offered by candidates along a programmatic-clientelistic spectrum, which involves variation along two axes: the recipient of the benefit (general or specific) and the time frame of the exchange (long-term or immediate). For Kitschelt and Wilkinson, who similarly see exchanges as payments, the passage of time between payment and voting poses the key problem around which their research coalesces: how to manage the 'threat of opportunistic defection, in which either the voter or politician reneges on the deal once he or she has been paid'. See Herbert Kitschelt and Steven I. Wilkinson, eds, *Patrons, Clients and Policies: Patterns of Democratic Accountability and Political Competition* (New York: Cambridge University Press, 2007), 8.

[36] Chatterjee attempts to navigate this terrain by theorizing 'community' groupings not in ascriptive terms, but as 'strategic' and post-political. Yet the kinds of political concessions that community groupings are able to 'extract' from the state in Chatterjee's formulation are suggestive of short-term welfarism rather than longer-term political projects. Chatterjee nonetheless insists on the democratizing, emancipatory potential inherent in 'political society' wherein he holds that 'the actual transactions over the everyday distribution of

The notion that the influx of money means that individual votes have now become freely exchangeable as marketable goods engages long-standing theoretical debates over the extent to which money possesses, as Bloch and Parry put it, 'an intrinsically revolutionary power which inexorably subverts the moral economy of "traditional societies"'.[37] By introducing a single measure of value into social spheres previously governed by other moralities or logics of valuation, money is theorized as having the potential to transform previously non-purchasable things into equivalent, freely tradable commodities: 'It is in the nature of a general-purpose money,' Paul Bohannan writes, 'that it standardizes the exchangeability value of every item to a common sale.'[38] Theorists of money from Marx to Simmel have emphasized money's particularity as an object of exchange that renders 'everything quantifiable according to one scale of value'.[39] Anthropologists have thus stressed the sociocultural effects of the introduction of money into previously non-economic spheres of life. By rendering comparable—that is, measurable by equivalent units of value—objects and relations that were previously governed by other logics or systems of value, these systems and moralities are held to deteriorate. The effects of this 'great transformation' on sociocultural life has been both celebrated and condemned: on the one hand, money's 'quality-less' quality has been feted for 'freeing' people from oppressive gender, caste, or other hierarchical institutions; on the other, this same quality-lessness has been cast as amorality, with money accused of undermining other sociocultural institutions, relations, and moralities.[40] 'If modern man is free—free because he can sell everything and free because he can buy everything—then he now seeks ...

rights and entitlements lead over time to substantial redefinitions of property and law within the actually existing modern state'. See Chatterjee, *The Politics of the Governed: Reflections on Popular Politics in Most of the World.*

[37] Jonathan Parry and Maurice Bloch, *Money and the Morality of Exchange* (Cambridge: Cambridge University Press, 1989), 13.

[38] See also Paul Bohannan, 'The Impact of Money on an African Subsistence Economy', *Journal of Economic History* 19, no. 4 (December 1959), 491–503. Cited in Parry and Bloch, *Money and the Morality of Exchange.*

[39] Bill Maurer, 'The Anthropology of Money', *Annual Review of Anthropology* 35, no. 1 (2006): 20.

[40] Maurer, 'The Anthropology of Money,' 19.

in the objects themselves that vigour, stability and inner unity which he has lost because of the changed money-conditioned relationships that he has with them,' writes Georg Simmel.[41] In the case of votes, liberal democratic theory holds that votes ought not to be exchanged for immediate monetary gain, but rather should be governed by logics of 'public good' and 'democratic accountability'. It is the presumed undermining of these democratic moralities that invites the condemnation of the exchange of votes for cash.

Yet conflating the presence of cash with 'vote buying' narrows the scope of inquiry to the narrow question of how voter 'compliance' with a presumed cash-for-vote 'contract' might be generated under conditions of voter balloting.[42] In what follows, we instead take an ethnographic approach to the subject of election-season cash transfer, thereby allowing other meanings of money to emerge. The following accounts of election-time cash flow probe some of the presumptions embedded in concepts of 'vote banking' and 'vote buying,' thereby unsettling the theoretical and normative frameworks through which practices of popular politics in contemporary India have been outlined. The ethnographies reveal multiple logics operative in election-time cash flows; actors involved with moving money have divergent and sometimes conflicting aspirations, motivations, and agendas, within which cash plays various roles simultaneously.

'VOTE BUYING' AND REGIONAL POLITICAL ECONOMY IN BIHAR

When 'following the money' that is distributed by a candidate to 'the electorate', the trail leads through a complex maze of brokerage since candidates do not distribute money themselves. What becomes clear when this web of brokerage is mapped is that the men who distribute

---

[41] Georg Simmel, *Philosophy of Money* (New York: Taylor & Francis, 2011), cited in Maurer, 'The Anthropology of Money'.

[42] Schaffer, for instance, differentiates between 'instrumental' and 'normative' compliance, where the former involves monitoring turnout and incentivizing fulfilment of the vote-buying 'contract', while the latter involves leveraging social resources such as 'gratitude' and 'personal obligation' to enforce compliance. See Schaffer, *Elections for Sale*.

money on behalf of candidates are more than mere conduits—they are local leaders who turn out to be central players in everyday interactions with state institutions and regional political economy. The local leaders who are 'networked' through the distribution of money are of varying types, but most are connected to regional political-economic networks that provide influence within the village. And while nobody really thinks that you can buy peoples' votes, everyone acknowledges that these local leaders are key to winning elections. To the extent that distributing money cements ties between the candidate and these local leaders, it is an important part of an effective electoral strategy. This is why the role of money in elections is not widely criticized—in fact, pre-election distribution is expected.

I (Witsoe) became interested in election-time cash distribution as part of a longer project on regional political economy, and especially sand mining, investigating the ways in which construction-driven growth in Bihar is transforming the region. What I quickly found was that sand-mining networks extend into all five of my research villages, and that politics at all levels in the region was increasingly shaped by struggles for access to sand profits. Examining exactly how cash generated through sand mining is used during elections provides a window into the ways in which a dynamic regional political economy is reshaping electoral practice and local politics.

In order to examine the broker networks through which election money is distributed, the next section turns to what locals term the 'sand mafia', which is such a central feature of the regional political economy of my research villages.

THE POLITICAL ECONOMY OF SAND

It is hard to imagine a better contrast between the ethic of 'vote buying' and that of liberal representation than the contest between Sanjay Surya, the sitting Bharatiya Janata Party (BJP) MLA and Satish Yadav, running on a Rashtriya Janata Dal (RJD) ticket, during the 2015 assembly elections in Bihar. Satish is a powerful figure in the region. His brother, and occasional rival, is an ex-MLA and the pair has connections to an extensive criminal network. Most importantly, Satish is a member of the 'syndicate'—the English term that everyone, include syndicate members, use—that controls sand mining in the region.

Sand from the Sone River—one kilometre from the village where I lived from 2002 to 2003 and have returned to for periods every year since—is considered to be the best quality in the state, known as 'yellow' or 'gold' sand (as opposed to white sand). The ghats on both sides of the river are the largest and most profitable source of sand in the state and alone contribute around 40 per cent of total sand royalties. As a result, sand mining is the most important non-agricultural economic activity in the region. Much of the money that is distributed before elections comes from profits related to sand mining—it is therefore not surprising that 'sand mafia' networks are central to election cash distribution.

The early history of sand mining was, in fact, shaped by the legacy of *zamindars* (landlords). Rajput zamindars held power over much of what is now Bhojpur District during the colonial period. Even after Independence, Rajput villagers owned a significant portion of agricultural land; they generally enjoyed strong relationships with local administrators and police, exercising what could be termed a 'regional hegemony'. During the Congress period, the political economy of sand mining reflected the late colonial political order and the regional dominance of Rajput ex-zamindars. Regional economic activity here reinforced the longstanding dominance of upper-caste landlords.

The 'sand mafia' emerged during the period of RJD rule, especially after the auction system began in 2002. Reflecting the dramatic change that had occurred in the state over the previous decade, mafia members were now only OBCs, without a single Rajput partner. The entry of lower-caste 'ganja mafia' groups was particularly important; earlier, Rajputs had mainly controlled drug smuggling in Bhojpur, a key regional distribution point. If, in 1991, OBC actors who possessed the qualities required to run sand-mining operations did not exist, by 2002, there was an entire group. An OBC caste network had been generated that now exercised considerable clout within regional political economy. And this network was crucial for providing leverage to a new class of lower-caste leaders in village contexts.[43] In short, the process of OBC

---

[43] See Jeffrey Witsoe, *Democracy Against Development: Lower-Caste Politics and Political Modernity in Postcolonial India* (Chicago: University of Chicago Press, 2013) for more details.

political empowerment involved challenging the longstanding dominance of upper-caste landlords in village contexts through leveraging
these regional networks.

The end of RJD rule and the election of an NDA government
under Nitish Kumar in 2005 changed the dynamics of the sand mafia
and its relationship with regional political economy significantly.
Nitish Kumar's desire to use state institutions to pursue his development agenda forced him to work with the upper-caste networks that
continue to exercise influence within public institutions. The end of
RJD rule meant the re-entry of the coal mafia into sand mining on
an unprecedented scale. So, while the RJD had been able to limit
the influence of the Rajput-controlled coal mafia for more than two
decades, this turned out to be only temporary. This re-entry further
criminalized the sand mafia as OBC groups inducted more powerful
criminals in order to compete with the coal mafia—this included the
biggest arms dealer of the region and a feared 'shooter' (assassin). And
rather than the sand mafia being part of the ruling party's political
project—as during the Lalu period—it increasingly became a gateway
into politics.

Growth in Bihar over the last decade has been driven largely by
construction—both public works such as roads, bridges, and schools
but also houses, apartments, and shopping complexes. Bihar's construction sector more than quadrupled during this period, and demand for
cement in Bihar has been growing faster than that of any other state.
All of this concrete requires a steady supply of high-quality sand—after
Bihar's bifurcation, sand is the largest source of mining revenue for the
state government. But sand is not equally dispersed—construction-
quality sand collects in certain areas of riverbanks, only some of which
have good transportation links. And specific groups exercise control
over these areas. The growing importance of sand mining has had a
profound impact on electoral practice in the region, as shall become
clear.

The economic logic of the syndicate is based on the system of
auctioning rights to mining. Rights to sand mining had been auc-
tioned every three years from 2011, and the group that wins the
bid holds the right to collect a fixed rate per cubic metre of sand.
This amount is collected from truck divers at collection points. By
forming a syndicate of powerful actors, rival bids are discouraged and

the winning bid can be much lower than would otherwise be the case. This is because bidding is different from controlling—there are significant 'barriers to entry', as a member of the syndicate explained. Only certain people have the capacity to enter this business. In particular, three qualities are needed. Only certain people have the authority required to smoothly collect payments and to 'manage local factors' (as a mining department official put it), possess the capital for the required auction bid, and can 'manage' government institutions including local police at the mining sites, police all along the transit routes, the block office, district magistrate, and the like. The logic of the syndicate is that, since there are a small number of actors who possess these qualities, and outsiders in particular cannot enter, the most profitable strategy is to reduce competitive bidding by organizing all of these actors into a single group—the syndicate. There are currently three groups of men (each with a separate registered company) who have joined together, with nine total members of the syndicate.

There are multiple groups of actors connected with managing sand-mining operations and thousands of labourers involved in sand-mining work. There are the owners of the trucks that purchase, transport, and sell the sand, with around hundred locally owned trucks, owners of excavating machines and boats used for mining; and the dozens of people employed by the syndicate to collect payments from trucks. In addition, groups of men who own or control access roads to the ghats collect a 'toll tax' from each truck. These men are almost always among the most powerful actors in their respective villages. And finally, there is a shadowy network of around 300 'investors'—each connected with a particular syndicate member—who invest money in the syndicate with high rates of return.

Each member of the syndicate has their own network, largely of people from their respective caste, and the syndicate itself serves to integrate these various networks at the regional level. As opposed to the open caste conflict of the Lalu period, the syndicate involves the cooperation of influential caste leaders and their networks for the sake of profit. These interlinked networks extend, to various degrees, into every village in the region, integrating village politics with the political economy of the region. And since many members of the syndicate are part of criminal operations such as drug smuggling and the 'coal mafia' that are often centred outside the state, the 'sand mafia' connects the local territorial dominance required to control mining operations with powerful translocal criminal networks. Looking at five panchayats that I have good knowledge of, for instance, four of the current *mukhias* were involved with sand mining before entering politics. In the 2010 assembly elections, two of the candidates were members of the syndicate. So, the sand mafia has become the key gateway into village and regional politics.

MAPPING BROKER NETWORKS: FOLLOWING THE MONEY

In an ironic inversion of the general trend of the 2015 election, where the BJP by all accounts spent a greater amount than the 'grand alliance', the RJD candidate Satish Yadav here distributed a great deal of his own money while the BJP's Sanjay Surya spent none. In a dramatic incident, Satish was reportedly nearly caught in a police raid to prevent 'vote buying'. Eyewitnesses described him grabbing a suitcase from his SUV and fleeing on foot, at one point falling and injuring himself before escaping on a supporter's motorcycle.

While Satish's story circulated almost as a heroic tale, what really baffled people—especially BJP supporters—was that Surya was reported to have not even spent all of the money that the party gave him to compete with Satish. People said, usually with amused disgust, that he returned a portion of this money. 'Why would he return money?' people asked with audible disdain. And this was usually stated as an explanation for why he lost by such a massive margin (in addition, of course, to the electoral wave that routed the BJP in much of the state). Virtually nobody praised Surya for his 'honesty' and there was also little discernible public critique of Satish's 'vote buying'. For instance, I heard very few allegations by BJP activists that the election had been unfairly bought, despite everyone's perception that Satish had distributed a large amount of money.

In the months before the election, Biju, a Dalit man, explained the logic of this disdain for Surya. He explained that he likes the BJP and especially Narendra Modi, describing the election of a BJP-led state government as having the potential to bring the economic modernity that he had witnessed in metros to Bihar. But, Biju was emphatic, if the election were between Surya and Satish, he would definitely vote for

Satish. When asked why, he said that Surya was 'useless' (*bekar*) while Satish did good work, such as providing him employment related to sand mining. Satish, and the brokers connected to him, could also provide loans, 'manage' the police, and provide protection or support in case of a conflict. If Satish ran, he said that he would be compelled to vote for such a 'good candidate'.

For Biju, what clearly made Satish a better candidate than Surya had nothing to do with the ability to 'represent' him in the state assembly, and certainly nothing to do with honesty. It was Satish's network—and his willingness to allow Biju to participate and benefit from this network—that mattered. Surya, in contrast, had no network despite being the sitting MLA in the constituency.

Not surprisingly, Satish's distribution of money flowed through the same networks that people like Biju value so much. 'Following the money' involves mapping the networks that link regional political economy—and especially sand mining—to local sites within villages. Most of the brokers to whom Satish gave money to distribute were involved in one way or the other with sand mining. For instance, informants told us that Satish's brother distributed money to Surinder Yadav, the ex-mukhia of one of my research villages and the most influential Yadav leader in the area, involved with sand transportation and owner of several trucks. One of the people to whom Arvind distributed money was Mandal Yadav, a small-scale contractor of government development projects who is also marginally involved in sand transportation.

Each of these people are asymmetrically tied to the person who gave them money to distribute and, in turn, are expected to distribute money to their supporters. So there is a chain of brokers here—all of the same caste and all involved with sand mining—extending from the candidate to specific localities within the village. Money distribution consolidates this network of brokers, but it's important to keep in mind that this network (the 'sand mafia') is also the source of the money. What this reveals is the increasing role of regional political economy in shaping electoral practice.

The key to effective money distribution is to consolidate the broadest network possible, one that includes as many 'nodes' (brokers) as possible. This enterprise can go badly. There were constant rumours that certain brokers were 'eating' the money instead of distributing it. Or the brokers can exclude key constituents who could otherwise be supporters. For instance, there was widespread anger in part of Surinder's village by Yadavs opposed to him who claimed that he was only distributing to 'his people'. Despite caste and party loyalty to Satish that brokers told us usually requires less cash distribution—with most distribution reportedly done in non-Yadav areas of the village—some of these voters openly threatened to vote for the BJP in response.

But this was minor compared to the widely perceived partiality by Surya's broker in the village, an elected party official with little clout in regional political economy and therefore an ineffective network. After an election rally (for BJP ally Ram Jitan Manjhi), conflict erupted with villagers threatening not to vote BJP ('BJP *nehi rahenge. Ham log koi value nehi hai*'). Surya mediated, telling people to resolve their disputes with him in private, not in public meetings.

PUBLIC SPECTACLES OF SUPPORT

Since consolidating an effective network is key to winning elections, many brokers and even voters want to be on the winning side as this will result in greater access to resources. A powerful patron who is a sitting MLA, all things being equal, is generally better than a powerful patron who is not. Brokers sometimes referred to this as 'wait and watch' (in English) when they were considering which side to support. This is why it is important to publicly signal the strength of one's network.

At village-level election rallies, the candidate speaks in the presence of affiliated local leaders, signalling their network to all who observe.[44] But these are usually one-off events. A more regular, and, therefore, publicly observable signal of network strength occurs at pre-election feasts where the supporters of a given candidate are provided food and often alcohol. Unlike cash payments, attendance at feasts generates very public pressure to support a candidate—it would be socially condemnable to be regularly seen at a feast in support of a candidate while vocalizing support for another candidate. These feasts, lasting as long as ten days before the election, therefore, produced social expectations about attendees' votes.

---

[44] Witsoe, *Democracy Against Development*.

Feasts are also considerably more expensive than holding a single rally and feeding supporters is where a significant portion of money distributed by candidates is spent. Some feasts are mostly attended by brokers, while more expensive feasts involve brokers bringing their supporters in a public demonstration of their own influence over voters. And there were scores of very local feasts held in specific areas of the village. Election feasts, of course, also publicly signal the influence of the host. The public spectacle of a widely attended political feast produces the public representation of an influential patron, someone connected with powerful men in the region, gathering supporters on their behalf, and doing so by 'sharing the wealth'. This serves as a very public representation of their influence while also demonstrating the local reach of the candidate. If the feast-giver is an influential person in the village, people may vote for the candidate primarily as an act of support for the proxy. Personal relationships are widely considered to be a sensible, and at least somewhat legitimate, reason to vote against the perceived interest of one's community.

Complicating the top-down 'chain' of brokers are local leaders who hold their own feasts on behalf of candidates using their own resources without taking money from a candidate. In my research villages, there were only two examples of these, and in both cases, the leader in question was a member of the syndicate. Leaders who wanted to signify their political clout but maintain equal status with the candidate had to utilize their own funds. This reveals the ways in which receiving money to distribute produces an asymmetrical relationship.

And since receiving money puts one in a position of subordination vis-à-vis the giver, this is only publicly acceptable if one is able to put others in a similar position—to become part of the chain of brokerage. This explains why 'vote buying' is popularly seen as more or less legitimate while 'vote selling' is not—this is because selling one's vote is selling perhaps the most tangible right of citizenship for most people in rural Bihar. Since it is through the vote that most lower-caste people have attained 'voice' (*bol*) and dignity, it would be humiliating to publicly acknowledge selling one's vote despite the uncertainty of the secret ballot. Nobody in my research sites acknowledged receiving money unless they were brokers who also distributed money, or held feasts.

While these feasts resemble the types of wedding and funeral feasts that erstwhile zamindars have long held, the backgrounds of brokers and feast-givers indicates that landholding as a basis of electoral influence is weakening—most of the brokers in my five research panchayats have relatively small landholdings or have purchased their land with cash earned through regional economic activities. Development brokerage, in fact, is more important for most brokers than land-based relationships with voters. But even as landholding as a basis of electoral influence is weakening, the centrality of caste identities is not, as regional political economy such as sand mining is organized around the caste-based networks of each syndicate member.

The next section examines how the distribution of cash is monitored and what this means for understanding the role of this distribution in electoral practice.

MONITORING ELECTORAL 'INVESTMENTS'

Before the assembly elections described above, elections were held for the member of legislative counsel (MLCs) in early 2015. This election had a restricted constituency made up of elected members of the panchayat system. Because it had such a restricted constituency, and because it ended up being a very close election, it serves as a good case for examining how cash 'investments' are monitored. The election was between two candidates, Charan, a lower-caste member of the sand-mining syndicate running on an RJD ticket, the brother of the notorious criminal politician Sunil Singh running on a Lok Janshakti Party (LJP) ticket (part of the NDA).

Singh entered the contest late, by which point Charan had already 'purchased' many votes. While panchayat members stated that the amount varied 'man to man', people put the purchase amount at around Rs 5,000 per vote. In an elaborate arrangement, voters who received money were asked for their ward member certificates as a 'security deposit' (*lachar*) and these certificates were collected and kept in various locations. Once Singh entered the contest, he tried to make up time in a similar operation, allegedly offering as much as Rs 15,000 per vote. It became possible for new 'deposits' to be collected, even from people who had already given up their ward member certificate, because of a rule change that now allowed voter identification cards to be used to verify identity at the voting booths.

On election day, the brokers who managed this operation returned the ward member certificates and voter identification cards that had been collected outside the booth. Panchayat members repeatedly told us that most people—70 per cent was a common estimate—took money from brokers affiliated with both candidates. These same people who distribute money were present at the voting booth, making sure that people who have been 'bought' turn out to vote. And people did report feeling pressure, especially since both of these candidates are very powerful regional figures. But since Charan started this process earlier, cementing ties, numerous people told us that that they felt compelled to vote for him, despite the fact that Singh was offering considerably more money. Despite Singh's much larger expenditure, Charan narrowly won the election.

What this case reveals is that although money was distributed for votes, and there were elaborate monitoring mechanisms put into place, the uncertainly surrounding how people would actually vote meant that the monitoring process was not about a straightforward enforcement of an economic transaction. Rather, the entire process of monitoring can be read as a way to exert 'pressure' (*dabao*), as people described it, a demonstration of the 'muscle' that candidates can exert through their networks. But despite so many people reportedly taking money from both sides, we couldn't find any examples of retribution despite the election being close and so much money being distributed. When asked why retribution did not occur, one ward member stated, 'Everyone took money. How many people can they kill?' So the coercion associated with cash distribution should be read as 'pressure' as opposed to the types of direct and open violence used during elections in the past. What this case also reveals is that just spending money is not how elections are won. Cash generates relationships and it is these relationships that ultimately win elections.

THE ROLE OF MONEY

Nobody thought that many votes were actually bought during this election. As a syndicate member put it, 'It didn't make any difference, *security key liye*' ('it was just for security'). It's also true that without giving money it would be difficult to win—and this does shape elections. And everyone agrees that the amount of money distributed during elections has increased dramatically in recent years.

This increase has occurred at the same time as governance of elections has become considerably tighter. Since 2005, paramilitary forces more or less ensure the anonymity of the secret ballot. It is no longer possible to directly control voting booths through either the old tradition of 'silent booth capturing' (wherein the poor were simply prevented from voting) of the Congress period or the often violent competitive 'booth capturing' of the Mandal period that pitted 'backward' against 'forward' castes in pitched struggles. Now, money is required to influence votes by consolidating networks that provide access to an expanding regional political economy.

In Srinivas's classic 'vote bank' model, regional networks enabled upper-caste landed elites to buttress their influence after Independence. After Mandal, new OBC networks—such as the sand mafia—provided leverage to a new class of lower-caste leaders in their efforts to displace upper-caste hegemony. In both of these cases, the central object of political struggle was control of the village. As India's non-farm economy has rapidly grown, regional networks have become increasingly important to everyday political life. Since these networks are all about making money, it is not surprising that the distribution of cash has become important in producing and reproducing these relationships.

An examination of the distribution of cash during the 2015 election reveals networks of brokerage linking localities with regional political economy that are increasingly central to everyday political practice. There is no longer—if there ever was—a dichotomy between 'the village' and 'the state' with brokers in between. Rather, regional political-economic networks extend from localities to state institutions and many other sites such as criminal networks and regional economic spaces. These are new forms of 'patronage', based not on traditional authority and land, or the violent competition between groups of the Mandal era—even though regional networks also played a key role here—but in providing voters with access to regional political-economic networks.

MUMBAI

Over the winter of 2011–12, I (Björkman) spent four months in Mumbai, carrying out ethnographic research in the run-up to and aftermath of the municipal corporation election.[45] I focused my inquiry on a few areas of the city with which I was quite familiar—neighbourhoods where I had already worked for more than two years, conducting research on the everyday politics of water.[46] The question that had pulled me back to Mumbai for the 2012 election emerged directly from that earlier research. I had set about studying water as a way to explore what I had been thinking of as *informal* politics: the everyday, myriad, un-institutionalized ways in which city residents interface with and encounter 'the state'—its official rules and procedures, its formal actors and representatives, its built forms and material infrastructures—outside of the formal, institutionalized practices that social scientists generally describe as 'politics' in representative democracy: the election. Once in Mumbai, however, what quickly became clear is that a tidy divide between 'formal' and 'informal' moments and modalities of politics was utterly untenable; the everyday politics of water access and the rhythms of electoral democracy were inextricably intertwined in both time and space. During the parliamentary and state legislative assembly elections of 2009, I had observed how the very actors and practices that I had been thinking of as uninstitutionalized forms of politics turned out to be key players at election time, often in innovative ways and to unpredictable ends. So it happened that I returned to Mumbai in 2012 to study 'the politics of elections'—to probe the co-constitutive relations and interpenetrations between the everyday workings of the city, and the rhythms of electoral democracy.

In 2014, I published an article in which I examined a two-part puzzle: first, while I had initially trained my eye on *water* as a currency of contestation, what I encountered instead were currents of *cash*; many of the people whom my earlier research had found to be part of the socio-material infrastructure that makes water flow (or not flow) now re-emerged at election time as conduits of cash.[47] What was the relationship between election-season flows of cash and the broader (both geographically and temporally) social, material, and infrastructural

---

[45] 'I' in this section refers to Björkman.

[46] Lisa Björkman, *Pipe Politics, Contested Waters: Embedded Infrastructures of Millennial Mumbai* (Durham: Duke University Press Books, 2015).

[47] Lisa Björkman, 'You Can't Buy a Vote: Meanings of Money in a Mumbai Election', *American Ethnologist* 41, no. 4 (2014): 617–34.

politics within which elections occur? And in the context of reportedly unprecedented flows of cash, what sense was to be made of the
fact that the final vote tally in ward ABC did not reflect monetary
expenditure? That (as I wrote then) 'the candidate who spent the most
money came nowhere near winning the election, while the candidate who won (by a landslide) spent nowhere near as much money as
some of her rivals.' In Ward 228, 16 candidates were on the ballot, of
which five were affiliated with registered political parties. While the
official limit for campaign spending stood at Rs 5 lakh (an inflation-
inspired fivefold increase over the 2007 election spending limit), actual
expenditures were reported to have been significantly greater.[48]
The English-language media—which doggedly pursued cash-related
stories—found that minimum campaign expenditures for serious
candidates started at 20 lakh, reaching as high as a crore for 'prominent
candidates'. My own research in Ward XYZ found similar figures, with
expenditures reported to range from Rs 15 lakh (then around $30,000)
to a crore (about $200,000).

Dispensing with popular and scholarly theories of 'vote buying',
I demonstrated two things: first, that the money that changed hands in
the run-up to the 2012 Corporation election flowed not between candidates and voters (as cash-for-vote theories would have) but between
candidates and brokers (popularly described as 'social workers'). As an
elected councillor put it, 'of the 45 lakhs now needed to contest a
[Municipal Corporation] election, half goes to the social workers and
the other half for election expenses; any money given to voters would
come from the social workers.' Second, I showed how money is 'productive and performative of sociopolitical networks that infuse everyday life far beyond election day; gifts of money [...] work much like
any other gifted good in producing relations of debt and obligation'.[49]

[48] Mumbai's 227 electoral wards were contested in 2012 by 2,233 candidates (an average of 10 candidates per ward); with the conservative assumption that of these, only half were 'serious candidates', and that each spent only
the minimum estimate of 20 lakhs then campaign expenditure over the two
weeks prior to the election reached more than Rs 2 billion ($44 million)
(Mankikar, S.U., 2012. 'Cashing in on the Election Fever', *Hindustan Times*,
2 February).

[49] Björkman, 'You Can't Buy a Vote', 619.

Having addressed the second of the two above-mentioned puzzles (that is, what is all that money *doing* if it is not buying votes?), I return here to the first: How does election-season cash flow relate to the broader context—to the longer-sighted and multi-scalar political economies and socio-materialities of everyday life in Mumbai? This puzzle can be disaggregated further into two interrelated puzzles: First, who are all these brokers, and what exactly is it that they broker—not only at election time, moreover, but more generally? What processes, histories, personal attributes, ascriptive characteristics, or identity categories (caste, linguistic community or locality, for instance) invite or impel particular figures into brokerage relations or situations during election season? Second, and relatedly, while election-time brokerage is nothing new in Mumbai (or in India more generally), the amount of cash that changed hands during the 2012 corporation was by most accounts unprecedented. Why is *cash* (as opposed to durable goods or luxury items as in the past) the medium by means of which relational chains of sociality and claims-making are increasingly being articulated? In what follows, I present ethnographic accounts that suggest some answers to these questions.

THE STAKES OF ELECTIONS

On 8 February 2012—a week before polling day—I received a frantic phone call from Seema,[50] the candidate on whose ultimately unsuccessful bid for office my research on the 2012 Municipal Corporation election had largely focused. Please come to her home straight away, Seema said; she had something 'serious' to talk about. When I arrived, she served me tea and nervously explained that the co-partisan MLA[51] in whose district Seema was contesting—a man named Mastan Aziz (popularly known as Mastanbhai) who by all accounts had been responsible for Seema's having been awarded the Nationalist Congress Party ticket—had phoned her up that morning, directing her to ask her 'university friend' (me, that is) to make an official press statement declaring that we are, in fact, 'friends'. Seema explained that an opposition party candidate, a man named Shaffir (who not only was Seema's next-door neighbour, but also a not-too-distant relative by marriage)

[50] All names have been changed.
[51] Member of the State Legislative Assembly.

had been spreading rumours about her tenure as elected councillor in
Ward ABC—a nearby constituency where Seema currently held elected
office, but from which she was now ineligible to contest due to a change
in the district reservation from 'Open Female' to 'OBC Open'.[52] Shaffir
and his campaign team had been spreading rumours, Seema explained,
that she had made a regular practice of making official 'complaints' to
the municipal authorities about so-called 'unauthorized constructions'
in ABC, and then extorting cash payments from residents in exchange
for withdrawing the complaints. Reports that Seema was a virtuoso
player of the 'complaint game' [*natak*]—a not-uncommon pastime in
Mumbai—was spreading through XYZ like wildfire, Seema told me
anxiously. Mastanbhai hoped that a statement from me to the press
on the subject of our 'friendship' might be helpful in shoring up her
flagging reputation.[53]

Seema's (and Mastanbhai's) desperate appeal and frantic effort to
rescue Seema's reputation gestures towards some of the most pressing
issues confronting voters not only in XYZ but in Mumbai's popular
neighbourhoods more generally: the vagaries and contradictions of the
policy frameworks governing built space and material infrastructures,
and the resulting vulnerability to the vagaries of 'law enforcement' to
which any investment (public or private) is thereby exposed. Electoral
ward XYZ itself, for instance, is a residential and small-scale industrial
neighbourhood in the city's eastern suburbs, home at the time of my
research to anywhere between 100,000 and 300,000 people (estimates
vary). Created as a municipal resettlement colony in 1976, when the
Emergency-empowered municipal authorities issued a demolition
notice to the nearby neighbourhood of Indira Nagar[54] (itself a resettlement colony) citing a need to reclaim the municipally-owned land for
another 'public purpose', Indira Nagar's households were each officially allotted 10 × 15 foot 'plots' on a swampy swath of public land on
the edge of the city—an area that had been zoned in the Development
Plan for 'public housing'. The official record (a thick file of correspon-
dences among various public and private offices between 1972 and
2014) reveals that land on which XYZ is situated was supposed to be

---

[52] Seema does not hold an OBC certificate.
[53] Needless to say, I declined the request.
[54] Name changed.

leased to the residents of Indira Nagar upon registration of cooperative housing societies; however, a tussle over the details of a hastily carried out land exchange among two government bodies in the context of the Emergency has resulted in a 40-year bureaucratic struggle between residents and various state offices over the status of the official lease. In the interim half century, the neighbourhood has grown through myriad processes, programmes, and schemes.

Meanwhile, the policy framework by means of which the area residents might have obtained an official land lease and entered the district collector's register as cooperative housing societies—alongside many other means by which tenure claims might be articulated—have been occluded by a new policy discourse and framework that treats the neighbourhood as a 'slum', a designation that in policy practice tends to be conflated with notions of 'illegality' and 'informality'.[55] This means that even though the neighbourhood that came to be known as XYZ has never been 'declared' a slum, which would render it officially governable according to the 1971 Maharashtra Slum Areas (Improvement, Clearance and Redevelopment) Act, the current political climate is such that the neighbourhood is treated by municipal authorities, for policy purposes, as a 'slum'. XYZ was even surveyed in conjunction with the Government of Maharashtra's 1999 Slum Survey. When I asked at the office of the district collector how the surveyors had decided which Mumbai neighbourhoods to include in the slum survey, an officer who had been involved with that survey recalled, 'we surveyed illegal areas'. When I pointed out that XYZ is not illegal, the officer nodded his agreement but shrugged helplessly, 'but it *seems* illegal'. He then further elaborated that of course they only surveyed illegal *single-storey* structures, not illegal *multistorey* buildings. While many high-rise buildings are constructed without proper authorizations, those illegal buildings cannot be counted as 'slums', he explained, because after all, 'how can you bring a [multistorey] building under a slum redevelopment scheme?'

Treating XYZ as a 'slum' effectively restricts the kinds of material investments that can be made in the neighbourhood's built environment—its structures and infrastructures—to wholesale

---

[55] For an explication of the politics of 'slum' in Mumbai, see Björkman, 'You Can't Buy a Vote', and Björkman, *Pipe Politics, Contested Waters*.

demolition and redevelopment under a market-driven 'Slum Rehabilitation Scheme' (SRS). Under this policy framework, the land in question would be handed over to a private developer who would rehouse 'eligible' residents (that is, those able to marshal the requisite battery of documentary proofs of eligibility) in multistorey tenement buildings, in exchange for which the developer would be rewarded with dramatically increased development rights on land freed up by the verticalization of the neighbourhood. Many of XYZ's residents have no interest in such a scheme, not least because of the ongoing battle over their own rights to the land, but also because rehousing under an SRS would shrink living spaces while rendering workshops and commercial enterprises unviable. In this reconfigured policy context, any material investment in the built space and infrastructures of the area—the homes, workshops, water taps, industries, businesses of this industrious middle-class neighbourhood—are rendered vulnerable to complaints of 'illegality'. The question of what is 'legal or illegal' is, therefore, a political rather than an empirical question.

In a transformed political-economic context in which the business of land, real estate, and construction are among the most lucrative in the city (as in the world more generally), the question of who can reside, build, produce goods, and do business in the city—where and how—is no small matter. The rumours of Seema's 'complaint' antics in ABC gesture towards the broader political and economic context and stakes of the election. The activities leading up to polling day in 2012—and the role of money in these activities—in other words, must be understood in relation to the materialities and political economies that infuse everyday life in Mumbai beyond election season. Given the legal vagaries and contradictions that characterize everyday life in Mumbai's popular neighbourhoods, both production and maintenance of a neighbourhood's physical form and infrastructure, as well all manners of business activity, generally involve some kind of mediation by someone who has access to various kinds of knowledge and resources that are necessary for navigating the physical, legal, and economic opacities of the city.[56] For instance, a broker is particularly sought after

---

[56] Elite Mumbaikars, incidentally, also rely on mediators for such things, albeit in somewhat different ways. Since such a high percentage of voters come from Mumbai's working classes, this research focuses on a non-elite neighbourhood.

when some required work requires proof of residency: a new water connection, for example, or inclusion in a slum rehabilitation scheme. This is especially true for the vast numbers of people living as renting tenants,[57] for whom proof of residency is exceedingly difficult to procure. In such cases, official applications are generally believed to have a better chance of being processed if they are accompanied by a letter from a politically connected person (a police officer or an elected official, for instance) verifying the address of the applicant. More important than the office or official position implied in the signature is the networks of power and authority that are implied in any particular signature. A powerful social worker, for instance, has no need for a corporator's signature, and conversely, an unknown corporator can accomplish very little without his social workers. A common popular and scholarly misconception is to assume that authority inheres in an official post itself. My research reveals that the direction of influence is the inverse, with the authority that an elected corporator is able to wield stemming from the fields of knowledge, authority, and influence from which he was elected. Hence, this prior question of *who* becomes corporator—or whom among social workers is awarded the party ticket—becomes quite interesting.

A SOCIAL WORKER WITH A PARTY TICKET

Ineligible to recontest in ABC due to the already mentioned change in reservation, Seema began the 2012 election season almost entirely unknown to XYZ's 40,000-voter-strong constituency. Seema was not alone; a newly implemented 50 per cent seat-reservation requirement for women (up from 30 per cent in 2007), in combination with the existing 30 per cent (combined OBC, SC, and ST)[58] caste reservations, unseated 70 per cent of Mumbai's sitting corporators during the 2012 election, while frustrating the aspirations of scores of would-be candidates. Moreover, on top of the gender and caste reservations, all of Mumbai's major political parties formed pre-poll alliances during the

[57] Tenants comprise an estimated 60 per cent of so-called 'slum dwellers', who themselves are estimated at more than 60 per cent of Mumbai's official population.

[58] Other Backward Class, Scheduled Caste, and Scheduled Tribe, respectively.

2012 corporation elections. Thus, while the party leadership hammered out seat-sharing agreements and candidate lists for the 227 wards, reports emerged from across the city (stories reported on gleefully by the city's excitable media) of bare-knuckled jockeying and threats of defection, with multiple social workers in each ward claiming it was 'their turn' to contest the election on the various party tickets.

Seema began campaign season not only entirely unknown, but faced with a sociopolitical landscape riven with deep wounds and fissures from the bitter fights over party tickets. In this context, the first order of business was to corral the support of the social workers, particularly those with Congress or NCP affiliations who were presumably amenable to alliance. Indeed, while Seema herself was unknown, her party of course, was not; the NCP boasted a strong network of social workers, many having longstanding personal loyalties to Mastanbhai, the standing MLA. Once her NCP candidature was announced, Seema thus found herself under the tutelage of a sprightly, diminutive, seasoned social worker named Hakim. Hakim's specialization was water and, before his kidneys failed, he used to spend long hours at the local water department office, pushing papers and negotiating hydraulic favours for area residents. Hakim was well known in XYZ—for his temper, his impatience, and above all for his unwavering work ethic. One well-known story has Hakim waiting for a municipal work crew that he had summoned to unblock a clogged drain. When the crew failed to arrive by midday (thereby putting Hakim's reputation on the line), the exasperated social worker is alleged to have leapt into the open drain, clawing out the muck and filth with his bare hands. Hakim's affiliation with Mastanbhai is longstanding, and his loyalty unwavering—particularly in the years since the MLA began picking up the bill for Hakim's monthly dialysis treatments. Indeed, not even when Hakim's own niece accepted a nomination from a rival party was Hakim's commitment to Seema's campaign called into question. This would not be the first time that Hakim would manage a campaign for a newcomer: Hasina's own victory a decade earlier is widely attributed to Hakim's reputation and networking skills.[59] Before that, Hakim had

---

[59] Hasina is an ex-councillor, also of Seema's party, who held the post two terms prior. Hasina had sought the party ticket from the standing MLA but was denied because, in the words of the MLA, 'her image was tarnished' from the business of 'running around making complaints.'

installed a woman named Sowmya in office on behalf of the Janata Dal.[60]
So it was with some confidence that, with Hakim at the helm, Seema
set out to build a network of support for her candidacy.

Thus, on a breezy night, early on in the campaign, our entourage
(comprised of Seema's immediate family, me, and Hakim) followed
Hakim to a meeting that he had arranged with a group of men—
butchers by profession—in the shade of the ramshackle tin roof of
the neighbourhood's open-air market, where I observed the following
exchange:

SEEMA: [addressing the men] What are your problems? Speak openly.

MAN A: Water!

HAKIM: Get your papers together and I'll arrange for new connections.

MAN A: We don't *have* papers.

HAKIM: Okay, there are other ways, but I can't talk about it here in the
open. Come to my home, we'll talk at my home.

MAN B: [animatedly] And demolitions!

SEEMA: Have I ever taken your money?[61] Never! See, I'll protect you,
you can trust me.

MAN B: [gesturing at the muddy uneven ground] We want to build a
new market hall, a proper [pukka] one. If you build it with your corporator fund, then no one can complain.

The legal status of built space and infrastructures sits at the heart
of area voters' concern, and the meeting thus gestures towards two
interrelated risks, on the mitigation of which the act of voting would
ultimately speculate: first, did Seema have access to networks of power
and authority that would enable her to successfully navigate the legal
contradictions governing the built space and infrastructures of their
neighbourhood? Making the rounds with Hakim—who was well known
in XYZ for his success in arranging municipal water connections for

---

[60] '*Hakimne usko jitaya*'—Hakim made her win—was how Sowmya's victory was generally explained.

[61] Here, Seema is referring to the practice of accepting money in exchange
for dropping an official complaint—a practice for which Hasina had become
infamous during her tenure two terms prior. Seema's rhetorical question—
'have I ever taken your money?—is an effort to distance herself from any
demolitions that may have occurred in the past.

residents who might not be in possession of the right combinations of documentary 'proofs' surely went some way (or at least attempted to) in producing some confidence that Seema's networks would extend inside key offices of the Municipal Corporation. But what was to say that Seema would use her authority and connections to make 'law' work in their favour rather than to their detriment?

Local brokers and community leaders sought to mitigate these significant risks in the run-up to the election both by forging reciprocal relations of obligation as well as by relying on already existing signs of shared values and areas of concern. Seema, for instance, initially began her campaign by reaching out to prominent leaders of community organizations affiliated with her husband's family's regional and linguistic group (as well, of course, to individual members of her extended family itself).

> We head over to the office of the XXX Welfare Society—an NGO run by members of the Tamil-speaking XXX community—where we're greeted by five men. One of the men, who appears to be a leader of sorts, tell us that 70 per cent of XYZ belongs to the XXX community. Since this is Seema's husband's community, I had expected to be greeted warmly ... but they're guarded, and receive us with open scepticism: 'We've never met you,' the man says flatly. It seems like an accusation.[62] 'I've been busy in Ward ABC,' Seema replies, without apologizing. The man responds (in the same slightly reproachful tone) that he'd heard there was a standing corporator in the neighbourhood; their society has had so many functions but they didn't invite her because they didn't know her. Now I can't tell if they're accusing her, or apologizing for not inviting her; maybe both. Seema nods and repeats 'I've been busy in ABC.' They seem to soften a bit ... but then one of the other men who hasn't spoken yet jumps in, 'You're not going to run around making complaints about illegal construction and demanding money like Hasina did, are you?' 'No, no!' Seema says quickly, anxiously, 'you can ask anyone in ABC whether I did that—absolutely not. [The MLA] has offered me the ticket [in his constituency] because of my good work in ABC.' She smiles, and laughs a little nervously, '[The MLA] told me he'd

---

[62] This conversation was conducted mostly in Tamil between Seema's husband and the Trust leaders. The translation was provided to me in Hindi by Seema's sister-in-law.

be behind me with a whip if I ever did that in his area.' They seem to accept this and nod. The first man says, 'Okay, the main problems here are water, blocked gutters, and we need more toilets.' Seema nods; this is nothing surprising. Then suddenly the second man starts talking about their group's programs—and now it seems they're selling themselves to Seema! 'We've given out schoolbooks, we gave out mutton on Eid, we give out sewing machines … and we've never take money from anyone!' Now it's Seema's turn to nod. After we're outside, I ask Seema to explain what the MLA had said to her about unauthorized construction. 'Is he opposed to making complaints and then collecting money? Does he instead want you to make complaints and then actually follow through?' She shakes her head vigorously. 'No, no,' she says, '[The MLA] says not to interfere; he says it's not my job.'

The palpable distrust that permeates this encounter is matched by the anxiety that runs through the exchange. The society leaders, for their part, tack back and forth between (on the one hand) trying to sell themselves to Seema—to convince the candidate, that is, of their standing in the neighbourhood, their status as benevolent patrons who 'never take money from anyone!'—and (on the other hand) attempting to assess, under conditions of absolute uncertainty, what Seema may or may not do if elected to office. The question posed to Seema, of whether she would run around making complaints, was clearly not a real question, but rather a straightforward expression of the deep uncertainty and unknowability that characterized the decision of whom to support.

Seema's newcomer status rendered her campaign highly vulnerable to the forces of rumour. Thus, the night after Seema's candidature was announced, Hakim counselled Seema that their first order of business was to sort out the troubled relations with local NCP and Congress party workers, Sushma, Hasina, Juned, and another long-time NCP party worker named Sonu who had sought the NCP ticket for his wife. Most important were Sushma and Hasina, who seemed open to collaboration; Juned and Sonu, who were reported to already have aligned themselves with the Samajwadi Party campaign, were quickly dismissed as lost causes. Despite Hasina's declaration of her niece's independent candidacy, she had made it known (through carefully spread rumours) that she would withdraw the application if only Mastanbhai would call her personally to seek her support for Seema's candidacy. As Seema explained to me, the only way that Hasina could rejoin the party while preserving her reputation and dignity (that is, her reputation as having strong networks independent of her association with Mastanbhai and his party) would be if she could proclaim that Mastanbhai himself had recognized the extent of her influence among area voters and had personally requested that she withdraw her niece's candidacy. Mastanbhai, however, was having none of it; as he explained to a gathering of 150 or so party workers a week before polling day, 'Hasina? The public rejected her. She asked for the ticket, but we did a survey in the area—her image was tarnished … We told her, "we'll give you other responsibilities and then next time we'll see." She said 'okay', but then put up her niece!' The standoff between Mastanbhai and Hasina was never resolved and Hasina did not withdraw her niece's candidacy.

As for Sushma, her reputation as a powerful social worker was rumoured to have an extended reach ('*Uski public bahut hai*', it was often said of Sushma—'she has a lot of public!') and Hakim counselled that Seema would do well to have Sushma on her side, or at least not campaigning against her. Indeed, after Sushma's initial phone call, during which she had apologized and pledged her support, the NCP ward president had been conspicuously absent and difficult to reach, having yet to come and meet Seema in person. Seema had requested a meeting earlier that very afternoon, but Sushma had put her off, telling her to 'come tomorrow'. Sitting in Hakim's home late that first night, Seema phoned Mastanbhai to ask his advice: 'Leave her behind,' Mastanbhai counselled, 'we'll get a new ward president. She's out of the party.' Seema, however, was not convinced and went to meet Sushma the following day. Mastanbhai had called a meeting of party workers for the following evening, Seema explained, and she needed a crowd; Sushma was the NCP ward president and 'her people' were needed.

Seema spent much of those first days in this way, rounding up social workers for the inaugural campaign meeting, where the strength of their various constituencies would be assessed. The evening before the meeting, we thus found ourselves (at the invitation of a childhood friend of Seema's husband) in the 5,000-voter-strong neighbourhood of Phule Nager, where Seema addressed a gaggle of social workers, instructing each of them to bring at least 50 women to Mastanbhai's inaugural party worker meeting the following evening. Thereafter,

Seema continued, she would need these women to work for her, to accompany her on rallies. 'They'll be fed and paid,' Seema explained, at the rate of Rs 200 each per day.' Seema clarified that the money would not go directly to the women, but rather as a lump sum paid to each social worker, to be distributed to the women as he or she saw fit. 'Bring your 50 women tomorrow,' Seema concluded, 'and we'll count them.'

People arrived in droves to the party meeting, and the 2,000 chairs rented for the occasion quickly proved insufficient to accommodate the crowds, who stood in lines along the back wall. Seema was visibly relieved at the impressive turnout. Seema's sister Razia explained, 'They're all *karyakartas*; this is a karyakarta meeting, not a *public* meeting. Most of the people here are paid to be here.' The people whom the various party workers brought were described as both karyakartas, as well as simply *log* (people). One party worker explained that 'in every lane, there will be some *main* person (*har ek gali me koi main rahega*) to whom people go when they need help; that's the person that we bring.' Indeed, Razia and a few other of Seema's relatives were standing at the entryway of the school grounds and circulating through the rows of seats to write down the names of social workers and count the number of supporters that each had brought. When Sushma's 'hundred women' turned out to number around 20, Seema's team set about speculating over whether this disappointing attendance was a sign of Sushma's weakness, or of her lack of commitment to Seema's campaign. Such assessments of party worker strength and loyalty—indicated by the numbers of each party worker's 'people' who turned up—was, Razia explained, the primary purpose of the meeting.

The first half of the two-hour meeting was thus devoted to inviting on stage a parade of prominent area social workers to be garlanded by Mastanbhai in the presence of the 2,000-person strong audience. Among those thus honoured, significantly, were a handful of high-profile defectors from rival parties: a senior party worker from the Republican Party of India (RPI) for instance, was summoned onstage along with—notably—four of her young karyakartas. Mastanbhai took care in recognizing each boy individually with a garland and a handshake, introducing him by name to the crowd. Mastanbhai made it clear that he intended for Seema to win, and the pomp and ceremony with which he recognized and honoured the social workers in the audience signalled that those among them who would help Seema win might in the future be able to leverage Mastanbhai's support—and his network of powerful contacts—in their future work.[63]

MONEY AS A SIGN OF TRANSLOCAL CONNECTIONS

During the two weeks leading up to polling day, Seema employed, at the rate of Rs 200 per day, anywhere from 15 to 1,000 people every day to attend rallies and to accompany her on parades around the neighbourhood. The crowds (of mostly women) were 'provided' by various social workers to whom Seema paid cash at the end of each day according to the number of people provided. Notably, since all the major campaigns were offering cash for a crowd, there is no reason to think that a woman receiving money from one or another party would have any reason to be inclined to vote in any particular way. While the women, of course, needed to be paid for their labour (many people having taken time off from regular jobs in order to make themselves available for this work), the real meaning of the money inheres in the transaction between Seema (or Seema's team) and the *social worker*, rather than the *voter*. The trust-building (as opposed to instrumental, exchange) function of the cash payments was further demonstrated when one of Seema's men eventually spotted Sushma (our elusive NCP ward president) at a Samajwadi Party rally. On that particular day, Seema had employed 40 of Sushma's women. After some hand-wringing over whether or not to pay these women for that day's work (Seema did eventually pay them), Seema explained to Sushma's women that their leader seemed to have switched parties, and instructed them to please not return the following day; there were other social workers eager to send women in their place.

If money works not as the medium of purchase, but rather, gift-like, as productive of longer-term relations and alliances, then

---

[63] This dynamic was again evidenced on the eve of the election when the neighbourhood's elected MP made an appearance in Seema's office. The half hour that this senior Congress party member spent in the little office was devoted to meeting and taking down the names of Seema's 15 or so most active campaign workers. The purpose of the list remained unspecified, but clearly suggested a promise of future favours.

what is the significance of *cash* as the substance of such gifts? Cash exchanges that took place in the run-up to the election worked as a sign of access to the most crucial kind of urban knowledge: of how to navigate the opacities, dangers, and promises of the city's little-understood but palpably real economies. Indeed, the contemporary city of Mumbai runs largely on cash—both rumoured and real. While the 2012 landslide victory of the incumbent candidate—a man named Fareed[64]—was credited by person after person to the reach and strength of the candidate's networks, discussions of the strength of the campaign almost invariably involved reverent references to Fareed's own business and personal wealth. While few people could account for the precise origins of Fareed's wealth or with what kind of business he might be involved, that he was rich was evidenced and signified both in the grand, three-storey palazzo that he has built at the heart of the working-class neighbourhood,[65] as well as in Fareed's liberality with cash: cash for marriages and dowries, cash for school fees, cash for medical bills, cash for home repairs. 'He is always very charitable,' one area resident explained, 'that's how he made a name for himself.' In the run-up to the 2007 election, a social worker named Raju (a long-time associate of Fareed's but who had joined Seema's campaign out of loyalty to the MLA, Mastanbhai) explained, Fareed was very liberal with cash: 'that time,' Raju told me, '*everyone* got money.' Raju explained that this time around it was not necessary to actually *distribute* cash, 'Fareed is the master of hype—even if he just gives a hundred rupee note, people run around saying "Fareed is distributing so much money!"' For Fareed, rumours of cash distributed are as good as distributions of cash itself, the work of the cash being less that of actual exchange, than of shoring up reputation.

In the weeks following the election, social workers, residents, and higher-level party officials invariably told me that Seema's bid for

---

[64] Or rather Fareed's aged mother; XYZ was reserved as a 'ladies ward' during the 2012 elections.

[65] Notably, Fareed no longer actually *resides* in this neighbourhood; he built the house around the time that he relocated to Navi Mumbai, suggesting importance of the house as a spectacle of wealth.

office failed because area social workers had advised their various 'publics' to vote for Fareed. Seema's 2012 loss thus mirrors her 2007 victory in Ward ABC, where—according to both Seema as well as area social workers—the seat had been gifted to her by defecting social workers formally affiliated with a rival party. Following a split among higher-ups in their own party, the ticket in ABC had been awarded to a candidate affiliated with the rival faction; should this person be elected, it would have jeopardized social workers' access to the offices of the Municipal Corporation, the police, and so on. In an effort to forge new lines of connection, the area's entire contingent of social workers had decided to throw their weight behind Seema's 2007 campaign. Seema, who was completely unknown, nonetheless won by a comfortable margin and, as Seema recalled, without spending a single rupee to pay social workers to marshal their 'publics' for campaign rallies.[66] 'Last time, *we* made her win,' one social worker explained, 'but this time, over there [in XYZ], all the social workers supported Fareed.' Indeed, for social workers who would live and do business in the neighbourhood no matter *who* won, betting on the right candidate is of crucial importance. At issue, in other words, is not so much the risk of revenge by the victor against areas from which he did not win support,[67] but rather the risk of putting someone incompetent, short-sighted, or vindictive at the helm of the ward.

WHAT MONEY CAN BUY

Less than two years into her term as elected corporator, Fareed's ailing mother passed away. A by-election was called, and a furious public—which had so recently demonstrated overwhelming support for Fareed but was now enraged at what was described as his

---

[66] In the 2010 legislative assembly election, the same contingent of social workers helped to hand the legislative assembly district to their new party—a party which had previously had almost no presence in the neighbourhood.

[67] Indeed, the aftermath of the election—not only in XYZ but across Mumbai—was notable for the absence of any retribution against neighbourhoods that booth-wise polling data showed to have voted the wrong way.

'disappearance' following his mother's election[68]—handed a landslide victory to an independent candidate, the wife of a young man named Santosh had contested in 2012 on a Samajwadi Party ticket, but who had recently been expelled from the Samajwadi Party after a video clip circulated through the city in which Santosh appeared in police custody, demonstrating how, using a small machine, he had been duplicating credit cards. Santosh (whose wife had outflanked Seema in the 2012 election by a few hundred votes, but still garnered less than a third of the votes that Fareed's mother got) had reportedly blanketed the neighbourhood in cash in 2012; inside sources report that his campaign spent double what Seema's campaign had. When I had expressed to one of his social workers my shock at the scale of this misplaced investment, the man shook his vigorously, 'No, no! He didn't expect to *win* that first time around. See, before the election he was known around here only as "duplicate-note-wala Santosh"; but after the election he became "electionwala Santosh"!' Santosh used the 2012 election to whitewash his reputation, establishing himself as a generous and reliable benefactor (following his failed 2012 bid, he hammered this point home by taking his entire contingent of campaign workers on a week-long holiday to Goa). And following another cash-infused bid for office, Santosh's wife won the 2014 by-election in a landslide victory. A long-time Congress-affiliated social worker summed up Santosh's wife's victory like this:

> For a candidate, the most important things are to have contacts with the police and with the BMC. If you have approach with these two, then you get the people. Santosh is a known criminal—duplicate notes, duplicate credit cards, plenty of cash. There's so much corruption that people here want [to elect] someone who has plenty of money to pay the police and the BMC. And Santosh showed he had plenty of money. See, there are groups that form at the time of elections, and Santosh was there—he was always around, talking to these groups, listening to their problems, and making promises and paying them money, lots and lots of money. See, Santosh and his brother are in construction business. Construction is a lucrative industry and is also a great way to whiten money. But to succeed as a builder, you need to keep your houses from getting torn down [by the authorities], and to do that, you need contacts.

---

[68] Fareed explained to me that he regretted having disappointed his constituents but he had been called away by his duty to care for his mother.

A local contractor named Karim explained to me what this means in practice. When he's preparing to start a new work, Karim tells me,

I call up everyone—the corporator, local offices of political parties, the various departments of the Municipal Corporation, the police, everyone. But still, people from the neighbourhood can complain—they can take a photograph and complain. When that happens, the BMC will call me and tell me to 'manage that person'. If that person is a serious complainer—if they follow up on the complaint—then I have a problem; in this case, the BMC will come and demolish a little bit. Then take their own photograph proving that they have responded to the complaint with this demolition. But, of course, then the BMC and the police officials are vulnerable, so they tell me 'go ahead but do the work fast'. Speed is key to the success of my work.

To be a successful contractor, in other words, requires not only that a contractor maintain networks of connections with local officials, but that in order to 'do the work fast', he must have reliable and on-demand access to all the materials required for construction: cement, sand, water, labour, and cash. These are materials and resources that are difficult to procure—particularly sand and water, the procuring of which is legally and infrastructurally complex. To be a successful contractor, in other words, requires elaborate networks of trust not only in the neighbourhood, but throughout the city and beyond.[69] Indeed, while Karim tells me that while he calls himself a 'contractor', his role is actually more that of a 'point man'. He explains that because his work has an ambiguous (even antagonistic) relation to formal law and urban policy, 'reputation' and 'guarantee' are very important. 'Other contractors, if there's a dispute, maybe they run off with the deposit or something. But with me, I've never had a dispute. I keep goodwill with everyone.' Maintaining 'goodwill', Karim explains, is the essence of the work of being a 'point man'. In the case of our contractor-turned-corporator's husband Santosh, all of which is to say, the imperviousness of his houses to the forces of 'complaint' demonstrated the strength and reliability of his networks, signalling to area social workers and voters

---

[69] Many construction materials are sourced beyond the territorial boundaries and administrative jurisdiction of the city.

that Santosh might indeed be a very good person to represent them in the municipal corporation.

★ ★ ★

These ethnographies of election-time cash distributions in very different field sites suggest four general conclusions.

First, cash exchanges cannot be described as 'vote buying' in Schaffer's sense of 'purchased delegation'—that is, in terms of 'short-term contracts—money for votes' in which 'once votes are paid for, politicians may feel free of any debt to their voters.'[70] Rather, what we find in both urban and rural ethnographies is that cash both produces and flows through enduring sociopolitical and material relations and obligations. In both Mumbai and in rural Bihar, we see how cash distributions articulate chains of 'brokers' who are influential and powerful local people without whose support it would be difficult to win an election. While candidates cannot 'buy' the support of these brokers, the cash gifts work to create and consolidate constituencies of support among networks of brokers.[71]

Second, while locality continues to matter in the expression of material and symbolic authority, we see in both Mumbai and Bihar that the basis of brokers' authority and power is increasingly tied to connections, networks, and processes that are translocal. In the research area in Bihar, a great deal of election-time cash is generated through sand-mining profits and this cash is distributed mostly through the networks of people connected to the 'sand mafia'. Similarly, in Mumbai, we see how the authority of local 'point men' like Karim and Santosh hinges upon connections to the multi-scalar networks that produce and protect the neighbourhood's structures and infrastructures.

As these first two points suggest, the chain of connections produced and described by cash cannot be characterized as vertical in structure as Srinivas's model suggests, with the party at 'the top' operating at a larger scale within which the brokers' authority is 'nested' and as the source of resources flow in a downward direction. Rather, we see

---

[70] *Schaffer*, Elections for Sale, 11.

[71] See Björkman, 'You Can't Buy a Vote,' for a more thorough discussion on these limitations.

that (first) the scales of authority have become asymmetrical, and (secondly) that resources flow in all directions. This means that relations among brokers and voters (on the one hand) and brokers and parties (on the other) are easily describable neither as straightforwardly 'vertical' as Srinivas's formulation suggests, nor as horizontal, as Guha, Breeding, and Chatterjee would have.

We see in both accounts that cash does not flow from candidates to voters *via* brokers, but rather cash is distributed by candidates *to* brokers who candidates believe and speculate might have influence over groups of voters. And contrary to Breeding's contention that, in the absence of enforcement mechanisms, these gifts are largely symbolic gestures given to 'already loyal supporters',[72] we see as well how the mechanism of cash gifting helps and hopes to produce these relations of obligation and mutual benefit. So, while Guha is correct in his observation that electoral reforms have shifted moral hazard to the candidate and/or the party, the story is more interesting than his simple reversal of the direction of influence suggests.

In addition—and contra the notion that the curtailing of coercion has freed voters from vertical relations and shored up *horizontal* social identities—what we see in the accounts is how the new political economies of rural and urban India are producing *new* forms of hierarchy, asymmetry, and coercion, and how these newer forms both articulate with and challenge older forms of power in complex ways. In Bihar, we saw that regional political economy is organized around caste-based networks and caste identities are still central to party support. Local politicians claim that less cash has to be distributed to the core caste supporters of parties—Yadavs and Muslims for the RJD and upper castes for the BJP, for instance. But the electoral influence of land appears to be weakening; most of the brokers and local leaders distributing money in our research villages in Bihar were not large landlords (or their land was purchased with money made in regional economic activities). But even as landholding as a basis of electoral influence is weakening, the centrality of caste identities is not and regional political economy such as sand mining is organized around caste-based networks. Similarly, in Mumbai, we saw how caste, language, and community continue to be important dimensions of local

---

[72] Breeding, 'The Micro-Politics of Vote Banks in Karnataka'.

networks of trust, but that language, caste, and community work in ways that are indistinguishable from other dimensions of identity that are of equal salience in the urban context: locality, for instance, which is the scale at which infrastructural claims and needs (water, sewerage, drainage) are expressed and experienced.

Fourth, and related to these points, the ethnographies show how an increase in *cash* as the election-season medium of gifting is related to two processes. First, cash signifies accesses to these translocal networks. Where patronage relations in Srinivas's formulation (echoed by Kothari, Yadav, and Kohli) are 'activated' at election times either by goods that index access to party and state resources (welfare programmes, for instance) as well as by the distribution of durable and luxury goods (saris or spirits), voters in both Bihar and Mumbai demonstrate that they're interested in money. And what's more, they're interested in money not (only or primarily) as a good in itself (that is, for the exchange value printed on the note), but rather as an index of the broker's access to broader, translocal political and economic networks. The ethnographies from both Mumbai and Bihar thus demonstrate the increasing importance of new economic activities, especially related to construction—suggesting the extent to which economic growth in both rural and urban India is reshaping both local and regional political economies in ways that are transforming everyday politics.

There are key differences as well that have emerged between the Mumbai and Bihar accounts. The shifts described above, for instance, articulate in different ways vis-à-vis caste identity. In rural Bihar, the translocal networks that election cash is part of reflect the dynamics of sociopolitical change. Regional networks buttressed the dominance of upper-caste landlords in the wake of zamindari reform. In the wake of Mandal, the emergence of OBC regional networks—especially criminal networks—provided leverage to a new class of OBC leaders, fuelling a 'backward-caste' struggle against 'forward-caste' dominance. Now, for the first time, these regional networks are no longer being used primarily in relation to efforts to maintain or contest dominance over the village. Rather, as regional economic activity booms while demographic pressure increasingly makes agriculture marginal, the direction of influence is reversing. Instead of regional networks being leveraged for struggles over local control, people are increasingly using local politics as a gateway to access the regional networks where economic opportunity resides. In Mumbai, by contrast, we see how caste, regional, and linguistic identities continue to matter at the local level in the sense that community centres and welfare societies perform brokerage functions in the neighbourhood, coordinating and facilitating access to state resources and offices. But we also saw that the role that these community networks play at election time, that is, in commanding political loyalty, is not really any different from the role played by associations that assemble around non-community and non-caste idioms.

The differences in the ethnographies from Bihar and Mumbai raise important and pressing questions: What difference does urbanism and urbanization make—why and how and to what end? How is urban growth transforming Indian politics and what are the implications for democracy? How might shifts in India's rural and urban economies either shore up or unsettle established hierarchies and uneven distributions of resources? What are the possibilities and limits of electoral democracy for shaking up entrenched class and caste inequalities and animating creative contestations over the future? The stunning influx of cash into Indian elections raises more questions than it answers— questions that, as we have shown, conventional contract-theory formulations are ill-equipped to answer. Making sense of the transformations characterizing India's political present will instead require theoretical and conceptual open-mindedness, creativity, and (most importantly) sustained research attention.

6 What Costs So Much in Indian Elections?

*Intuitions from Recent Electoral Campaigns in Mumbai**

Simon Chauchard

Elections are rumoured to be *very* expensive in India, and analysts frequently speculate that the costs of campaigns are spiralling up.[1] Various pieces of anecdotal information have been brandished as evidence to support these claims. While this does not constitute systematic evidence,[2] recent ethnographic studies[3] suggest that many

* I thank the editors, Lisa Björkman, and Irfan Nooruddin for interesting discussions. Thanks to Dinesh Dubey, Kaushik Koli, and Hanmant Wanole for research assistance and translations.

[1] See, for instance, Ajit Ranade, 'Money Flow in Civic Elections', *Mumbai Mirror*, 11 February 2017. 'Campaign Finance in India: Black Money Power', *Economist*, 4 May 2014.

[2] We so far lack systematic data allowing us to properly evaluate these recurrent claims, and it remains unclear whether the cost of electoral campaigns in India is large on a per-voter basis, or whether it is large compared to other democracies in which the enormous costs of electoral campaigns have been well documented, such as Indonesia or the United States. For data on Indonesia, see for instance Jeffrey A. Winters, 'Oligarchy and Democracy in Indonesia', *Indonesia*, no. 96 (2013). For data on American elections, see http://www.opensecrets.org.

[3] Anastasia Piliavsky, ed., *Patronage as Politics in South Asia* (Cambridge, UK: Cambridge University Press, 2014).

candidates, both in rural and urban settings, distribute gifts to voters on a large scale, and that candidates and political actors in general distribute large amounts of cash during elections. Second, these studies and other anecdotal tallies that appear in the press during electoral campaigns suggest that the *real* total cost of campaigns by far surpasses the *legal* limits fixed by the Election Commission of India (ECI) for state and national elections or by the various state election commissions for local elections. While different studies provide different numbers, both ECI bureaucrats and political operatives on the ground easily acknowledge that winning candidates (and especially serious contenders) spend *many times* more than the legal limit, sometimes by a factor of 30 or 50, but regularly by a factor of 10 or more. While political actors—including ECI officials—almost universally acknowledge that these legal limits are too low to allow modern campaigns to take place, this spending is read as evidence that elections are indeed expensive in India. Finally, candidates and political operatives generally agree with the idea that campaigns have been getting increasingly costly over time. For what they are worth, these complaints may suggest that the costs of campaigns are indeed spiralling up.

These various pieces of evidence—however incomplete or imperfect they might be—raise many questions regarding the role that money now plays in Indian elections. Why are elections so expensive? What motivates candidates to provide gifts? What explains variations in costs across candidates, constituencies, and states? Finally, what has changed over the past 30 years and for what reasons have elections become more expensive? Other chapters in this volume, as well as related work by the author, frontally explore some of these questions.[4]

While it indirectly relates to these questions, this chapter focuses on *what* costs so much in electoral campaigns in India, and on what candidates concretely spend their money during these presumably expensive campaigns. Specifically, I am interested in two questions. First, to what extent is this expenditure illegal—that is, unaccounted for—in official reports? Second, and more importantly, to what extent is this unaccounted spending directed towards illegitimate tactics or tactics that potentially threaten the fairness of elections?

---

[4] Simon Chauchard, 'Electoral Handouts in Mumbai: The Cost of Political Competition', *Asian Survey*, 58, no. 2 (March/April 2018).

To address these questions, this chapter relies on three types of data. First, it draws on the official guidelines and 'compendiums of instructions on expenditures' of the ECI. Second, this chapter incorporates material from a long-term ethnographic project that has led me to follow and repeatedly interview political operatives from several parties, in a single neighbourhood of Mumbai, since 2014, including during several electoral campaigns.[5] Specifically, I rely on daily observations of several groups of party workers during the weeks leading to the 2014 Maharashtra assembly elections and the 2017 Mumbai municipal elections.[6] I also rely on discussions with over 80 party affiliates in this constituency, whom my collaborators (Kaushik Koli and Hanmant Wanole) and I repeatedly interviewed since October 2014, including during and after the 2017 municipal elections.[7]

These affiliates belong to all parties playing a significant role in the constituency—the BJP, INC, Shiv Sena (SS), NCP, and the Maharashtra Navnirman Sena (MNS)—and serve at a variety of levels within their parties or within their parent organizations (youth wing, women's unit, regional unit, and so on). While most of them are low-level party workers (*karyakartas*), serving as presidents or vice-presidents at the booth or ward level, this sample also includes, for the three main parties (INC, BJP, and SS), the party's candidate in a recent election

[5] To protect the anonymity of my interlocutors, all names in what follows have been changed and I will simply refer to this competitive assembly constituency of greater Mumbai as Savli. There is no constituency called Savli in Maharashtra.

[6] In this chapter, I especially—though not exclusively—draw on the time I spent shadowing the efforts of this team of INC workers in ward ABC during the 2014 campaign. This crew operated out of the office of Ravindran, a popular INC politician in several wards of Savli. During the weeks leading to the campaign, his karyakartas conducted strategy meetings on a daily basis at Ravindran's office, and generally spent most of their time there, unless they were dispatched to a meeting, a rally, or to canvassing. Dinesh Dubey (my first collaborator on this project) and I spent most of our time following the life of this office during the weeks leading to the election.

[7] Though some of these discussions resembled 'semi-structured interviews', they were more spontaneous discussions during the first few months of research. Most importantly, these discussions typically took place over several meetings and a variety of topics were addressed during these discussions.

(either the 2009 or the 2014 assembly elections, or the 2017 municipal elections), as well as district-level position-holders and members of the candidate's direct entourage.

While official expense reports provide a sense of legal and accounted expenses, this strategy provides rare, on-the-ground perspectives on the cost of campaigns and the allocation of campaign budgets—the real object of interest in this chapter. This allows me to learn not only about legal and accounted expenses, but also about illegal, illegitimate, and unaccounted expenses, and to estimate the relative amounts spent by candidates on each type of expense.[8]

The evidence provided in the next few pages overall lead me to make several important points about the campaign expenses of candidates in Mumbai, and beyond, and what might have led campaigns to become so expensive in the city. Though this will be obvious to most readers with some knowledge of Indian politics, I document that the legal and accounted expenses of candidates only represent a miniscule fraction of their real expenses. I also show that actual expenses include, as is often suspected, a large number of gifts and handouts to voters and/or local influencers, in line with suspicions that votes are routinely being bought and sold in Indian elections. However, I also show, *contrary* to the belief that unaccounted expenses are expenses allocated towards the purchase of votes, that gifts and attempts at buying or influencing the choices of voters are neither the only nor even the primary reason why electoral campaigns are expensive in Mumbai. Other kinds of expenses, such as the short-term wages that candidates pay to their workers and to the crowds these workers recruit, or even basic logistical costs, place even more important constraints on candidates. While some voters or communities do receive costly gifts, campaigns are increasing in cost because they are getting bigger, more ambitious, sophisticated, and professional. Furthermore, I argue that gifts are rather unlikely to change the results of elections.

---

[8] A major caveat comes from the fact that my work takes place at the local level. As a result, I do not have good intuitions or data regarding the portion of political parties' spending that is not channelled through candidates (presumably a majority of this spending). This is worth noting insofar as parties' centralized spending indirectly contributes to local races, for instance by paying for advertising in local newspapers.

These observations have two important implications. The first is that expensive campaigns cannot be equated with illegitimate or corrupt tactics. The second implication derives from the first. Since illegal and illegitimate tactics such as electoral handouts do *not*, in and of themselves, explain the large cost of campaigns, the frequent perception among political actors that campaigns have been getting increasingly expensive over time does not necessarily imply that handouts have become more frequent. It may instead, as I argue, have to do with more structural changes in the context of democratic elections in the country, namely, their increasingly competitive nature, which drives the aforementioned changes in the scope of campaigns.

The rest of the chapter proceeds as follows. In the next section, I draw on official texts on expenditures and on analyses of expenditure reports across India to describe the legal expenses of candidates during campaigns. In the third section, I estimate the size of the discrepancy between legal and real expenses, drawing on two elections in Savli. The fourth section, the core of this chapter, details what candidates in Savli spent their money on during these campaigns. In this section, I rely on my qualitative data and on repeated interviews of political workers to detail what specific kinds of expenses lead to the large discrepancy between accounted expenses and actual expenses, and the relative size of each type of expense in a candidate's aggregate budget. The fifth and final section develops the implications of these observations.

LEGAL EXPENSES OF CANDIDATES

As documented in the chapter by Sridharan and Vaishnav in this volume, candidates in Indian elections are not free to spend as much as they like on their campaigns. The law states that the total election expenditure shall not exceed the maximum limit prescribed under Rule 90 of the Conduct of Election Rules, 1961 (if it did, it would theoretically amount to a corrupt practice under section 123 (6) of the Representation of the People Act [RPA], 1951). These funds can come from three sources: the candidate, the party, or any third party. While there are neither limitations as to how much of these funds have to come from each of these three sources nor limitations as to how much third parties (who may be persons, companies, firms, or associations) can lend or gift, candidates theoretically have two obligations. First, they have to report from which of these sources their funds come from. Second, their total expenses from these three sources have to remain below the legal limit.

The limit for election expenditure is revised from time to time and varies by state, and, in some cases, by rural/urban status of constituencies. As of 2014, the limits set by the ECI for Mumbai were Rs 70 lakh for parliamentary elections and Rs 35 lakh for assembly elections. In addition, the limit for municipal elections (decided by the State Election Commission of Maharashtra) were Rs 10 lakh[9] per candidate as of 2017.[10] While it is difficult to benchmark these amounts, they are small when measured on a per-voter basis. ECI data suggest that parliamentary constituencies possessed an average of 1.5 million eligible voters in 2014, and that Maharashtra assembly constituencies were home to roughly 290,000 eligible voters, on average. This suggests that candidates were legally able to spend Rs 4.6 (seven cents in USD) per voter in Lok Sabha elections and about Rs 12 per voter (18 cents in USD) in Vidhan Sabha (state assembly) elections. Even taking in to account the cost of living in India, these official limits do not allow for extravagant campaigns.

Under section 77 of the RPA, 1951, every candidate participating in a national or state election is required to keep a separate, accurate account of all expenditure incurred or authorized by the candidate or his election agent between the date of nomination and the day results are announced. The ECI has the authority to audit these accounts during the course of the campaign. Once the results are declared, every candidate has to produce a report on said account within 30 days. Since 2014, candidates are also required to open a separate bank account dedicated to paying campaign expenses, to facilitate the monitoring efforts of the ECI, and (theoretically, at least) to e-file their expenses.

[9] In USD as of June 2017, respectively, $107,692, $53,846, and $15,384.

[10] Given that parliamentary constituencies include over five assembly constituencies on average and that assembly constituencies include over seven municipal wards on average, these official limits imply that authorities recognize that local elections are much costlier on a per-voter basis than higher-level elections. This is an intuition that the vast majority of my political interlocutors on the ground in Savli confirmed.

Under section 10A of the RPA, 1951, if the ECI finds that a candidate has failed to lodge an account of election expenses within the time and in the manner required without an adequate justification for the failure, it has the power to disqualify the candidate for a period of three years from serving in either house of Parliament or in the state legislative assembly or legislative council.

As detailed in the ECI's latest 'Compendium of Instructions on Election Expenditures',[11] a sophisticated machinery working around the powerful returning officer (RO) has developed over the years in order to monitor the expenditures of candidates. This machinery includes field components, such as flying squads (FS) and static surveillance teams (SST), liquor monitoring teams and video surveillance teams (VST), as well as back-office elements, such as the video viewing team (VVT) and an accounting team. On the ground, at the constituency level, all of these actors typically report to assistant expenditure observers (AEOs), who themselves report to expenditure observers (EOs) and ROs—all of whom are members of an 'expenditure monitoring cell'. In addition to reviewing the accounts of candidates (both during and after the campaign), these actors decide on the rates of various expenses to be recorded by candidates (before the campaign), keep track of the visible spending of candidates (by shadowing candidates, randomly auditing their expenses, and taping events), respond to complaints from the public, and regulate the transport of cash and liquor during elections (leading to numerous and typically heavily publicized seizures). To carry out these functions, they coordinate with various law enforcement agencies. While a discussion of the efficiency (or lack thereof) of this monitoring framework is beyond the purview of this chapter, it is worth noting that a sophisticated monitoring structure exists.

Within this legal framework, what are candidates allowed to spend on? The answer to this question can be found in the instructions provided by the ECI as well as in the official expenditure reports filed by candidates after the elections.[12] These legal expenditures can be

---

[11] I refer here to the September 2016 version of these instructions. 'Compendium of Instructions on Election Expenditures', Election Commission of India, Document 6 Edition 2, September 2016, http://eci.nic.in/eci_main1/E-Book/Compendium_%20EEM_Sept2016/index.html#/0.

[12] See annexures 15 and 16 of the aforementioned instructions.

divided into six categories (though the sixth is very much a residual category):

1. Expenses related to the cost of public meetings, rallies, processions, and the like. These are very diverse and potentially include:
    a. Vehicles for transporting visitors.
    b. Costs related to the erection of stages, or to podiums and stage furniture (this may, for instance, include red carpets, tables, and chairs).
    c. Expenditures on chairs *for the audience*.
    d. Arches and barricades.
    e. Flowers and garlands.
    f. The hiring of loudspeakers and microphones, and the like.
    g. Posters, pamphlets, banners, cut-outs, and hoardings. In recent times, this may also have included erasable tattoos and paper facemasks.
    h. Beverages like tea, water, cold drinks, and juice, *to be distributed to political workers and speakers*.
    i. TVs, screens, projectors, display boards, and 3D displays (the latter possibly for the display of holograms).
    j. Expenses on celebrities, musicians, and artists.
    k. Illumination-related items.
    l. Expenses on transport of material and guests (other than cars).
    m. Power consumption/generator charges.
    n. Rent for venues.
    o. Guards and security charges.
    p. 'Boarding and lodging expenses of self, celebrity, party functionary'.
    q. 'Other expenses'. This may be where firecrackers and other miscellaneous expenses not already listed here fit.

[Note that special procedures exist to report expenses of events featuring leaders listed as 'star campaigners'.]

2. Campaign materials other than those used in meetings, rallies, or processions. This refers to expenditures used during canvassing (in the presence of the candidate or not) or distributed at the candidate's headquarters or during any other type of legitimate campaign activity that is not a meeting, a rally, or a procession,

as in the first point. Many of the legal expenses included under this category are already listed in the first point earlier: handbills, pamphlets, posters, banners, amplifiers, and loudspeakers.

3. Expenditure on print and electronic media including cable network, bulk SMS, or Internet or social media for candidate.
4. Expenditure on campaign vehicles. This may include hiring cost as well as fuel, driver's charges, and so on. This may concern both the candidate's vehicles and display vehicles mounted with screens or banners.
5. Expenditure on campaign workers/agents. This may concern honoraria and salaries for campaign workers, as well as boarding and lodging in some cases. Importantly, the rules do not precisely define who counts as a campaign worker and also use the word 'agent'. Accordingly, this may be interpreted to refer to a variety of positions: office manager, peons and cooks, personal assistants, personal bodyguard for the candidate, social media 'community manager', accountant, treasurer, secretaries, and the many workers or karyakartas that work alongside the candidate to spread his message and convince voters.
6. 'Any other campaign expense.'

While this is already a fairly exhaustive list, it is important to clarify what is absent from it and what other instructions from the ECI explicitly forbid. As seen in the above list, part of a candidate's budget can be allocated to beverages and food *for campaign workers*. But neither food nor beverages (especially alcoholic beverages) can legally be distributed *to voters*.[13] Indeed, any kind of transaction or gift, either in kind or in cash (see next), between political agents and voters is strictly forbidden during the campaign.

Official expenditure reports filed by candidates after the election, assuming they were honest representations of candidates' real expenses, would give us a sense of the relative amounts spent on each type of expenditure listed here. While they are rarely posted online, these expenses can typically be obtained through a Right to Information (RTI) request. For what it's worth, the Association for Democratic

---

[13] Note that this in practice would require a clear distinction between voters and political workers, which may not be that easy in practice.

Reforms (ADR) recently attempted such an analysis of the expenditure reports of newly elected MLAs in the 2017 Punjab elections.[14] According to their analysis, 42 per cent of expenses were incurred on meetings, processions, and so on; 20 per cent were spent on campaign materials; 20 per cent were spent on vehicles; 7 per cent on campaign workers; 7 per cent on other expenses; and 4 per cent were spent on media.

While these numbers may be informative (the fact that candidates declare spending so little on media, for instance, might be comparatively interesting), there are several reasons to pay scant attention to the data contained in these reports. As suggested by ADR, these reports filed by winning candidates (and, hence, candidates who likely ran among the most expensive campaigns in their constituencies) strongly suggest that the monitoring machinery of the ECI fails at controlling the expense of candidates, and that candidates do not feel strongly pressured to provide realistic accounts of their spending. As noted by the report, for instance, 38 per cent of winning candidates in Punjab declared that they did not spend *any* amount on meetings or processions, which seems highly improbable (and relatively easy to check). Besides, these newly elected MLAs only declared total expenses that averaged at 55 per cent of the legal limit, which is highly suspicious given that this limit is already low. Of course, these suspicions are compounded by two of the worst kept secrets of Indian politics, on which I expand in the following sections: that candidates spend exponentially more than they report, and that some of these additional (and hence illegal) funds are spent on activities explicitly prohibited by the ECI, and potentially on tactics that threaten the overall fairness of the electoral process.[15]

Accordingly, in order to make useful inferences on the campaign expenses of candidates in India, it is necessary to go beyond these reports and to estimate: (a) how much candidates really spend; and

---

[14] 'Analysis of Election Expenditure Statements of MLAs—Punjab Assembly Elections 2017', Association for Democratic Reforms and Punjab Election Watch, 28 April 2017, accessed 8 June 2017, http://adrindia.org/content/analysis-election-expenditure-statements-mlas-punjab-assembly-elections-2017.

[15] It should be noted here that these expense reports have all been validated by the ECI as of June 2017, in spite of these problematic numbers.

(b) what they really spend their money on. While doing this on a large scale would require considerable resources, ethnographic methods and patient fieldwork in one constituency of Mumbai allow me to provide a window into the real expenses of candidates in a single site.

HOW MUCH DO CANDIDATES *REALLY* SPEND? AN ILLUSTRATION

Much of my time shadowing candidates during both the 2014 assembly elections and the 2017 municipal elections in Savli—the two elections on which I draw here—was spent devising a method to estimate the real amounts spent by the main candidates.

Estimating the amounts disbursed by candidates with precision is obviously hard, for several reasons. This is, unsurprisingly, because the amount of cash spent by candidates is not readily observable by keeping track of campaign events. While part of the money is certainly spent in a very visible manner—as I explain subsequently—most of it is not. Besides, political workers did their best to prevent my collaborators and me from observing excessive spending first-hand—except in a handful of cases. Therefore, observing all transactions was impossible. In addition, attempting to observe transactions could have later compromised my access to the campaign crews I followed.

This does not mean, however, that it is altogether impossible to estimate candidates' spending patterns. To the contrary, rumours about the spending of the various candidates were common topics of discussion among political workers in Savli, and most of our interlocutors had a surprisingly confident opinion of the amount spent by each of the main candidates. And since low-level party workers were rather open to describing the spending patterns of their own candidate—often to complain about them—as well of other candidates, we chose not to observe and monitor the spending of candidates first-hand, and rather to rely on these discussions to estimate the spending of candidates.

Thus, in what follows, I rely on subjective estimates provided by these political workers. Concretely, in the months following the 2014 elections, I asked 8 to 12 workers of each of the main parties that had competed in the assembly constituency (INC, BJP, INC, Shiv Sena), over the course of broader and repeated discussions on politics and on their own political experience, to estimate the total spending of their candidate as well as of the other three main candidates. While other methodologies may be equally appropriate, I simply asked these workers to provide me with intervals for each of the candidates. In this section, I present an interval for each candidate that takes into account the estimates of each of these political workers.[16] In follow-up questions, from which I draw below, I subsequently questioned them on the kind of expenses that candidates had engaged in order to reach the stated amount, which allowed me to get a sense of these workers' perceptions of candidates' budget allocations.

Several elements lend relative credibility to these estimates, even though workers may not always be knowledgeable about the details of their candidate's spending, and even less so, of other candidates' spending. First, even though these discussions did not provide me with precise estimates, the intervals provided by these different workers overlapped and frequently converged. Second, workers attached to different parties tended to converge on the ranking of the various candidates in terms of spending. Third, not a single one of my interlocutors pretended that their own candidate had respected the official limits set by the ECI for an assembly election. On the contrary, in spite of the fact that they were well aware of these limitations, as well as of the penalties their candidates would incur if they were convicted of violations, *all* admitted that their candidate might have spent *at least* three or four times the legal limit, and often much more than that.

Overall, the estimates that emerged from discussions with Savli political workers regarding the 2014 assembly elections suggest the following: The Shiv Sena candidate—a serious contender in the race[17]—had clearly spent the least of all serious candidates, somewhere between Rs 1 and 2 crores (between $153,000 and $306,000, or three to six times the legal amount). The BJP and the INC candidates, also serious contenders in the race, had spent far more (estimates vary from 1 to 5 crore for the BJP candidate, and from 2.5 to 6 crores for the

---

[16] Altogether, across party lines, my collaborators and I interviewed 51 workers. The lower bound of the interval I present below is the lowest of the lower bounds I was given across workers, while the higher bound is the highest of the higher bound I was given.

[17] I deliberately refrain from providing final vote shares to maintain the anonymity of the study.

INC candidate).[18] The NCP candidate, who was not a contender at the beginning of the race—the NCP is traditionally very weak in Savli—but ended up with a vote share in the high single digits, surpassed all of these candidates, with estimates ranging from Rs 9 to 16 crore (that is, between 27 and 45 times the legal limit).

I subsequently repeated this exercise with my contacts in the weeks and months that followed another election, the February 2017 Brihanmumbai Municipal Corporation (BMC) election in ward ABC of Savli, in which I had already spent much time during and after the 2014 Assembly elections. In this ward, there were four serious contenders (one from each of the INC, Shiv Sena, and BJP, plus an independent), each of which ended with a vote share above 10 per cent.[19] I collected the following estimates for this election: The Shiv Sena candidate once again reportedly spent the least of all, with estimates ranging from Rs 60 lakhs to Rs 1.1 crore (between 6 and 11 times the legal limit). The independent candidate had reportedly spent between Rs 40 lakhs and 1.5 crore (between 4 and 15 times the legal limit).[20] The INC and the BJP candidates had in all workers' opinions spent the most, each between Rs 2 and 3 crore (that is, between 20 and 30 times the legal amounts).

As was often emphasized during these discussions, these amounts do not include the sums that most, if not all, of these candidates would have had to shed in order to obtain a party ticket.[21] These sums

---

[18] So, between 3 to 15 times the legal amount for the BJP candidate, and between 7 and 18 times the legal amount for the INC candidate. Also, I deliberately refrain from naming the winner of the race here to maintain the anonymity of my interlocutors.

[19] I similarly refrain from naming the winner of the race here to maintain the anonymity of my interlocutors.

[20] Estimates around that candidate were especially noisy because he had reportedly spent enormous amounts in the months that preceded the campaign rather than during the campaign, which led to discrepancies across estimators, who were unsure as to whether these early amounts should be considered.

[21] While money is not the only factor that parties base their ticket distribution on, all of our interlocutors confirmed that it is customary for candidates to pay a large sum of money to their party before or after they have been granted the ticket. As far as I can tell, this was equally true of all four parties described in this section.

however included the legal campaign expenses listed above (car rentals, chairs and stage rental for meeting, printing costs, and so on) as well as various types of illegal expenses that I detail as follows.

While they are noisy, these estimates suggest three important things. First, and as noted above, all major candidates massively exceeded the legal spending limit in Savli.[22] In both elections, major candidates spent large amounts relative to the legal limits, but also in some cases, per voter. Second, there were important differences across candidates (and maybe across parties, though two data points may not be sufficient to be sure of this). Third, in Savli at least, one challenger (the NCP candidate) spent far more than any other candidate. This behaviour quickly earned him the derogatory reputation of a 'money-based can-didate' or 'money-power candidate', referring to the fact that he did not have a pre-existing record or reputation as a politician to uphold (he was a wealthy developer by profession), and perhaps to the belief that much of this spending was done in an obnoxiously visible manner during the campaign.

Subsequent discussions with party workers suggest that such patterns are not exceptional. As mentioned earlier, that the main contenders in Mumbai elections spend far more than what ECI rules authorize is not a secret among journalists and officials. It is equally well known among political workers that candidates should not bother seeking a ticket unless they know they can spend large amounts of cash. For one, no party would give a ticket to a candidate who promises to spend around (or less than) the 35 lakhs authorized (for assembly elections) or the 10 lakhs authorized for municipal elec-tions. Besides, such candidates would not be likely to be able to afford the price tag for a ticket (that is, the gift to be paid to the party in exchange for the ticket).

Such implicit rules are common knowledge among party workers, all the way down the hierarchy of parties. This is best illustrated by my exchange with Aditya Yadav (AY below), a commission-based insurance salesperson serving as ward-level vice-president for the BJP.

---

[22] Another frequent observation was that these amounts had increased in comparison to the last assembly elections in 2009 or to the last municipal election in 2012.

When I inquired after the 2014 elections about his electoral ambitions, the following exchange took place:

> 'AY: I'm not sure I'll be able to run. There is no point even trying unless you have the money....
>
> SC: Well ... do you have a sense of how much you need?
>
> AY: Yes, of course. Everyone knows! You need to have *minimum* $50,000 to spend if you want to run for corporator, and *minimum* $200,000 for MLA [that is, more than three times the legal amount]. We have been told that also. Not sure I can do that. If [the seat] is reserved for OBCs, maybe I can because then the BJP may have no one better than me. But if it is a general seat, for sure it is not happening....'[23]

The presence in Savli of what may be called a super-spender (or 'money-based candidate') during the 2014 assembly elections appears equally unexceptional. Similar cases came up frequently in discussions about other constituencies or about corporation elections. In 2014, many of my interlocutors (including strong BJP loyalists) compared the case of the NCP candidate *in* Savli to that of a BJP candidate in an adjacent constituency.[24] In 2017, many low-level BJP workers had similar complaints, both about their candidate in ward ABC—who was both rich and 'dynastic'—and about the party's general preference for rich candidates across the city.

WHAT DO CANDIDATES SPEND THEIR MONEY ON?

These patterns in Savli in both 2014 and 2017 suggest that most, if not all, serious candidates spend many more times than what they are legally allowed to during campaigns. Since all candidates spend

[23] Emphases are his. He answered directly in dollars, maybe to make it easier for me to understand. His dollar estimates however seem consistent with the amounts in rupees described above, and in other interviews, though they actually look slightly on the low side.

[24] Workers ranted against the fact that both candidates had reportedly gotten their tickets 'because of money', even though they knew neither karyakartas in their own party nor voters. In both cases, this led to the same narrative. Namely, that the showering of cash orchestrated by these candidates was a desperate attempt at compensating for this initial handicap.

much more than they are allowed to, what do they spend their money on?

'Black Money', Electoral Handouts, and Illegitimate Influence

The most common answer to this question among observers of elections in India today relates to the now ubiquitous concept of 'black money', which I broadly understand to mean unaccounted funds (in this context, funds unreported in official expenditure reports or funds used in addition to those reported). In this narrative, 'black money' is often equated with illegitimate or corrupt tactics: candidates vastly overspend mainly because they attempt to unduly influence voters with illegal funds. In this narrative, the tone is often alarmist, as 'money power' is said to be used on a large scale around elections in myriad ways.

The ECI itself considers this to be the single biggest threat to the electoral process in the country. A vast portion of the aforementioned 'compendium of instructions on expenditures' of the organization is now dedicated to the identification of such practices and how best to combat them. Besides, leaders and former leaders of the organization[25] now easily recognize that such practices are common, and that candidates are creative in the ways they use 'black money' or 'money power'. A great example of this awareness is the following list, titled 'Forty Ways of Use of "Black Money" in Elections', distributed to expenditure observers by the ECI during a 2013 workshop.[26] I reproduce this list in full to illustrate the wild diversity of practices on the ground, across India, which ECI officials have presumably grown aware of and tend to include under this label:

1. Cash in envelopes in morning newspapers pushed beneath the door of the voter.

[25] S.Y. Quraishi, *An Undocumented Wonder: The Making of The Great Indian Election* (Delhi: Rupa Publications, 2014).

[26] This was part of a presentation during a workshop on Election Expenditure Monitoring organized by the ECI in September 2013 at the Delhi Secretariat ahead of the Delhi legislative assembly elections. The PowerPoint presentation 'Monitoring of Election Expenditure' was retrieved from the ECI's website on 20 May 2017.

2. Inside morning milk pouch, along with cash in an envelope to the voter.

3. Through self-help groups (SHG) for onward distribution among women voters.

4. Through pawnbrokers by reimbursing the short-term loan taken by voters, by mortgaging jewellery.

5. Paying cash as incentive for not casting vote by the committed voters of other rival candidate, if such voter shows his finger without indelible ink after election.

6. Cash given in advance before notification of elections to the local leaders for distribution among voters.

7. Cash given through community feasts under the plate or banana leaf.

8. Cash given in the name of Mahatma Gandhi National Rural Employment Guarantee Act (MGNREGA), Development of Women and Children in Rural Areas (DWACRA), or other government projects.

9. Cash given to dummy candidates for using the permission obtained by them for the campaign vehicles or political agents.

10. Cash given to certain non-serious persons of a locality to contest to divide votes of rivals.

11. Cash given to leaders of rival political parties or rival candidates not to seriously campaign in elections.

12. Black money raised by party/candidate in the name of coupon sale.

13. Cash given to the polling agents of rival's candidates, to be silent, during counting.

14. Cash given to village head for ensuring votes.

15. Cash given to village fund on the eve of elections for construction of road or temple or school, and the like.

16. Distributing cash among the ladies who come for *aarti* to candidate.

17. Distributing cash to those who come to attend public rally arranged by party or candidate.

18. Making cash payments for the vehicles or trucks for ferrying the voters to the place of rally or to the polling booth.

19. Cash given to journalists or media persons to write positively about the candidate or to write pessimistic news of rivals.

20. Cash given to journalists/media persons to blackout the news about the rivals or to publish negative news.

21. Cash transferred through real-time gross settlement route of banks to the accounts.
22. Cash given to the youth clubs on the eve of elections for organizing cricket match, football match.
23. Cash given for charity like organizing medical camp, melody party, theatres, and the like, on the eve of elections.
24. Distributing TVs, video recorders, and projectors to village clubs.
25. Giving cash for constructing toilets and tube wells, or mobile phone with top-up cards or laptops to the voters or local leaders.
26. Organizing mass marriage functions during election process and bearing the entire cost of marriage.
27. Distributing SUVs or luxurious vehicles to appease local party leaders.
28. Reimbursing fuel bills through negotiated deals with petrol pumps.
29. Promising jobs for the unemployed youth in the academic institutes or companies of the candidate.
30. Organizing religious functions like 'Prabachan', 'Ramayan', 'Hanuman Chalisha', and the like before elections.
31. Distributing free books to the students, just before elections.
32. Free admission to children of influential voters of a locality in engineering college or medical college run by the candidate.
33. Distributing free cows or buffalos among voters before election.
34. Distributing free agriculture seeds and manures among the voters.
35. Distributing free solar lamps among the rural voters.
36. Distributing diaries, calendars, purses, t-shirts, sarees, and vanity bags.
37. Using '*Aarthiyas*' (commission agents) for distribution of cash among farmers or waiving his commission demanded from the farmers.
38. Cash given to religious leaders or leaders of a caste for ensuring votes of their followers.
39. Distribution of liquor, drugs, and poppy husks among the voters.
40. Organizing rallies with film stars, musicians, orchestra, and important personalities in aircrafts or helicopters to the constituency and not showing the correct expenditure.

This list is interesting for several reasons. While it is—in numerical terms—overwhelmingly concerned with practices related to gift-giving, electoral handouts, and possibly 'vote-buying,'[27] it is notable that it also includes practices that do not entail a transaction between candidates and voters, even indirectly. Items 9 to 11 are concerned with the use of illegal funds to finance proxy candidates; item 17 relates to a widespread practice that may be called 'paid political participation' on which I expand below; items 19 and 20 relate to the practice of 'paid news' which has concentrated much of the ECI's attention over the past decade; and item 40 simply describes the use of unaccounted funds towards extravagant campaign expenses, though not necessarily illegitimate ones provided they were on the books. This diversity illustrates the vagueness of the concepts of 'black money' and 'money power', and suggests that illegal and unaccounted funds are used for more than just electoral handouts. Second, the fact that these practices are here grouped with practices that are obviously illegitimate and corrupt (such as electoral handouts) implies that they might be equally illegitimate, problematic, or dangerous, which may or may not be the case. Third, the near absence from the list of expenses on the authorized items listed earlier implies that 'black money' is largely devoted to the funding of illegitimate or corrupt tactics.

Are these reasonable assumptions? More generally, how are unaccounted funds spent? To answer this question, I return to Savli. Drawing on my observations during the 2014 campaign and on subsequent interviews, the next subsections describes the main ways in which unaccounted funds were likely spent in the constituency.

Unaccounted Electoral Expenses in Savli in 2014: Gifts and Handouts

In line with what the above 'black money' list of the ECI emphasized, electoral handouts and gifts played a major role in the 2014 campaign in Savli. According to estimates I collected from party workers during interviews, the various aforementioned candidates had spent between 19 per cent (for the Shiv Sena candidate) and 64 per cent (for the

---

[27] For nuances between these concepts, see Chauchard, 'Electoral Handouts in India'.

NCP candidate) of their large budgets on gifts to voters or to groups of voters.[28]

According to workers, the way in which most of these gifts were disbursed in Savli during the campaign[29] was through a lump-sum payment to influential citizens (housing society presidents, temple and mosque association presidents, and regional or caste association presidents). While Björkman observes such a transaction first-hand, a young Congress karyakarta (named Mohammad) inadvertently provided us with a stylized description of these remarkably common events as we met him at the candidate's office on a busy Sunday afternoon.[30] I reproduce here my field notes on this episode:

> As Mohammad was waiting to be called in the office of the candidate, several groups of men bypassed the line and went for the door. While they were unannounced, they were not pushed back the way other people are. Visibly incensed at this point, Mohammad started telling Dinesh what was likely going on. According to him, the first group of men was composed of leaders of a big housing society in xxxx. They were visiting the candidate to pledge the votes of members of their society and to get money in exchange. According to his description, this is what happens during elections in Savli. […] In the weeks leading to the elections, society presidents approach candidates to pledge their votes. In some cases, candidates approach presidents. While candidates do not always believe that these presidents actually have these votes— 'everybody knows you can't control voters today,' Mohammad says— they usually come up to an agreement. A few days later, a discreet visit is organized and someone from the inner-circle of the candidate, usually accompanied by a karyakarta from that area, delivers a big amount.

Importantly, this account converges with most other accounts I collected. The somewhat coherent account of these transactions that emerges from our notes suggests that these transactions take place

---

[28] These are averages across estimators.

[29] Some funds appeared to have been distributed throughout the calendar year leading to the campaign, for instance, during religious functions or marriages. While I do not describe such events here for an obvious reason—I was not there—such spending is theoretically included in the estimates of my interlocutors.

[30] Lisa Björkman. 'You Can't Buy a Vote: Meanings of Money in a Mumbai Election', *American Ethnologist*. 41, no. 4 (2014): 617–34.

ahead of the elections, though not at the last minute. Either the candidate herself, or typically a very close associate of the candidate—often even a family member—arranges for the delivery of the cash. Because the constituency is large, a senior karyakarta often accompanies him, though this is not always the case, and lower-level karyakartas are almost never involved in these high-level transactions. While lower-level workers are usually aware of transactions of this type in their area, these transactions remain discreet and understandably take place out of the public eye.

While I did not observe such a transaction first-hand during the time I spent with Ravindran's crew, these high-level transactions were a constant source of discussion among the karyakartas present in the office. Insofar as at least one other candidate was known to have engaged in such payments in societies of ward ABC—their very own societies—Ravindran and his workers were worried. While the NCP candidate had no political background, and his party was generally non-existent in Savli, his liberal spending led many Congress workers to believe that the NCP might win the vote in ABC. As the election was approaching, these perceptions grew stronger among low-level workers. Being aware of such transaction in their own area, many workers started predicting the NCP candidate's victory in private interactions. While Ravindran himself never said so, his concern was palpable as he organized an emergency meeting two days before the election. In front of a room full of karyakartas, where tensions ran high, Ravindran and a senior karyakarta had the following exchange:

RAVINDRAN: We have to tell people what [the INC incumbent] has achieved during five years. Many people just do not know and....

SENIOR KARYAKARTA: Sir, if I may. It is not the problem. [NCP candidate] has been giving money all around and what do we do …?

RAVINDRAN: I know, I know. Listen! This is why you also have to tell them that they do not have to vote for the NCP even if they get money, or if someone tells them they will get money if they vote for the NCP. You have to tell them loud and clear: 'TAKE THEIR MONEY BUT VOTE FOR US.'

Contrary to what this dialogue may suggest, it is not clear that the INC incumbent had himself refrained from distributing cash to local

leaders of ward ABC. Several discussions among low-level workers of
Ravindran's crew in fact suggested that he had definitely not refrained
from doing so, and these workers frequently blamed him for having
done so. This was, for instance, a frequent aside of Mohammad and Anil,
who both blamed their candidate for his strategy: instead of distributing cash through the party's existing network of karyakartas, he had put
his sons in charge. They had followed the same strategy as the NCP
candidate, and to make things worse, they had done it poorly. While
his opposition was not on moral grounds, Mohammad objected to his
candidate's strategy on three counts, which were somewhat contradic-
tory. The first two related to efficiency. First, he blamed the candidate
for having spent too little or for having spent cash in the wrong areas.
More importantly, he blamed his candidate for not having understood
that society presidents did not really have the power to convince many
people in their society, and that they were likely to 'keep most of the
money for themselves'. His last objection, while connected, related to
issues of fairness within the party: 'Instead of wasting all this money,
they should pay us better, since we work days and night to get him
elected.'

Another, more basic form of 'influence money' existed in Savli, as in
many other constituencies in India.[31] In addition to targeted payments
to 'influential citizens', money from several of the candidates trick-
led down party networks, which led to gifts and cash handouts being
showered on voters in a relatively indiscriminate manner during the
last day and the last night of the campaign. Contrary to observations
made in other contexts, this type of indiscriminate distribution was
restrained to very specific areas within ward ABC (namely, the poorest
areas and the ones in which voters were the least organized).[32]

Because this is the only form of influence that the ECI and police
forces can really hope to crack down on, observing such distribution
was equally challenging, as the local slums were filled with police that

---

[31] Shivam Vij, 'An Election in Matsura', *Caravan*, August 2010; Anastasia
Piliavsky, 'India's Demotic Democracy and Its Depravities', in *Patronage as Poli-
tics in South Asia*, ed. Anastasia Piliavsky (Cambridge: Cambridge University
Press, 2014); see also ECI list earlier.

[32] This may suggest that this type of cash distribution takes place when
parties are unable to arrange for the lump payments described earlier.

night. Discussions with party workers on election day, however, hinted at the fact that the much joked-about 'rat meetings' during which such handouts are delivered had occurred at several locations the night prior to the vote.

One place in which this form of distribution was likely to happen was Fatima and Ali's area, an unorganized squatter's camp threatened with eviction, which was notorious for its drug addicts, its population of public sanitation workers, and more generally, for high levels of misery. While Fatima never mentioned having been involved in any of this during our subsequent discussions, Ali, her 'freelancer' neighbour readily confirmed that the night had been busy when we met him the morning of election day. He had had several meetings and he had received not one but two cash handouts, and was waiting for a third one that had been promised by Srinivasan.[33] When I asked him, rather puzzled by this nocturnal hyperactivity, why candidates had waited till the last minute to do this, even though cops were all around, his answer was rather straightforward: 'For maximum impact!'

The fact that workers did not estimate both types of gifts to voters to jointly constitute the majority of candidates' expenses—except for the NCP candidate, who had reportedly spent a small fortune—suggests that important sums were dedicated to budgetary items other than gifts. While my material does not necessarily allow me to provide precise estimates of the relative share of each of these items in candidates' budgets, it is significant that two types of large and illegal expenses were mentioned over and over during my interviews with workers after the campaign. I refer to them in the following paragraphs as 'work money' and as 'politics-as-usual money'.

'Work Money'

Besides gifts and handouts, much of the illegal expenses of candidates were on wages, honoraria, and remuneration for diverse groups of

---

[33] Including a handout from a small candidate enjoining him to vote 'against the BJP'. The existence of this type of cash distribution in Fatima's settlement was confirmed later that day by BJP workers, who had observed it and reportedly 'tried to alert the police after [they] caught NCP workers red-handed'.

people. The concept of 'work money' simply refers to the wages that political candidates pay during the campaign. Since these wages are paid in exchange of a task, they are theoretically different from gifts. Gifts to voters are normatively problematic because they come with an expectation that the gift will yield a vote. By contrast, wages are likely less suspicious and problematic insofar as the recipient of the money has provided work in exchange for this payment, and is hence less likely to feel pressured to give away his vote in exchange for the gift. This is presumably why payments to workers and campaign employees are perfectly legal (as noted in the ECI list).

In Savli, candidates' payments to their workers constituted a major expense. While these estimates are less reliable than the ones presented above—since this was a particularly sensitive question to be asking to political workers themselves—political workers estimated that candidates on average spent over 10 per cent of their real budgets on these wages to their staff. Given the size of these real budgets, this implies that serious candidates may be spending several times more than the overall spending limit on wages to their workers alone.

According to party workers, Savli candidates typically provided large amounts to mid-level workers, who were then in charge of sharing it among their crew. While workers presented this money as compensation for campaign-related expenses (shifts at their 'regular jobs' not taken, rounds of tea offered, meals taken out of the house while canvassing, and so on), it is clear that many workers expected to make money—and not merely even out—with these compensations. Accordingly, part of the 'work money' spent by candidates is also directly meant for karyakartas, as salaries. The fact that political work was paid had acquired the nature of a norm among workers. As one of the oldest BJP workers in Savli—echoing a concern Ravindran and the BJP candidate himself later voiced—spontaneously told me when I asked him what had changed in the party since his time (the 1970s and 1980s): 'You simply cannot run a campaign without paying people nowadays. This has changed and it is a big problem. We used to give karyakartas only tea and samosas. If you do not pay them nowadays, many won't even come out of their house'.[34]

---

[34] While this is somewhat beyond the scope of this article, he interestingly attributed this trend to the progressive demise of the Congress post-1980.

This suggests that a major part of the unaccounted funds illegally spent by candidates goes not towards attempts at buying or unduly influencing votes but towards the functioning of their organization.[35] This may eventually have the same objective as gifts directly doled out to voters: candidates may wish to hire the workers that are best able to convince or influence voters, through a variety of means, including illegitimate ones. In that sense, they may attempt to buy influence on the ground rather than directly attempt to buy votes. Nonetheless, this remains less directly problematic overall than attempts at directly providing gifts to voters.

The normative case, however, becomes more complicated when the recipient of 'work money' wages are not workers but simple citizens who are not affiliated to the candidate or to her party. In Mumbai, as I suspect in most of India (see ECI list above), much of what political scientists refer to as 'political participation' (participating in processions, attending rallies or meetings, engaging in door-to-door canvassing, and the like) is contingent on these sums. While this may not be the case elsewhere, the norm for most campaign events in Mumbai is to pay participants. When I argued that this was unconventional, an influential party worker named Srinivasan dryly rationalized, 'If we didn't, almost no one among the public would show up and it would look really bad for the candidate.'

While these practices are easy to spot during Indian campaigns, excerpts from our field notes detail how this paid political participation unfolded in constituency ABC. As Ravindran's crew met to prepare a big 'bike rally' through the constituency five days before the election, the following scene took place:

> This morning Ajay called up all the karyakartas of ABC in small groups to the office, presumably by area ... After hearing a number of their grievances, Ravindran—with Srinivasan behind him—explained that each karyakarta present could bring up to 15 people to the rally that was scheduled at 2 p.m.. He asked that they bring good people, willing

---

The narrative goes like this: as the Congress started losing elections, they started paying their workers in order to prevent them from working for other parties. Soon other parties had to follow to remain an attractive prospect.

[35] Whether or not these attempts are effective is beyond the purview of this chapter.

to work, and that they should not leave until the end of the rally, contrary to what happened the previous week....

A few hours later, as we attempted to meet Fatima—one of the workers present at the meeting—at her house, we observed the following:

> Fatima is away somewhere, but we find her older son and a neighbour seated on plastic chairs in the middle of the main path ... As we sit down to smoke a cigarette with Ali, we observe the scene. They hold an open notepad and are approaching most young men passing by on their bike. The son is also making calls. They carefully explain the job: 'You have to be there at 1 so that you can get the flags fixed on your bike', 'Then the job is from 2 to 4', and finally 'You get 400 rupees for that. Petrol included'. When one of them says yes, they write down his name and phone number. As far as we can tell, they recruit anyone willing to go. Ali, who has himself organized 'the public' for the SP candidate, confirms this: 'Poor people will go to anything, it does not matter'.

While we do not attend the bike rally that day, we observe the following scene at the end of a procession for the INC candidate two days later:

> The rally ends under the bridge. As Ravindran and [the candidate] are still shouting slogans on the jeep (the sound was really bad today), tired participants start to evaporate or gather in little groups in shady areas. At this point we see a Tempo vehicle backing up; the trunk is full of individual boxes, which we later learn contain biryani. We approach closer to the spot to see the distribution. Behind one of the pillars of the bridge, a tall Tamil Congress karyakarta we have seen but never saluted is calling up names listed on a piece of paper. Mainly women. He hands a few notes to each of them. (200, maybe 300 rupees). They grab notes and biryani, and go.

Subsequent interviews confirm that such scenes are likely common during electoral campaigns in Mumbai, and political workers in Savli made no attempt to conceal this point: the people occupying most, if not all, of the seats during meetings were only there because they were paid. Evidence that this was the norm may be inferred from the fact that low-level karyakartas stubbornly refused to sit during meetings, and often frequently refused to walk during processions, not to be mistaken for members of 'the public'. When I asked him why he did not want to sit next to me on an unoccupied chair during a particularly tedious meeting, Anil, a karyakarta working two jobs in addition to his 'political work', immediately responded, 'Chairs are for the public! I'm a karyakarta and it would look bad....'[36]

Overall, such 'paid political participation' reportedly accounted for an even larger share of the expenses of Savli candidates in 2014: party workers estimated the overall amounts that the various candidates spent on hired crowds to range between 10 and 40 per cent of their overall expenses. This implies that considerable amounts in illegal spending were allocated to paying the salaries of poor citizens—often women and youth—occupying chairs at meetings and holding flags during processions.

While it is formally illegal, this 'paid political participation' did not appear to me to be as normatively problematic as the gifts that are sometimes doled out to voters during campaigns, or to constitute an urgent threat to the fairness of elections. This is because, as interviews later revealed, party higher-ups mostly do not expect the hundreds of voters whom they pay to wave flags or sit during meetings to support their candidate. In Savli, these people were recruited because they were poor and available. This was implied during a discussion I had during a BJP meeting with Rikhil, an influential ward-level president in Savli:

SC: So are all these people seating here [at a meeting] BJP supporters?

RIKHIL: These? I don't know. I don't think so. I have no idea who they are actually, but they just probably got something to be here ... poor people.

SC: So [BJP candidate] is giving this long speech in front of people who are not even likely to vote for him?

RIKHIL: No, hopefully they will ... but yes, you are right. See, the problem is that poor people around here are still addicted to the Congress and the NCP ... so we hope but it is very unlikely.

---

[36] While they do not like to be confused with members of hired crowds, party workers however tend to 'take a cut' on the sums disbursed by candidates in order to generate 'the public'. Ali, the aforementioned neighbour of Fatima, for instance, made a comfortable living in that manner during campaigns. A small-time freelance operator for *several* parties—except the BJP, which he pledged never to collaborate with—Ali was well known in ward XYZ for his ability to generate a public in a matter of minutes. In his own words, this was easy money: 'I get the party to give me 300 per person and I give each of them only 200. You can easily make thousands during campaigns.'

Judging from statements of this type, one can hypothesize that the objective of this 'paid political participation' was not to influence attendees themselves but to generate as much *tamasha* (spectacle) as possible in order to impress others (onlookers and bystanders). In that sense, it does not necessarily seem dissimilar or more morally ambiguous than advertising, which the ECI happens to authorize. While payments of this type to citizens are illegal and illegitimate according to the ECI (hence their inclusion in the 'black money' list), they may not deserve to be seen as equally problematic from a normative or moral standpoint. In my opinion, this constitutes further evidence that much of the funds illegally spent by candidates are not allocated to activities whose direct objective is to subvert the democratic process.

'Politics-As-Usual' Expenses

Finally, beyond normatively problematic electoral handouts, and maybe less problematic 'work money' expenses, a large part of the illegal funds mobilized by candidates were spent, contrary to what the alarming ECI list might suggest, on perfectly boring items such as the ones listed above. See the section 'What do Candidates Spend Their Money On?' in this chapter. In other words, a large share of the real budget of candidates—a share estimated by political workers to range between 20 and 30 per cent of their real expenses, which were themselves large—was spent on material for rallies and processions, vehicles, speakers, chairs, tables, posters, and so on ... that is, on items that would not be illegal nor illegitimate if the total spending of the candidate had remained inferior to the legal limit.

Over the course of my discussions with political workers, the need to allocate amounts far larger than what the legal limit allowed to campaign events appeared obvious to the workers of the main candidates. Workers frequently derided the low limits fixed by the ECI, even after these were just revised in 2014, as completely unrealistic.

Interestingly, and maybe counterintuitively, these complaints did not always delve on the high costs of gifts and handouts to justify the fact that candidates needed much larger budgets than the ones they were legally allowed to spend. Workers also frequently complained about the rising costs of materials, and about the need to generate ever louder and ever more visually appealing campaign events, as well as increasingly creative pamphlets and cut-outs, in order to keep up with their main competitors. They also frequently noted the need to hedge their bets and engage in multiple campaign strategies in order to reach young and mostly apolitical voters that they thought were deserting political events. Rikhil, the aforementioned BJP leader, for instance, started organizing BJP-sponsored kabaddi tournaments in order to attract younger voters that he was worried not to see at more traditional political events, both before and during the campaign. Others insisted on the need for campaigns to better staff themselves with social media teams and community managers. Each of these new activities, since they did not replace the need for more traditional campaign tactics such as meetings and processions, added to the already heavy burden of candidates. Finally, many of these complaints were purely numerical and referred to the spending per voter that was authorized. Fatima best expressed how demographic factors made it practically impossible for candidates to spend less than the legal limit when she said, 'there are now over 450,000 people living in the constituency, and we do not always know who is a voter and who is not. So 35 lakhs [the legal limit] is probably not even enough for us to provide a pamphlet to every voter!'

Altogether, this suggests that campaigns are getting more expensive not only because voters or communities receive gifts, but also because they are getting bigger, more ambitious, more sophisticated, more professional, and more competitive.

IMPLICATIONS

While the legal and accounted expenses of candidates only represent a small fraction of their real expenses, estimates from two recent Savli campaigns suggest that gifts and attempts at buying or influencing the choices of voters are neither the only nor the main reason why electoral campaigns are expensive in Mumbai. Other kinds of expenses, such as the short-term wages that candidates almost universally pay to their workers and to the crowds these workers in turn recruit, or even simply 'politics as usual' expenses, place equally important constraints on candidates. This suggests that the perceived increase in the cost of campaigns does not have one cause but several, and that the current narrative assigning the rise in the cost of campaigns to increasingly illegitimate tactics may be simplistic, or simply erroneous.

There are two important implications to these observations. The first one is that it would be a mistake to simply equate expensive campaigns with illegitimate or corrupt tactics. While no one contests that candidates spend a lot more than they are legally allowed to, it does seem to be the case that many of these unaccounted expenses are allocated to otherwise perfectly legitimate tactics—buying flags, distributing flyers, renting vehicles, hiring a drum band, or other strategies geared towards generating as much tamasha as possible, over a very short period of time. In other words, forms of 'politics-as-usual'. Other unaccounted funds are allocated towards budgetary lines that fall in somewhat of a grey area in terms of legitimacy—for instance, payments to political workers who quit their regular jobs to dedicate themselves fully to campaigns or payments to crowds filling seats at political events. But the point remains: while both the popular and the official discourse has tended to equate 'black money' and above-the-limit expenses with 'vote buying' and tactics that potentially threaten the fairness of elections, this is not necessarily true. Or at least, I argue, things are more complicated than that.[37]

The second implication derives from the first. Since illegal and illegitimate tactics such as electoral handouts do not in and of themselves explain the large cost of campaigns, the frequent perception among political actors that campaigns have been getting increasingly expensive over time does not necessarily imply that handouts have become more frequent. It may instead, as I argue, have to do with structural changes in the context of democratic elections in the country. Regardless of the ubiquity of gifts and handouts (whose normative importance this chapter does not intend to minimize), a number of alternative factors might explain why campaigns are getting more expensive in India. These factors may explain why both handouts and less problematic expenses are on the rise.

---

[37] Although this is beyond the scope of this chapter, it should be noted here that the portion of that spending that is indeed spent on such tactics may not succeed in influencing voters, and this is for diverse reasons, as noted by a flurry of recent works on handouts. Though this is not my objective here, I also note that both Björkman and my own work on Mumbai argue that gift-givers mostly fail to buy votes.

First, steady increases in the size of constituencies likely play a role. Simply put, larger populations require candidates to spend more. Concretely, candidate likely need to print more pamphlets and organize more meetings. Besides, campaigns in more populous constituencies require the involvement of an ever-larger number of intermediaries in order to reach and convince voters. A larger population and a denser habitat may in addition make it more expensive for them to identify voters, to reach them, and to attempt to convince them, regardless of the strategy used towards that objective.

Second, there may be generational changes that affect the cost of campaigns. In Mumbai, the rising number of young educated voters, beyond the reach of parties' influence and increasingly independent from their families' partisan preferences, is widely described by workers as heralding the progressive disappearance of 'vote banks'. According to many party workers I interviewed, young urban voters are increasingly difficult to read, as they sort amongst candidates on their own merits rather than on caste or party labels, or are frankly disinterested in the political process. Political workers lament these changes, as they increasingly break down the natural connections that existed between members of some groups and some parties. This forces candidates to deploy new strategies—for instance, social media strategies—in addition to the traditional campaigning strategies they have long engaged in. This places a heavier burden on them.

Third, and most importantly, a steady rise in political competition has contributed to making campaigns exponentially expensive, regardless of the number of gifts that are doled out by candidates. More candidates automatically mean more uncertain elections, and hence costlier ones for candidates forced to match the expenses of their competitors. In that sense, increasingly costlier elections are less likely due to lower levels of morality in the political class or to the rise of handout politics than to the fact that candidates now face fierce competition at the polls.

7 Whose Money, Whose Influence? Multilevel Politics and Campaign Finance in India

Jennifer Bussell[*]

Elections are pivotal moments in democracies, not only because they determine who wins elected office, but also because they can shape who acquires influence over those who take office. Recent work on campaign finance suggests that the character of election support can determine who most easily interacts with elected officials,[1] as well as the policy priorities of those in office.[2] If this is the case, then evaluating the character of support for politicians during elections, including both financial and non-monetary contributions, is of prime importance for

[*] I thank Disha Banik and Vaibhav Srikaran for research assistance; Bhartendu Trivedi and the team at MORSEL for their assistance in data collection; and Milan Vaishnav, Devesh Kapur, and the participants in the Carnegie Endowment for International Peace and Center for the Advanced Study of India Election Finance Workshop for their comments on an earlier draft.

[1] Joshua L. Kalla and David E. Broockman, 'Campaign Contributions Facilitate Access to Congressional Officials: A Randomized Field Experiment', *American Journal of Political Science* 60, no. 3 (2015): 545–58.

[2] Stephen Ansolabehere and James M. Snyder Jr., 'Soft Money, Hard Money, Strong Parties', *Columbia Law Review* 100, no. 3 (2012): 598–619; Eleanor Neff Powell, 'Legislative Consequences of Fundraising Influence' (working paper, University of Wisconsin-Madison, 2015).

understanding the actions of elected officials. Yet, in many contexts, especially developing countries such as India, we have little insight into the nature of campaign support in general, let alone campaign finance.

In this chapter, I provide new data and analyses to shed light on three key aspects of campaign dynamics in India: relative differences in the costs of campaigns across levels of Indian government; variations in the importance of different funding sources across levels; and the role of various actors, including politicians, in providing other forms of campaign assistance to candidates at different levels of government. In doing so, I also bring attention to the prevalence of illegal activities in Indian election campaigns, in the form of reliance on illicit funding sources, or 'black money', and the attempts of politicians to influence voting behaviour through giving gifts to voters.

In order to examine these topics, I draw on unique surveys of politicians at all levels of government in three Indian states: Bihar, Jharkhand, and Uttar Pradesh. While not representative of the entire country, the experiences of politicians in these states—which I characterize in greater detail below—give us a new and unique view into the dynamics of election finance in highly competitive electoral environments. These surveys provide us with direct insights into the ways in which politicians view campaigns, both their own and that of their peers. In order to account for potential issues related to social desirability bias in responses, I use a combination of direct and indirect question techniques to elicit responses. I also combine the results of these surveys with additional public information on respondents, including data on their assets and open criminal cases drawn from election affidavits.

I find, first, that financial support from political parties is relevant only in national and state legislative elections, not at the three levels of elected councils within states—the district, block, and village councils.[3] At these lower levels, personal resources play a more dominant role, as do donations from family and friends. Nonetheless, and second, when asked what the most common source of funding is, a substantial portion of all respondents highlight the role of illicit funds in campaigns, with

---

[3] As I discuss in greater detail below, it is illegal for candidates for office at the village level to campaign on party tickets. However, parties are allowed to be involved in campaigns at the block and district levels.

state and national legislators highlighting this more than any other form of funding. Third, in terms of non-financial campaign support (for example, helping to mobilize voters on election day or handing out gifts), higher-level politicians are highly reliant on support from local politicians, party workers, and non-party fixers, while lower-level politicians are more dependent on local village and neighbourhood associations. State legislators are also much more likely than other respondents to say that they help other candidates by handing out gifts. Fourth, when candidates comment on the 'typical' campaign costs at their level of office, this is, on average, double what they report spending on their own campaign. Finally, gift giving, while illegal, is reported to be a substantial portion of the typical campaign, making up between one quarter and one hundred per cent of spending.

In the remainder of this chapter, I begin by setting the stage for an analysis of campaign finance and support activities with a discussion of important related findings in other contexts. I then offer a brief overview of campaign laws in India, particularly with regard to finance and limits on the size and nature of spending. In the subsequent empirical section, I consider two broad sets of questions related to (a) who gains influence over politicians via campaign donations and other forms of campaign support and (b) what is the character of spending by politicians. I conclude with thoughts on the implications of my findings for our understanding of the motivations of politicians when in office and potential areas for further research.

SOURCES OF INFLUENCE AND THE ROLE OF GIFT-GIVING IN CAMPAIGNS

To frame the analysis of campaign finance and related activities across India's five levels of elected office, I consider three sets of relevant findings in the existing literature. These analyses of campaign finance in other contexts, including both other developing countries and the United States, suggest potential paths forward for uncovering the dynamics of competing in elections in a setting such as India. Specifically, I discuss work on the relevance of party money, the direct contributions of time or money by various state and non-state actors more generally, and the relevance of vote buying to campaign dynamics.

Distinguishing between party money and candidate money in financing campaigns is of key importance for understanding overall patterns of campaign finance. This distinction is relevant due to the influence that the former may have on other aspects of democracy, such as through providing 'a counter-weight to the inequity between individual candidates' resources, most notably the discrepancies between the financial positions of incumbents and challengers'.[4] Similarly, money from a central party organization may provide important resources to state parties, helping to balance resources across sub-national units while also supporting voter mobilization by state units.[5] Finally, party money may also induce greater party discipline in policymaking.[6] The extent to which these same dynamics, investigated primarily in the United States, exist in Indian politics is unknown, largely because we have little understanding of the degree to which candidates receive money from their parties and the characteristics of those who merit party support.

There is also increasing evidence that providing campaign contributions increases access to, and influence over, politicians when they are elected,[7] and that this applies to donations from both private donors and politicians who make contributions to the campaigns of their peers.[8] This raises at least two questions for the Indian case: Who are the actors contributing to individual campaigns, particularly given the historical limits on corporate financing that I discuss below, and how do politicians support each other? The answers will be suggestive of different paths by which various individuals and groups within society may exert influence over politicians once they take office.

Finally, giving gifts to individual voters—in the form of cash payments or physical items such as food or clothing—is understood to be a key element of campaign dynamics in many developing countries. Whether these payments are made to influence the character

---

[4] Ansolabehere and Snyder, 'Soft Money, Hard Money,' 607.

[5] Ansolabehere and Snyder, 'Soft Money, Hard Money,' 607.

[6] Ansolabehere and Snyder, 'Soft Money, Hard Money,' 607.

[7] Kalla and Broockman, 'Campaign Contributions Facilitate Access'; Powell, 'Legislative Consequences of Fundraising.'

[8] Eric S. Heberlig and Bruce A. Larson, 'Redistributing Funds by U.S. House Members: The Spiraling Costs of the Permanent Campaign', *Legislative Studies Quarterly* 30, no. 4 (2005): 597–624; Powell, 'Legislative Consequences of Fundraising.'

of voting,[9] turnout,[10] or something else,[11] the illicit use of cash and gifts is perceived to be both prevalent and potentially relevant to election outcomes. In the discussion below, I use the term 'gift giving,' to encompass all forms of vote buying, turnout buying, and other forms of inducement intended to influence political behaviour. Examples of this activity in the Indian context include the handing out of cash to voters, often late at night on the evening before the election; distribution of alcohol, clothing, and other personal goods; and the hosting of large public meals.[12]

A demand for gift giving is relevant to work on campaign finance, because it may influence pressures to draw on illicit, non-traceable funds to finance gifts. This also suggests a potential connection to the emerging literature on criminal politicians in India.[13] The illicit funds supporting gift giving may be more accessible to those with criminal connections. To what extent are these dynamics present in Indian elections, does the use of such tactics differ at different levels of elected office, and what role do various state and non-state actors play in the process? The answers to these questions may have important implications for the character of influence both during and after elections.

THE EMPIRICAL CONTEXT: CAMPAIGN FINANCE IN INDIA

To provide the relevant context for an evaluation of campaign spending and related activities, I provide here a brief review of the official

[9] Susan C. Stokes, 'Perverse Accountability: A Formal Model of Machine Politics with Evidence from Argentina', *American Political Science Review* 99, no.3 (2005): 315–25.

[10] Simeon Nichter, 'Vote Buying or Turnout Buying? Machine Politics and the Secret Ballot', *American Political Science Review* 102, no. 1 (2008): 19–31.

[11] F. Daniel Hidalgo and Simeon Nichter, 'Voter Buying: Shaping the Electorate Through Clientelism', *American Journal of Political Science* 60, no. 2 (2015): 436–55.

[12] Anastasia Piliavsky, 'Introduction', in *Patronage as Politics in South Asia*, ed. Anastasia Piliavsky (Cambridge, UK: Cambridge University Press, 2014): 1–38.

[13] Milan Vaishnav, *When Crime Pays: Money and Muscle in Indian Politics* (New Haven: Yale University Press, 2017).

rules for campaign finance put forward by the Election Commission of India. I also discuss rules related to party participation in elections, as may be relevant to campaign finance activities. I then briefly discuss disclosure requirements related to household assets and pending criminal cases.

Perhaps most importantly, the Election Commission of India sets rules related to the amount of money individual politicians are allowed to spend on their campaigns. The specific figures differ by state, according to size, with limits for the 2016 national parliament election ranging from Rs 5,400,000 to Rs 7,000,000 (approximately $90,000 to $116,667) and the limits for state elections ranging from Rs 2,000,000 to Rs 2,800,000 (approximately $33,333 to $46,667).[14] To place these limits in the context of *actual* spending on campaigns, estimates during the last national election placed total spending for a parliamentary seat at approximately ten times the official limit.[15]

One reason that overall spending can be so much higher than the individual limits is that these limits do not directly apply to spending by political parties, which face no limits on campaign spending, or that by other actors on behalf of a candidate. This implies that candidates could feasibly benefit from substantial licit spending on the part of other actors. However, this could also create incentives for politicians to redirect their own resources in ways that mask the true origin of funds. Similarly, another recent analysis suggested that politicians spend money in their constituency prior to declaring their candidacy[16] and outside the official period of the campaign, which is typically a rather short two-week window.

Parties also have more flexibility than candidates in the receipt of donations. While corporate donations have been variably regulated over the post-Independence period, the 2017 Finance Act eliminated

[14] Throughout the chapter, I use the exchange rate of Rs 60 = US$1.

[15] Sruthi Gottipatti and Rajesh Kumar Singh, 'India Set to Challenge U.S. for Election Spending Record', *Reuters*, 9 March 2014, accessed 10 March 2016, http://www.reuters.com/article/us-india-election-spending-idUSBR EA280AR20140309.

[16] Saritha Rai, 'Candidates Exploit Loopholes to Skirt Spending Limits', *India Ink* (blog), *New York Times*, 16 April 2014, accessed 2 August 2016, http://india.blogs.nytimes.com/2014/04/16/candidates-exploit-loopholes-to-skirt-spending-limits/?_r=0.

caps on corporate giving. Parties also have only minimal limits on disclosure of donations, which can be given with no identifying information as long as the total amount is less than Rs 20,000. This again implies that parties can collect funds from illicit sources (as long as the individual payments are relatively small) and then use this money to support candidates. As one analysis put it, once the money is collected, 'the only hurdle to moving it into the pockets of the voters is the physical transfer of the banknotes'.[17]

The role of parties is legally limited, however, at the lowest level of elected office. In most Indian states, political parties are not allowed to support candidates directly in elections for the village-level councils and candidates are not allowed to identify themselves with particular parties. This is intended to encourage apolitical elections at the local level. In practice, there is evidence that parties do play a role at this level,[18] or at least that candidates are often affiliated with a particular party,[19] but this is outside the legal norms.

Another important regulation of campaigns has been the introduction of an affidavit requirement, which obliges candidates to submit information on their contact details, personal assets, and any pending criminal cases against them. While the requirement to provide this information may not directly affect the character of campaign finance, we can use the declarations to investigate whether certain types of individuals display differing tendencies in their campaigns.

MULTILEVEL CAMPAIGN FINANCE IN INDIA

The analysis of campaign finance discussed here draws on a set of politician surveys conducted in two rounds in three Indian states,

---

[17] 'Campaign Finance in India: Black Money Power', *Economist*, 4 May 2014.

[18] S. Rajendran and Nagesh Prabhu, 'Politics Creeps into Gram Panchayat Elections', *Hindu*, 24 April 2010, accessed 1 August 2016, http://www.thehindu.com/todays-paper/politics-creeps-into-gram-panchayat-elections/article755277.ece.

[19] Thad Dunning and Janhavi Nilekani, 'Ethnic Quotas and Political Mobilization: Caste, Parties, and Distribution in Indian Village Councils', *American Political Science Review* 107, no. 1 (2013): 35–56.

Bihar, Jharkhand, and Uttar Pradesh. These states are in the Hindi-speaking belt of North India, one of the least developed regions of the country. The states are known for high levels of corruption[20] and criminal participation in politics,[21] as well as highly competitive elections. As a result, the nature of campaigns in general, and campaign finance in particular, may differ in these states from that in other parts of the country. At the same time, because electoral rules are largely constant across the country, and because both high levels of electoral competition and highly expensive elections are reported across the country, basic characteristics of campaign finance described here may still be relevant for thinking about what may be occurring in other parts of the country.

The survey sample includes politicians at all levels of elected office: village, block, and district councils (in ascending size), and state and national legislative constituencies. In the first round of surveys, I randomly chose respondents through a nested selection process. First, districts were randomly selected in each state. Within districts, blocks were then randomly selected. The president of the council and one council member were chosen in each block and district. For legislators, the blocks and districts in the sample were mapped to state and national constituencies and all politicians whose constituencies fell in the overlapping areas were included in the sample. Village council respondents include the council president and two council members, of whom one must be Scheduled Caste or Scheduled Tribe and another a woman.[22] In a second round, I attempted to survey all of the state and national legislators who were not included in the original random sample, in order to approximate a census of politicians at these levels. These procedures resulted in a total sample of 2,577 politician respondents. Summaries of the sample and respondent demographic statistics are provided in Appendix A (Table 7.A1). I take advantage of the multilevel character

---

[20] Jennifer Bussell, *Corruption and Reform in India: Public Services in the Digital Age* (New York and New Delhi: Cambridge University Press, 2012).

[21] Vaishnav, *When Crime Pays.*

[22] Village councils within selected blocks were chosen via a regression discontinuity design based on the reservation of council president seats for Scheduled Castes. This design was employed in a separate study using only the citizen and local council surveys and is not germane to this analysis.

of the data to examine differences in each of the analyses described below across politicians at all levels of government.

I first examine what types of actors may gain access to—and potentially garner influence over—politicians, through their roles as providers of campaign funds or other forms of assistance during campaigns. Related to this, I then consider politicians' responses about how they support other candidates, and thus gain their own supplementary influence within the political system. Finally, I evaluate the overall size of spending, comparing politicians' reports on their own campaigns to that of the 'typical' election at their level, and the relative contribution of gift giving to total costs. The questions used in the survey to generate the data analysed here are provided in Appendix B, in English and Hindi, in the order discussed below.

Influence via Funding and Assistance

In the first set of analyses, I present the results of a set of questions asking politicians about their receipt of financial support from their parties as well as their other sources of funds.

WHAT ARE CANDIDATES' SOURCES OF FUNDS?

The responses shown in Table 7.1 are politicians' reports about whether or not they received campaign funds from a variety of sources. This includes their political party as well as their personal resources, donations from friends and family, and contributions from bureaucrats or representatives of the private sector. A key initial observation is that state and national legislators (MPs and MLAs) are substantially more likely to report receiving funds from their party than any respondents at lower levels of government. The same trend is observed, though in a somewhat less dramatic manner, for donations from friends and family. In general, village council presidents seem substantially more dependent on their own resources, relative to contributions from other types, than do politicians at higher levels of office. This is perhaps unsurprising, given laws against formal party support in village council elections. Yet, this is only one view into the sources of funds, and I provide an alternative perspective on the most common sources of funding after reviewing in more detail the character of party contributions.

TABLE 7.1   Sources of Campaign Finance

Position of Politician	National Parliament (MP) (in per cent)	Legislative Assembly (MLA) (in per cent)	District Council President (in per cent)	Block Council President (in per cent)	Village Council President (in per cent)
Political party	69	64	6	2	2
Personal resources	88	88	97	96	89
Friends & family	78	76	64	47	28
Private sector/ companies	16	7	0	2	1
Bureaucrats	4	2	0	0	0

Source: Author's survey.

Note: Responses to the questions: Did your party provide campaign funds to you when you ran for your current position? Where did you obtain funds for your election campaign, other than a political party?

Among those politicians who reported having received funds from their party, the average amount received by MPs was Rs 1.6 million, or approximately $27,000. State legislators reported receiving Rs 500,000 rupees, on average, or approximately $9,000. None of the small number of district council presidents who reported receiving party funds answered the question about the amount received, while the two block council presidents receiving funds reported garnering an average of Rs 125,000 ($2,000). For the 21 village council presidents who reported receiving party funds, the average amount was Rs 13,000 (around $217).

Are the characteristics of candidates correlated with receipt of funds from parties and how much is received? Perhaps surprisingly, a range of individual-level characteristics do not seem to be associated with either whether a politician reports receiving funds from the party or the amount reported received. Multivariate regressions including measures of both demographic characteristics and party-related characteristics suggest no clear predictors of party funding, other than being an MP or MLA (See Appendix A, Table 7.A4). Of particular interest, given recent work on the incentives for parties to run candidates with

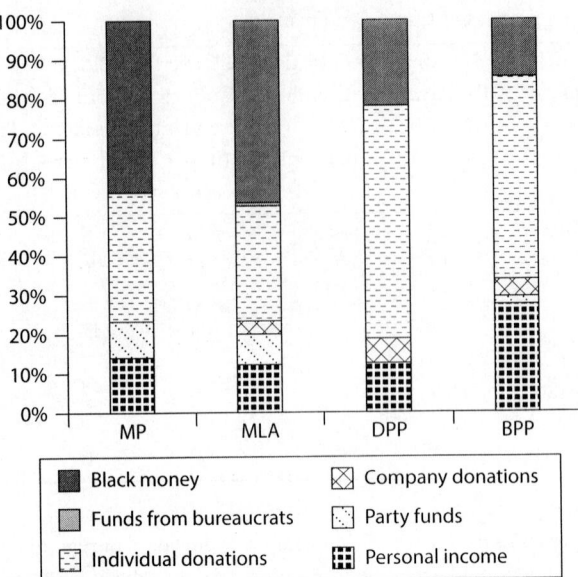

FIGURE 7.1   Perceived Most Common Source of Funding for Peer Politicians
Source: Author's survey.

criminal records,[23] there is no association between number of open criminal cases and receipt of party funds among senior politicians. This is interesting, because we might expect parties to give less money to candidates accused in criminal cases, if one of their appealing characteristics is the ability to fund their own campaigns. Yet, we do not observe such a difference in these data. With regard to the *amount* of money received among those who did receive party funds, there is no difference between MPs and MLAs versus lower-level politicians, on average, though the small sample size in the latter group may be masking actual differences. Other Backward Class (OBC) respondents do report lower funds received than do forward castes, and this difference is statistically significant at standard levels.

Perhaps more illuminating are respondents' answers to a question about what they think is the *most common* source of funding for their peers (see Figure 7.1). When asked to think about their peers' campaigns and forced to choose one option from a set of common

[23] Vaishnav, *When Crime Pays*.

funding sources, high-level politicians—state and national legislators—chose 'funds gained through corrupt activities/black money' more than anything else, followed by individual donations, personal income, and party funds, respectively. In contrast, district and block council presidents were most likely to report individual donations as the most important source of funds, followed either by black money or personal income. This highlights quite starkly the strong presence of illicit funds in campaigns across levels of elected office. Even more importantly, these data also underscores the diminishing influence of individual donations, in relative terms, at higher levels of government. While block and district politicians rely predominantly on individual donations, and thus may be expected to respond to the demands of individual voter supporters while in office, state and national politicians seem more likely to be beholden to whomever provides them access to corrupt rents.

WHO PROVIDES ASSISTANCE TO CANDIDATES?

In addition to campaign finance, other forms of assistance may play an important and related role in ensuring the success of a candidate and, thus, acquiring access to the levers of power. This assistance may involve activities such as organizing campaign events, going door-to-door to promote a candidate, or encouraging people to vote. As a part of any activities, those assisting a campaign may also play a role in distributing cash or other forms of inducements to encourage support for a particular candidate or party.

Survey respondents were asked who they look to when they need assistance with an election campaign in villages. Response categories were not mutually exclusive, so politicians could include multiple sources of assistance in their replies. The potential responses included a range of state and non-state actors, as shown in Figure 7.2.

The mean responses highlighted in Figure 7.2 suggest a shift in the range and forms of support across different types of politicians. In general, MPs and MLAs report having access to a wider range of actors for assistance in their campaigns compared to politicians at lower levels, yet, there is important variation in the predominance of certain types of actors. While a large number report utilization of caste, village, and neighbourhood associations as a part of their campaigns, these numbers are substantially lower than those noted for party actors and

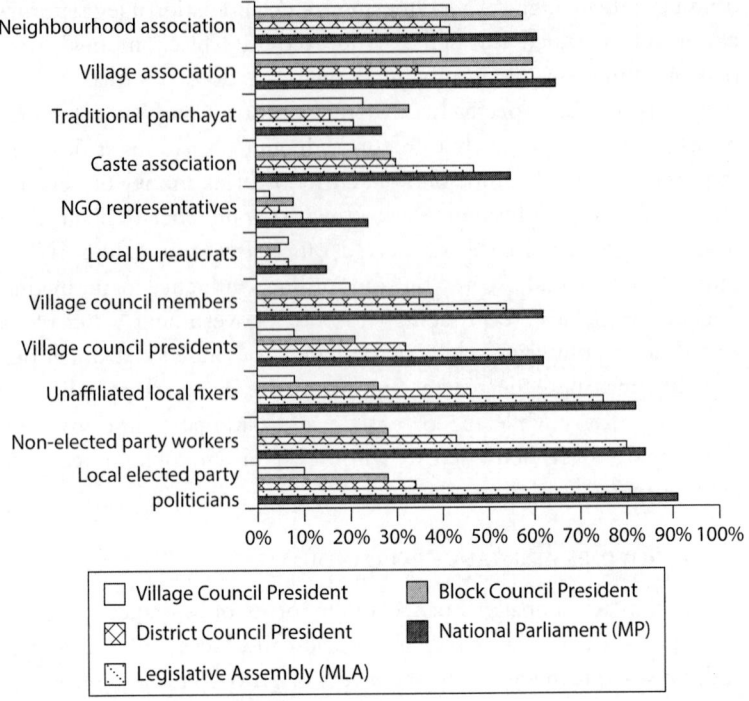

FIGURE 7.2 Sources of Campaign Assistance
Source: Author's survey.

individual fixers. For local politicians (at the village and block council levels), though they report similar levels of support from local associations as do MPs and MLAs, their reliance on individual actors is substantially lower. The one exception is village council members, in that 20 per cent of village council presidents report relying on them for assistance. Thus, in relative terms, lower-level politicians are more reliant on local organizations than are state and national politicians, and they are also less likely in general to report having access to support from the full range of actor types. Additionally, local bureaucrats and non-governmental organizations are the least likely to receive requests to assist with campaigns, based on reports of politicians at all levels.

What are the potential implications of these tendencies for the influence of party and non-party actors on politics at different levels of government? In line with the patterns of campaign finance, parties seem to play a more dominant role in facilitating the campaigns of state and national politicians than politicians at more local levels. That said, parties are not invisible at these lower levels and party workers clearly have some role to play in local campaigns. This suggests that parties are, at least in some cases, establishing their presence in areas through direct participation in, if not funding of, local elections.

With regard to non-state actors, and especially local associations, while state and national politicians in most cases are more likely to report relying on these actors than lower-level politicians, the relative importance of associations to local politicians is striking. Because sub-state politicians are so much less likely to rely on parties or individuals for assistance, these associations, especially village and neighbourhood associations, are the dominant sources of assistance for these actors. Whereas high-level politicians will have to balance the access and influence they offer to all of the individuals and groups who may have supported them, local politicians can more easily privilege these associations, and their interests, over less common sources of support.

WHO PROVIDES ASSISTANCE BY GIVING GIFTS TO VOTERS?

An analysis of 'assistance' in general tells us very little about the specific activities that different actors engage in to support a candidate. To gain leverage on this aspect of the question, I examine in greater detail a specific form of assistance closely tied to campaign finance—the distribution of gifts to voters prior to an election. Subsequent to being asked a question about the typical spending of candidates at their level on gift giving (discussed in more detail below), respondents were asked who actually gives these gifts to voters.

Responses shown in Figure 7.3 highlight a similar pattern to that reported for assistance in general. Politicians at high levels are the most likely to say that local party workers and politicians, as well as non-party fixers, play a primary role in gift giving. However, here we also see that district and block presidents report relying on these same actors more than they would rely on local associations.[24]

---

[24] The question differentiated between a number of different kinds of locally based associations, including neighbourhood, village, and caste associations and traditional panchayats. We also asked about non-governmental organizations, which referred instead to non-state organizations based outside the village area, but perhaps with some local operations.

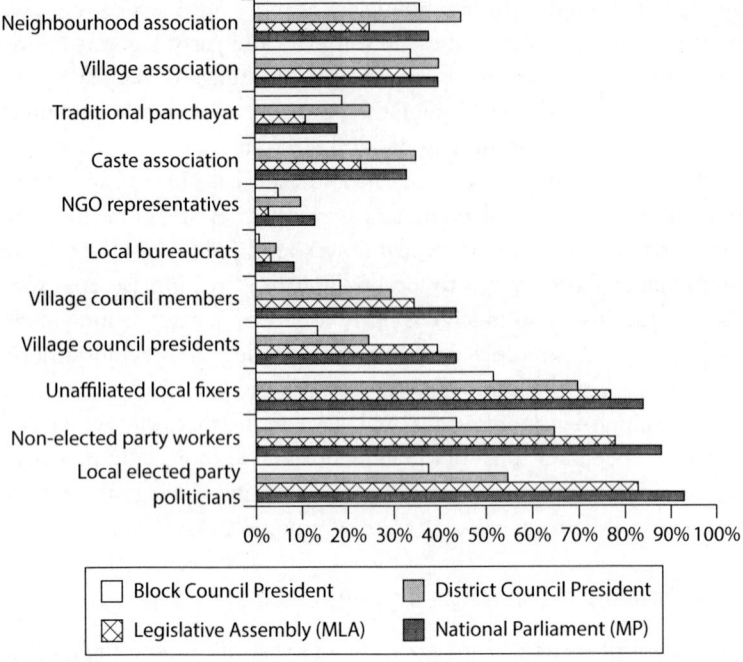

FIGURE 7.3 Assistance with Gift Giving to Voters
Source: Author's survey.

This suggests that a key role for party workers in local elections is to facilitate the distribution of gifts, while other types of associational actors are more likely to offer different, and perhaps more licit, forms of assistance.

WHAT ROLE DO POLITICIANS PLAY IN CAMPAIGNS AT OTHER LEVELS?

A final perspective on the role of different actors in facilitating campaigns comes from politicians' reports of what they do to help their fellow candidates. Respondents were asked first whether they support other politicians in their campaigns, including those at other levels of office. As shown in the top row of Table 7.2, a large majority of MPs and MLAs responded in the affirmative, as did approximately half of district and block officials. Only village council presidents were relatively unlikely to say that they provide assistance to others.

TABLE **7.2**   Supporting Other Politicians

Position of Politician	National Parliament (MP) (in per cent)	Legislative Assembly (MLA) (in per cent)	District Council President (in per cent)	Block Council President (in per cent)	Village Council President (in per cent)
Do you support other candidates' campaigns?	97	88	50	55	23
If yes, how?					
Mobilize turnout	96	97	94	97	86
Promote candidate	94	95	84	98	85
Distribute gifts	7	28	5	5	10

Source: Author's survey.

Note: Responses to the questions: Do you provide support during election time to other politicians from your party, for instance, candidates for the Block or Zilla Panchayats, MLAs, or MPs? What sort of support do you provide during election times to these other politicians from your party?

In terms of what politicians do to support other campaigns, both mobilizing turnout and promoting the specific candidate to voters were frequent responses across all types of politicians. Respondents were less willing to say that they participate in distributing gifts to voters on behalf of another candidate, with most groups reporting this activity at less than 10 per cent. An important exception was state legislators, nearly 30 per cent of whom acknowledged that they help to pass out gifts. This latter finding is important not simply because it highlights, again, the potential relevance of gift giving in campaigns, but also the role for MLAs in this process. While MLAs were not a specific response category for the previous questions about assistance and gift giving, and thus might not be thought to be a relevant part of that process, a sizeable number have self-identified as participating in this process in response to this separate question. This also suggests that MLAs may have a form of illicit influence over those to whom they are giving assistance, due to their knowledge about the gift giving involved in specific campaigns.

The Nature of Spending

The analyses to this point highlight the role of various individual and group actors in providing funds and assistance to campaigns. But what is the total magnitude of these efforts? In this last set of analyses, I examine politicians' reports about the absolute size of campaign spending and the degree to which gift giving contributes to these totals.

HOW MUCH DO POLITICIANS SPEND, AND WHAT PROPORTION DOES GIFT GIVING MAKE OF TOTAL SPENDING?

When asked how much they themselves spent on their own most recent election, the total amounts respondents reported spending decrease dramatically as we move down the hierarchy of elections to the village council (Table 7.3, row 1). It is this relative comparison that is of greater interest than the absolute numbers, given that politicians are reporting, on average, total spending numbers well below the official limits for their level of office. When, instead, respondents were asked to estimate the total cost of a typical election to their level of office in their state, the reports were significantly higher, but still lower than the official limits (row 2). In this latter case, we continue to observe a decrease in the average reported cost of elections as we move from the national parliament to local village councils.

The comparison between what respondents report spending and their views of total spending in typical elections also reinforces the importance of additional sources of financial support in campaigns above the level of village council. While the difference between these two measures of spending is negligible at the village council level, indicating that candidates themselves are responsible for most of the spending, the gap increases substantially as we move up the hierarchy of offices. Interestingly, this changes somewhat when we get to state and national legislators, with state legislators reporting similar total campaign costs as national legislators, but indicating that they cover a smaller portion of these costs themselves. This suggests that state legislators may be somewhat more beholden to their financial backers than national legislators.

Regression analyses, detailed in Appendix A, suggest that a small number of individual-level characteristics may predict election spending (Table 7.A6, first two columns). Most obviously, winning MP and

TABLE 7.3 Campaign Spending

Position of Politician	National Parliament (MP)	Legislative Assembly (MLA)	District Council President	Block Council President	Village Council President
Respondent's own reported campaign spending	2,043	1,037	317	99	28
Estimated *total* spending in 'typical' election	4,512	4,211	737	338	26
Per cent of peers who benefit from spending of illicit funds	64	57	64	41	32
Peers feel pressure to give gifts (in per cent)	92	83	86	71	51
Estimated amount spent by peers on gifts for voters	1,395	1,709	687	512	164
Estimated per cent of voters who receive gifts	34	26	4	31	25

Source: Author's survey.

Note: Responses to the questions: What was the total amount of rupees that you spent on your most recent election campaign for your current position? How much money do you think is spent on a typical election for office at your level in this state including funds spent by the candidate's party and friends? (Amount in Rupees). What portion of your peers do you think benefits from the spending of illicit income during election campaigns, either by themselves or others? (Amount in per cent). Do you think that your peers feel pressure to provide gifts to voters prior to an election? How much do you think the average candidate for office at your level spends only on money and gifts for citizens in a typical election? (Amount in Rupees). What portion of eligible voters would you guess receives money or another gift from a politician or political party before elections at your level of office? (Amount in per cent). Absolute amounts shown are in '000 Indian Rupees (INR).

MLA candidates spent more on their elections than did winners at lower levels. With regard to caste groups, among MP and MLA respondents, OBC winning candidates and their scheduled caste peers spend less on campaigns in general than those from forward castes, even when holding position and total assets constant. Perhaps most interesting is that, in general, neither total assets nor open criminal cases are strongly associated with reported spending. The same is generally the case for reports of perceived total spending in a 'typical' election at respondents' level of government (Table 7.A6, last two columns), with the exception that among MP and MLA respondents, scheduled caste representatives report higher perceived costs than do forward castes.

It is the analyses reported in the next four rows of Table 7.3 that are the most striking and possibly indicative of the true character of elections in these three states. Across district presidents, MLAs, and MPs, and in line with the findings highlighted in Figure 7.1, respondents perceive that more than half of their peers benefit from spending illicit funds. Block presidents and village council presidents also report only slightly lower numbers. Perhaps related to this, more than half of all respondents, and upwards of 80 per cent among the highest-level politicians, perceive that their peers feel pressure to give gifts at the time of elections. This pressure results in perceived spending on gifts alone at the constituency level of between $2,700 in village council elections to more than $23,000 in state and national elections. These absolute figures do not necessarily suggest that a very small number of voters are the recipients of this largesse. In the final row of the table, we see that politicians estimate that more than a quarter, and in some cases upwards of one-third, of voters receive gifts in a given election at their level of office. Considering that elections are held for each of these levels, and even taking into account overestimates on the part of these respondents, that amounts to a substantial portion of voters who may be receiving gifts in advance of elections.

This chapter set out to provide new descriptive insights into the character of campaign finance in India, by examining politicians' own perspectives on the nature of their campaigns and those of their peers. This type of fine-grained data on elections is rare in studies of Indian politics and sheds new light on the sources of funding and support, as well as potential patterns of influence post-campaign.

Building on recent findings in the literature on campaign finance more generally, I have suggested, first, that the character of funding sources and the nature of assistance provided in campaigns may have important implications for which actors are able to influence politicians once they have won office. While I do not provide evidence for that claim here, I offer suggestive evidence about which actors are likely to have influence at different levels of government. In general, political parties in these states are likely to have direct influence only over elected officials at the state and national levels. At lower levels, party financial contributions are quite limited, suggesting, at least, that any power parties weld at these levels stems from alternative forms of influence. This suggests both that there are likely to be major financial discrepancies across incumbents and challengers at these levels of office and that parties will have only limited ability to shape the behaviour of those who win office.

Instead, other individual actors or associations may be the dominant sources of influence at lower levels. Regarding individual actors, I highlight that party workers and individual non-party fixers are likely to be influential with politicians at higher levels of government, in particular MPs and MLAs, but also district and block presidents, to a lesser extent. Local associations, and especially village and neighbourhood associations, in contrast, while also relevant to high-level politicians, should have relatively more influence at lower levels of government. As a result, if particular groups or powerful individuals within a community dominate these local organizations, those same actors are likely to have the greatest influence over local elected officials.

Second, I highlight the importance of illicit funds and activities in the context of elections at all levels of government. While again most common at the highest levels, all types of respondents highlight the preponderance of illicit funds as a part of overall campaign funding. This implies that actors who are the sources of these funds, or activities that may create new sources of potential funds, may be emphasized during a typical politician's time in office, perhaps to the detriment of the broader public. Surprisingly, however, this does not seem related to the criminal background of politicians, at least in terms of open criminal cases.

Finally, I instead find suggestive evidence of a demand for black money campaign funds to support election gift giving. The substantial absolute numbers that politicians report as estimates for the value of gift giving, which we might still reasonably interpret to be underreports, suggest significant pressure to cultivate non-traceable sources of funds that can then be spent in ways that are also not tracked by election officials. Given the high levels of pressure that politicians relate, it is difficult to imagine that this aspect of campaigns is likely to change in the near future. If this is the case, then we should expect continued stress by politicians on the cultivation of illicit rent sources, even where this may impinge on their other responsibilities as elected officials.

These insights are drawn from unique surveys of politicians and highlight the limited forms of data we possess on the nature of campaign finance. Many further and related questions could be explored with efforts to build similar forms of data and complementary firsthand reports of spending on the ground during campaigns. It is only with these kinds of detailed and yet comprehensive data collection that we will begin to parse apart the complicated character of campaign finance in India.

Appendix

APPENDIX A: ADDITIONAL DATA AND ANALYSES

TABLE 7.A1 Sample Demographic Statistics

Politician Type	Sample Size (n)	Age	Per cent Male	Education Level*	Monthly Income ('000 rupees)*	Per cent Hindu	Per cent Forward Caste	Per cent Other Backward Class
Village Council President	562	N/A	63.0	Class 9 (9.2)	N/A	N/A	N/A	N/A
Village Council Member	1154	N/A	50.4	Class 7 (7.7)	N/A	N/A	N/A	N/A

(Cont'd)

TABLE 7.A1 (Cont'd)

Politician Type	Sample Size (n)	Age	Per cent Male	Education Level*	Monthly Income ('000 rupees)*	Per cent Hindu	Per cent Forward Caste	Per cent Other Backward Class
Block Council President	117	40.6	41.0	Class 10 (10.0)	7–8	93.2	24.8	52.1
Block Council Member	133	39.1	57.9	Class 9 (9.1)	4–5	92.5	22.6	55.6
District Council President	37	39.5	29.7	Intermediate (11.3)	9–10	86.5	10.8	64.9
District Council Member	41	42.0	61.0	Intermediate (10.7)	8–9	87.8	26.8	55.2
Member of Legislative Assembly	448	47.6	87.7	Intermediate (12.0)	10+	88.2	40.4	41.3
Member of Parliament	85	54.2	85.9	Intermediate (12.2)	10+	84.7	45.9	28.2
Politician AVERAGE*		45.3	72.8	Intermediate (11.2)	8–9	89.0	34.2	45.2

Source: Author's survey.

Note: *The Politician Average excludes gram panchayat members and presidents. For education and income levels, responses were coded on a scale for which each number represented a range of education level or income. The respective range for the average score on the scale is shown in the cell, with the average for years of education in parentheses. N/A = Not available.

TABLE 7.A2 Sources of Campaign Assistance

Position of Politician	National Parliament (MP) (in per cent)	Legislative Assembly (MLA) (in per cent)	District Council President (in per cent)	Block Council President (in per cent)	Village Council President (in per cent)
Local elected party politicians	91	81	34	28	10
Non-elected party workers	84	80	43	28	10
Unaffiliated local fixers	82	75	46	26	8
Village council presidents	62	55	32	21	8
Village council members	62	54	35	38	20
Local bureaucrats	15	7	3	5	7
NGO representatives	24	10	5	8	3
Caste association	55	47	30	29	21
Traditional panchayat	27	21	16	33	23
Village association	65	60	35	60	40
Neighbourhood association	61	42	40	58	42

Source: Author's survey.

Note: Percentages calculated from politician reports.

TABLE 7.A3 Perceptions of Peers' Most Common Sources of Campaign Finance

Position of Politician	National Parliament (MP) (in per cent)	Legislative Assembly (MLA) (in per cent)	District Council President (in per cent)	Block Council President (in per cent)
Personal income	14	12	13	27
Party funds	9	8	0	2
Company donations	0	4	6	4
Individual donations	33	29	59	52
Funds from bureaucrats	0	1	0	0
Black money	44	47	22	15

Source: Author's survey.

TABLE 7.A4 Receipt of Party Financial Support

Position of Politician	Received Support (1)	Received Support (2)	Amount of Support (1)	Amount of Support (2)
MP	.09 (.48)			
Senior Politician		2.62*** (12.15)	1,047,544*** (5.35)	521,035 (.69)
Age	.01 (1.08)	.01 (1.01)	15,128* (2.20)	18,915** (2.88)
Male	−.15 (−.83)	−.14 (−.87)	210,965 (1.12)	180,864 (1.01)
OBC	−.04 (−.24)	.04 (.33)	−337,633* (2.24)	−335,957* (−2.334)
SC	−.04 (−.24)	.14 (.84)	−167,753 (−.84)	−199,236 (−1.07)
ST	.28 (.76)	.20 (.68)	465,747 (1.38)	523,905 (1.69)
Past Central Minister	.46 (1.01)	.57 (1.31)	−258,971 (−.69)	285,598 (.78)
Past State Minister	−.03 (−.16)	−.05 (−.04)	−91,944 (−.52)	100,264 (.58)
Past Different Party	.00 (.04)	.03 (.37)	−190,598 (−1.34)	−141,515 (−1.06)
Assets in Lakhs	−.00 (−1.54)		−152 (−.92)	
Criminal Cases	−.02 (−1.00)		−12,431 (−.53)	
Constant	.24 (.76)	−2.49 (−7.99)	−89941 (−.25)	−738,210 (−.89)
Pseudo/Adjusted R-squared	.01	.37	.16	.07
N	463	827	254	278

Source: Author's survey.

Note: Received Support 1 and 2 are probit models with coefficients in cells and z-ratios in parentheses. Amount of Support 1 and 2 are OLS models with coefficients in cells and coefficients in parentheses. Only MP and MLA respondents are included in the first and third models and MLAs are the excluded respondent group. Block council members are the excluded respondent group in the second and fourth models. Forward castes are the excluded caste category in all models. * = p < .05, ** = p < .01, and *** = p < .001.

Jennifer Bussell

TABLE 7.A5   Sources of Gift-giving Assistance

Position of Politician	National Parliament (MP) (in per cent)	Legislative Assembly (MLA) (in per cent)	District Council President (in per cent)	Block Council President (in per cent)
Local elected party politicians	93	83	55	38
Non-elected party workers	88	78	65	44
Unaffiliated local fixers	84	77	70	52
Village council presidents	44	40	25	14
Village council members	44	35	30	19
Local bureaucrats	9	4	5	1
NGO representatives	13	3	10	5
Caste association	33	23	35	25
Traditional panchayat	18	11	25	19
Village association	40	34	40	34
Neighbourhood association	38	25	45	36

Source: Author's survey.

Note: Percentages calculated from politician reports. Question not posed to village council politicians.

TABLE 7.A6 Receipt of Party Financial Support, Additional Tests

Position of Politician	Own Election Cost (1)	Own Election Cost (2)	'Typical' Election Cost (1)	'Typical' Election Cost (2)
MP	771,529*** (4.17)		−61,250 (−.11)	
Senior Politician		986,469*** (10.72)		3,795,263*** (13.86)
Age	7,744 (1.23)	7,644* (2.04)	25,496 (1.31)	18,366 (1.61)
Male	−100,771 (−.53)	−123,895 (−1.27)	−858,094 (−1.94)	−221,888 (−.76)
OBC	−303,233* (−2.11)	−252,537** (−2.85)	472,031 (1.09)	338,564 (1.29)
SC	−516,462* (−2.74)	−297,169* (−2.55)	−102,951 (−.17)	244,930 (.68)
ST	−49,593 (−14)	−106,278 (−.55)	2,262,661* (2.18)	1,051,451 (1.76)
Past Central Minister	1,505,977*** (3.66)	2,032,453*** (6.36)	−128,709 (−.11)	121,192 (.14)
Past State Minister	−134,805 (−78)	18,599 (.14)	435,584 (.84)	540,425 (1.36)
Past Different Party	−38737 (−.37)	11,911 (.16)	−521,857 (−1.75)	−287,184 (−1.38)
Assets in Lakhs	129 (.95)		−409 (−1.08)	
Criminal Cases	5864 (.34)		9,598 (.19)	
Constant	964,892 (2.91)	40,061 (.23)	3,769,040 (3.72)	−451,982 (−.86)
Adjusted R-squared	.10	.23	.01	.29
N	479	851	370	655

Source: Author's survey.

Note: All models are OLS with coefficients in cells and coefficients in parentheses. Only MP and MLA respondents are included in the first and third models and MLAs are the excluded respondent group. Block council members are the excluded respondent group in the second and fourth models. Forward castes are the excluded caste category in all models. * = p < .05, ** = p < .01, and *** = p < .001.

APPENDIX B: SURVEY QUESTIONS

Questions are listed according to the order discussed in the body of the article. The original question numbers are retained, and thus may appear below out of numerical order.

Table 7B.1

34. Did your party provide campaign funds to you when you ran for your current position?
    0. No (go to question 36)
    1. Yes (go to question 35)

99. Does not know/Did not reply (go to question 36)

34. इस वक्त जिस पद पर आप हैं, उसके लिए जब आप चुनाव में खड़े हुए थे तो क्या आपकी पार्टी ने आपको प्रचार अभियान के लिए पैसा दिया था?
    0. नहीं (प्रश्न 36 पर जाएं)
    1. हाँ (प्रश्न 35 पर जाएं)
    99. नहीं जानते/उत्तर नहीं दिया (प्रश्न 36 पर जाएं)

35. How much funds did your party provide to you during your most recent election?
    99. Does not know/Did not reply
35. आपके द्वारा लड़े गए पिछले चुनाव में आपकी पार्टी ने आपको कितना फंड दिया? (उत्तर दिया)
    99. नहीं जानते/उत्तर नहीं दिया

36. What was the total amount of rupees that you spent on your most recent election campaign for your current position?
    99. Does not know/Did not reply
36. अपने इस पद के लिए लड़े गए चुनाव में आपने कितना धन चुनाव अभियान पर खर्च किया?
    99. उत्तर नहीं दिया

Figure 7.1

37. Where did you obtain funds for your election campaign, other than a political party? (Interviewer—please read each option)

37. राजनीतिक पार्टियों के अलावा, आप प्रचार अभियान के लिए फंड की व्यवस्था कहां से
    करते हैं? (हर ऑप्शन पढ़ें)

    37a. Own funds
    0. No
    1. Yes

    99. Does not know/Did not reply
    37ए. अपना फंड
    0.   नहीं
    1.   हां
    99.   नहीं जानते/उत्तर नहीं दिया

    37b. Donations from friends and family
    0. No
    1. Yes

    99. Does not know/Did not reply
    37बी. मित्रों और परिवार से मिली मदद
    0.   नहीं
    1.   हां
    99.   नहीं जानते/उत्तर नहीं दिया

    37c. Donations from private sector/companies
    0. No
    1. Yes

    99. Does not know/Did not reply
    37सी. निजी क्षेत्र/कंपनियों से मिला दान
    0.   नहीं
    1.   हां
    99.   नहीं जानते/उत्तर नहीं दिया

    37d. Funds obtained from bureaucrats
    0. No
    1. Yes

    99. Does not know/Did not reply
    37डी. नौकरशाहों/अफसरों से लिया गया धन

0. नहीं
1. हां
99. नहीं जानते/उत्तर नहीं दिया

37e. Funds gained through corrupt activities/unfair means
0. No
1. Yes

99. Does not know/Did not reply
37डी. भ्रष्ट/गलत तरीके से एकत्र किया गया धन
0. नहीं
1. हां
99. नहीं जानते/उत्तर नहीं दिया

37e. Other

(Please specify _____)
0. No
1. Yes

99. Does not know/Did not reply
37ई. अन्य .... विवरण दें
0. नहीं
1. हां
99. नहीं जानते/उत्तर नहीं दिया

41. Considering your peers in the same political office as you, what would you say is the most common source of funding for their campaigns?
[read options]
   1. Personal income from other professional occupations
   2. Funds from their political party
   3. Funds from company donations
   4. Funds from individual donations
   5. Funds from bureaucrats
   6. Funds gained through corrupt activities/black money
   7. Other (Please specify _____)

41. जिस राजनीतिक पद पर आप हैं, उसके समकक्ष पद के लिए आपके विचार में चुनाव अभियान के लिए पैसा जुटाने का सबसे सामान्य तरीका क्या है? (ऑप्शन पढ़ें।)
1. दूसरे पेशेवर व्यवसायों की कमाई
2. उनकी पार्टियों से लिया गया फंड
3. कंपनियों से लिया गया डोनेशन
4. व्यक्तिगत रूप से लिया गया दान
5. नौकरशाहों/अफसरों से लिया गया धन
6. भ्रष्ट गतिविधियों से कमाया गया धन/काला धन
7. अन्य .... विवरण दें

Figure 7.2

40. When you need assistance with your election campaign in villages, to whom do you look for help? (Interviewer—please read out options]
40. जब आपको गांव में चुनाव अभियान के दौरान मदद की जरुरत पड़ती है तो आप किससे मदद के लिए पूछते हैं? (सभी ऑप्शन पढ़ें!)

40a. Local elected politicians from your party
0. No
1. Yes
99. No answer
40ए. आपकी पार्टी का चुनाव में चयनित स्थानीय नेता
0. नहीं
1. हां
99. कोई उत्तर नहीं for help? (Interviewer—please read out options)
40. जब आपको गांव में चुनाव अभियान के दौरान मदद की जरुरत पड़ती है तो आप किससे मदद के लिए पूछते हैं? (सभी ऑप्शन पढ़ें !)

40b. Non-elected party members
0. No
1. Yes
99. No answer
40बी. पार्टी सदस्य, जो चुना नहीं गया हो
0. नहीं
1. हां
99. कोई उत्तर नहीं

40c. Local fixers—*naye neta*—who are not officially affiliated with
a party
0. No
1. Yes
99. No answer
40सी. नया नेता/ छुटभैय्या नेता, जो पार्टी से आधिकारिक रूप से जुड़ा न हो
0. नहीं
1. हां
99. कोई उत्तर नहीं

40d. Gram panchayat president
0. No
1. Yes
99. No answer
40डी. ग्राम पंचायत अध्यक्ष
0. नहीं
1. हां
99. कोई उत्तर नहीं

40e. Gram panchayat member
0. No
1. Yes
99. No answer
40ई. ग्राम पंचायत सदस्य
0. नहीं
1. हां
99. कोई उत्तर नहीं

40f. Local bureaucrats
0. No
1. Yes
99. No answer
40एफ. स्थानीय नौकरशाह
0. नहीं
1. हां
99. कोई उत्तर नहीं

40g. NGO representatives

0. No

1. Yes

99. No answer

40जी. गैरसरकारी संगठन के प्रतिनिधि

0. नहीं

1. हां

99. कोई उत्तर नहीं

40h. Caste association representatives

0. No

1. Yes

99. No answer

40एच. जाति संघ के प्रतिनिधि

0. नहीं

1. हां

99. कोई उत्तर नहीं

40i. Traditional panchayat representatives

0. No

1. Yes

99. No answer

40आई. परम्परागत पंचायत के प्रतिनिधि

0. नहीं

1. हां

99. कोई उत्तर नहीं

40j. Village association representatives

0. No

1. Yes

99. No answer

40जे. ग्रामीण संघ के प्रतिनिधि

0. नहीं

1. हां

99. कोई उत्तर नहीं

40k. Neighbourhood association representatives

0. No

1. Yes

99. No answer

40के. मोहल्ला संघ के प्रतिनिधि

0. नहीं

1. हां

99. कोई उत्तर नहीं

40l. Other

0. No

1. Yes (Please specify _____)

99. No answer

40एल. अन्य

0. नहीं

1. हां .... विवरण दें

99. कोई उत्तर नहीं

Figure 7.3

49. When other candidates give gifts to voters, who actually distributes the gifts to citizens prior to an election? (Interviewer—please read out options)

49. जब दूसरे उम्मीदवार मतदाताओं को चुनाव से पहले उपहार बांटते हैं तो वास्तव में कौन उपहार बांटता है? (साक्षात्काकर्ता-ऑप्शन पढ़ें)

49a. Local politicians from your party

0. No

1. Yes

99. No answer

49ए. आपकी पार्टी के स्थानीय नेता

0. नहीं

1. हां

99. कोई उत्तर नहीं

49b. Non-elected party members

0. No

1. Yes

99. No answer

49बी. नहीं चुने गए पार्टी सदस्य
0.　नहीं
1.　हां
99.　कोई उत्तर नहीं

49c. Local fixers—naye neta—who are not officially affiliated with a party
0.　No
1.　Yes
99. No answer
49सी. नया नेता/छुटभैय्या नेता, जो आधिकारिक रूप से पार्टी से नहीं जुड़े हैं
0.　नहीं
1.　हां
99.　कोई उत्तर नहीं

49d. Gram panchayat president
0.　No
1.　Yes
99. No answer
40डी. ग्राम पंचायत अध्यक्ष
0.　नहीं
1.　हां
99.　कोई उत्तर नहीं

49e. Gram panchayat member
0.　No
1.　Yes
99. No answer
49ई.ग्राम पंचायत सदस्य
0.　नहीं
1.　हां
99.　कोई उत्तर नहीं

49f. Local bureaucrats
0.　No
1.　Yes
99. No answer
49एफ. स्थानीय नौकरशाह

0. नहीं
1. हां
99. कोई उत्तर नहीं

49g. NGO representatives
0. No
1. Yes
99. No answer
49जी. गैर संगठन के प्रतिनिधि
0. नहीं
1. हां
99. कोई उत्तर नहीं

49h. Caste association representatives
0. No
1. Yes
99. No answer
49एच. जाति संघ के प्रतिनिधि
0. नहीं
1. हां
99. कोई उत्तर नहीं

49i. Traditional panchayat representatives
0. No
1. Yes
99. No answer
49आई. परंपरागत पंचायत के प्रतिनिधि
0. नहीं
1. हां
99. कोई उत्तर नहीं

49j. Village association representatives
0. No
1. Yes
99. No answer
49जे. ग्रामीण संघ के प्रतिनिधि

0. नहीं
1. हां
99. कोई उत्तर नहीं

49k. Neighbourhood association representatives
0. No
1. Yes
99. No answer
49के. मोहल्ला संघ के प्रतिनिधि
0. नहीं
1. हां
99. कोई उत्तर नहीं

49l. Other
0. No
1. Yes (Please specify _____)
99. No answer
49एल. अन्य
0. नहीं
1. हां .... विवरण दें
99. कोई उत्तर नहीं

Table 7.2

38. Do you provide support during election time to other politicians from your party, for instance, candidates for the block or zilla pan-chayats, MLAs, or MPs?
    0. No (go to question 40)
    1. Yes (go to question 39)

99. Does not know/Did not reply (go to question 40)
65. चुनाव के दौरान क्या आप अपनी पार्टी के दूसरे पदों के उम्मीदवारों की चुनाव प्रचार में मदद करते हैं, जैसे-ब्लॉक पंचायत, जिला पंचायत, सांसद या विधायक ?
0. नहीं (प्रश्न 40 पर जाएं)
1. हां (प्रश्न 39 पर जाएं)
99. नहीं जानते/उत्तर नहीं दिया (प्रश्न 40 पर जाएं)

39. What sort of support do you provide during election times to these other politicians from your party? (Interviewer—please read each option) (number)

39. चुनाव के दौरान आप अपनी पार्टी को किस तरह की मदद देते हैं? (हर ऑप्शन पढ़ें। उत्तर संख्या में)

39a. Help to mobilize voters to turn out to vote

0. No
1. Yes

99. Does not know/Did not reply

39ए. चुनाव प्रचार में जिससे ज्यादा से ज्यादा लोग वोट दें

0. नहीं
1. हां
99. उत्तर नहीं दिया

39b. Help to convince villagers to vote for the candidate/party

0. No
1. Yes

99. Does not know/Did not reply

39बी. गांव वालों को समझाने में मदद, जिससे गांव वाले उम्मीदवार/पार्टी को वोट दें

0. नहीं
1. हां
99. उत्तर नहीं दिया

39c. Distribute gifts to voters

0. No
1. Yes

99. Does not know/Did not reply

39सी. गांव वालों को उपहार देकर

0. नहीं
1. हां
99. उत्तर नहीं दिया

39d. Other

(Please specify _____)

39डी. अन्य .... विवरण दें

Table 7.3

36. What was the total amount of rupees that you spent on your most recent election campaign for your current position?

99. Does not know/Did not reply

36. अपने इस पद के लिए लड़े गए चुनाव में आपने कितना धन चुनाव अभियान पर खर्च किया?

99. उत्तर नहीं दिया

42. How much money do you think is spent on a typical election for office at your level in this state including funds spent by the candidate's party and friends? (amount in rupees)

42. आपके विचार में जिस पद पर आप हैं, उस पद के चुनाव के लिए आमतौर पर कितना पैसा खर्च हो जाता है, जिसमें उम्मीदवार की पार्टी और उसके मित्रो का धन भी शामिल है? (उत्तर रुपए में)

45. What portion of your peers do you think benefits from the spending of illicit income during election campaigns, either by themselves or others? (amount in per cent)

45. आपके समकक्ष सारे नेताओं में कितने प्रतिशत नेता खुद या दूसरे व्यक्ति द्वारा गलत तरीकों से इकट्ठा किये गए धन का इस्तेमाल चुनाव प्रचार में करते हैं? (उत्तर प्रतिशत में दें)

46. Do you think that your peers feel pressure to provide gifts to voters prior to an election?
    0. No
    1. Yes
    99. No answer/Can't say
46. आपके विचार में क्या आपके समकक्ष नेता चुनाव से पहले मतदाताओं को उपहार देने का दबाव महसूस करते हैं
    0. नहीं
    1. हां
    99. कोई उत्तर नहीं

48. How much do you think the average candidate for office at your level spends only on money and gifts for citizens in a typical election? (amount in rupees)
48. आपके विचार में आपके बराबर पद का नेता आमतौर पर चुनाव में कितना पैसा उपहार और पैसा बांटने पर खर्च करता है? (उत्तर रूपए में)

47. What portion of eligible voters would you guess receives money or another gift from a politician or political party before elections at your level of office? (amount in per cent)

47. आपके विचार में आपके समकक्ष पद के चुनाव से पहले नेताओं और राजनीतिक पार्टियों से कितने प्रतिशत मतदाता पैसा या दूसरे उपहार पाते हैं? (प्रतिशत में)

Conclusion

Implications for Research and Policy

Devesh Kapur, Eswaran Sridharan,
and Milan Vaishnav

In this concluding chapter, we set out to do five things. First, we offer several stylized facts that summarize the current realities of India's political finance regulatory ecosystem. Second, we briefly review an important recent development on the policy front for political finance: Prime Minister Narendra Modi's sudden and dramatic decision to 'demonetize' the Indian rupee in November 2016. Third, we discuss the motivations for pushing for deeper legal and regulatory changes and outline the central tenets of a 'grand bargain' for electoral reform that combines both carrots and sticks in order to curb some of the most distortionary impacts that money is having. Fourth, we briefly assess the question of whether the Aam Aadmi Party (AAP) represents a new model of politics that combines internal party democracy with greater transparency in electoral funding, as some analysts have argued. Fifth, we conclude with some thoughts on a future research agenda. The research on money in politics, in India and across the developing world, is still in its infancy. It is our sincere hope that this volume will motivate other researchers to advance the research frontier. Quite simply, there is much more to be done.

CURRENT STATE OF PLAY

The chapter by Sridharan and Vaishnav in this volume outlined the legal and regulatory framework governing money in Indian politics. Drawing from that chapter, we offer the following five stylized facts, which make clear the severe infirmities associated with the status quo.

First, while a democracy cannot function without elections, India's democracy risks becoming defined solely by elections as the institutional foundations of the Indian state struggle to discharge their functions.[1] Broader institutional weaknesses have led elections to become the sole yardstick to measure India's democracy, a burden that comes with an increasing price tag.

Second, contemporary Indian politics is a cash-intensive business. Given the premium placed on anonymity and undocumented transfers, it is not surprising that cash reigns supreme when it comes to political finance. Indeed, political parties report the vast majority of their donations as cash gifts and politicians—as the chapters by Chauchard and Björkman and Witsoe demonstrate—regularly engage in the large-scale distribution of cash or other material inducements on the eve of elections. While cash does not equal black money, a heavy reliance on cash does facilitate a natural nexus with black money.

Third, details concerning political contributions are few and far between. In the majority of cases it is impossible to identify who is making contributions, and to whom. Since contributions below a Rs 20,000 threshold need not be disclosed under Indian law, there are incentives to repackage contributions below this arbitrary cut-off. As one of us has written, 'The oldest trick in the book is for donors to break up their offerings into bite-sized chunks, thereby obscuring their fingerprints.'[2]

Fourth, political parties are not subject to any system of independent audit. This does not mean that parties' accounts are not audited. To the contrary, parties are required to submit audited accounts to the

---

[1] For a recent analysis of this issue, see Devesh Kapur, Pratap Bhanu Mehta, and Milan Vaishnav, eds., *Rethinking Public Institutions in India* (New Delhi: Oxford University Press, 2017).

[2] Milan Vaishnav, 'Purify the Parties', *Indian Express*, 6 January 2017.

Election Commission of India (ECI) on an annual basis. However, they are under no obligation to subject their finances to independent, third-party scrutiny. In fact, many politicians privately admit that party finances are usually given the 'Good Housekeeping' seal of approval by a handpicked chartered accountant who will sign off on just about anything presented to him or her.

And fifth, the ECI is badly outgunned when it comes to taking on those who seek to circumvent existing campaign finance laws and regulations. The agency does not have adequate power or resources to sanction candidates and parties for even blatant misrepresentation on disclosure forms such as candidate affidavits or election expenditure statements. For instance, the law requires that candidates submit expenditure statements to the ECI within 30 days of an election, but many either fail to do so in the time prescribed or submit these forms with misleading or missing information. Currently, the commission lacks the statutory authority to levy even a slap on the wrist, let alone the sort of punitive penalties that are essential to ensure behavioural changes from those who openly flout the rules on the books.

Demonetization

2016 and 2017 were eventful years as far as money in Indian politics is concerned. The Modi government's demonetization gambit, which initiated a high-stakes crackdown on black money, merits special discussion given its relevance for the subject at hand. The chapter by Sridharan and Vaishnav covers the second major development in 2017, a slew of initiatives to 'reform' political finance passed as part of the Finance Act.[3] To avoid repetition, we focus here on the demonetization announcement.

---

[3] There was also a third development that deserves mention: amendments contained in the 2016 Finance Act retrospectively changed provisions in the Foreign Contributions Regulation Act (FCRA) that define what a 'foreign' company is. The changes were enacted in order to circumvent a 2014 Delhi High Court ruling that the BJP and the Congress had illegally accepted donations from the London-based multinational, Vedanta. Under FCRA (prior to the 2016 amendments), foreign contributions to political parties were strictly prohibited. To avoid embarrassment, India's two leading parties joined hands to rewrite the law rather than risk legal jeopardy.

On the evening of 8 November 2016, Prime Minister Narendra Modi addressed a hastily organized news conference to declare to a nation-wide television audience his government's intent to 'demonetize' the Indian rupee. With almost immediate effect, the government announced the existing five-hundred- and one-thousand-rupee notes—which together accounted for roughly 86 per cent of outstanding currency—would cease to function as legal tender. For a specified window of time, Indians could deposit the old currency in their bank accounts or exchange old notes for newly designed five-hundred- and two-thousand-rupee notes embedded with new security features.

The move fulfilled a campaign promise made by then-candidate Modi in 2013 and early 2014 to address the scourge of black money in the Indian economy, a significant share of which (at least in its liquid manifestation) is allegedly held in high-denomination currency notes.[4]

Among official explanations for the benefits of demonetization were curbing the use of undocumented cash for elections. Critics alleges that the move was intended to disadvantage smaller, regional parties with large cash holdings ahead of crucial assembly polls scheduled for early 2017. Although the ruling party might also suffer if it possessed undocumented cash, it would stand to gain in relative terms given the fact that national parties have access to diversified sources of income (unlike many of their smaller rivals).[5] Whatever the motivations, at first glance, demonetization did not lead to a marked decline in the reliance on cash or other material inducements during elections. In early 2017—just months after demonetization was announced—five states (including Uttar Pradesh, India's most populous state) went to polls.

---

[4] For instance, then-candidate Modi once proclaimed, 'When we bring back the black money, we will give it to regular salary holders. We must honour their patriotism. Till the time we don't bring back black money, such thefts will continue. So to stop new thefts and such cases, all black money should be brought home to teach one and all a lesson.' See 'Flashback: Here's What Modi Promised India on Black Money', *Rediff*, 29 October 2014, accessed 20 June 2017, http://www.rediff.com/news/report/flashback-heres-what-modi-promised-india-on-black-money/20141029.htm.

[5] Some commentators have even speculated that the Modi government provided its BJP party colleagues with advance warning, allowing them to take appropriate measures to minimize the party's cash exposure. There is no definitive evidence we know of that supports or refutes this claim.

According to India's chief election commissioner, these state elections saw an 'unprecedented number of seizures of all manner of inducements to the voter'. The total haul of undocumented cash, liquor, and drugs seized during the run-up to the election surpassed Rs 350 crore, more than three times the amount seized during the previous assembly polls in 2012.[6] While at least some of this increase could be a reflection of enhanced enforcement, the numbers certainly do not indicate the obsolescence of cash. Indeed, in Uttar Pradesh alone, the ECI sized more than Rs 115 crore in cash during the campaign, three times the cash recovered in the previous state assembly election.[7] As one Election Commission official concluded, 'The massive and unprecedented cash seizures from the poll-bound states prove that demonetization has had no effect on use of money power in elections.'[8]

The debate over the precise impacts of demonetization is beyond the scope of this book. However, the short run evidence suggests that, as far as political finance is concerned, the effect on money in politics has been minimal. By design, demonetization has the greatest potential impact on the stock of black money, but it does little to address the flow. As one writer pointed out, demonetization is like liposuction: it represents a one-time reduction in body fat. But if the body wishes to maintain its new physique, a healthy diet and regular exercise are required.[9]

WHY REFORM?

Before wading into the details of a possible reform package, one needs to stop and ask why reform is needed in the first instance. In our view, there are at least four reasons.

---

[6] Nistula Hebbar and Devesh K. Pandey, 'Leaders Must Tell Voters Not to Take Bribes, Says CEC Nasim Zaidi', *Hindu*, 9 March 2017.

[7] 'Assembly Elections 2017: Cash, Liquor Seizures Go Through the Roof', *Press Trust of India*, 26 February 2017, accessed 20 June 2017, http://www.livemint.com/Politics/O7fPAf4qxMTDfjyGqxplRP/Assemly-elections-2017-Cash-liquor-seizures-go-through-the.html.

[8] Bharti Jain, 'Despite Note Ban, Dirty Cash Flows for Elections', *Times of India*, 21 February 2017.

[9] Milan Vaishnav, 'Why India's Demonetisation Alone Won't End Dirty Money in Politics', *Alphaville* (blog), *Financial Times*, 28 November 2017.

278 Devesh Kapur, Eswaran Sridharan, and Milan Vaishnav

First, there are major positive and normative implications of rising financial barriers to run for political office in India. It is becoming increasingly difficult to be a viable candidate for elected office, especially at the state and national levels, without either being independently wealthy or having access to large pools of liquid financial resources. While there is nothing inherently wrong with well-resourced individuals contesting and holding office, the concern arises when *only* individuals who are financially well off are able to win political office and serve as the peoples' representatives. On the one hand, this has an adverse selection effect on the quality of candidates willing to run for office. And, on the other, by sharply narrowing the pool of potential candidates who can run for office, the equality of participation that is essential for the substantive content of democracy suffers. As research from other countries has shown, the composition of the political class is inextricably linked to their policy preferences and, therefore, policy outcomes.[10]

Second, the opacity of political finance has numerous ramifications for electoral politics. It provides an avenue for the generation and transmission of black money, which deprives the state of resources due to the loss of tax revenue. It facilitates corrupt exchange because those seeking to influence politics can finance campaigns without any public trace. Furthermore, the lack of transparency strengthens the power of party elites at the expense of rank-and-file members, eroding internal party democracy and the institutional integrity of political parties.

A third important ramification has to do with public trust. The perception that elections can be bought and sold can inflict lasting damage on democratic legitimacy. Even if money has diminishing returns, there is no doubt that money does influence political outcomes (for instance, as discussed above, by determining who enters the electoral fray and who does not).

Fourth, the profusion of political parties (in 2015, 1866 parties were registered with the ECI) and the opacity of political finance are not

---

[10] Martin Gilens, *Affluence and Influence: Economic Inequality and Political Power in America* (Princeton: Princeton University Press, 2013); and Larry Bartels, *Unequal Democracy: The Political Economy of the New Gilded Age,* 2nd ed. (New York: Russell Sage Foundation and Princeton; NJ: Princeton University Press, 2016).

coincidental but causal. Many political parties are simply conduits for money laundering. Consequently, it is not just that black money undermines the electoral process, but political parties themselves are important players in nurturing the black money ecosystem. In December 2016, the Election Commission delisted 255 political parties that existed only on paper and had not contested a local body, assembly, or Lok Sabha election since 2005.[11] Many political parties in India today exist in name only; they derive tax benefits yet have no intention of contesting elections seriously.

But even if citizens find reforming political finance to be a worthy objective, the next question to ask is why political parties would ever want to reform the system, especially given the fact that the prevailing opaque equilibrium is so deeply entrenched. One possibility is that reforms might reduce the costs of campaigns for which politicians need to raise funds. Privately, many politicians fret about the rising costs of elections and even honest, well-intentioned *netas* acknowledge that one needs to find ways of making money while in office if only to pay for the next election. As one aspiring politician in the state of Andhra Pradesh lamented to one of the authors in 2014, 'If I am lucky enough to win [election], next time I'll need even more money. How does one remain honest and succeed in politics in this country?'[12]

Parties and candidates also recognize the fact that money, while an important factor, often does not win elections on its own. Indeed, India is notable for its high turnover in office at both the central and state levels. While state-level anti-incumbency declined in the decade of the 2000s (especially compared to the politically tumultuous 1990s), incumbency at the level of the individual candidate is still markedly low, compared to advanced democracies such as the United States.[13]

---

[11] 'Election Commission Delists 255 Political Parties Existing Only on Paper', Indo-Asian News Service, 23 December 2016, accessed 20 June 2017, http://www.hindustantimes.com/india-news/election-commission-delists-255-political-parties-existing-only-on-paper/story-aYb0McyM1KWpwwy-acxKedI.html.

[12] Milan Vaishnav, *When Crime Pays* (New Haven: Yale University Press, 2017), 117.

[13] See the discussion of anti-incumbency showing that incumbents who have an advantage in raising political funds in a rent-seeking political economy are regularly voted out of office in E. Sridharan, 'Electoral Finance Reform:

There is another reason politicians might find political finance reform in their self-interest: the reduction of entrenched corruption can actually be politically rewarding. One needs to look no further than Prime Minister Modi's demonetization exercise for evidence. After demonetization was announced in early November, it endured a rocky rollout. The government and Reserve Bank of India (RBI) repeatedly tweaked the rules governing the implementation; by one count, there were 54 changes in just 42 days.[14] Newspapers carried images of bank queues on a daily basis, while reporting suggested a poorly conceived and executed strategy for reconfiguring old ATMs and injecting a fresh supply of newly fashioned rupee notes into circulation. Be that as it may, the move proved to be electorally popular (or, at the very least, minimally damaging). In the state polls that followed demonetization, the ruling BJP did exceptionally well, forming governments in four of five states on offer. The party won a three-fourths majority in the biggest prize—Uttar Pradesh—where the implementation issues were most likely the most acute, given its size and largely rural character.[15]

Anecdotally, many voters cheered the move. Millions of Indians appeared willing to stand in serpentine queues because someone else higher up the food chain was getting squeezed. As one farmer remarked to the *Financial Times*, Modi 'may have hit us in one eye, but

---

The Relevance of International Experience', in *Reinventing Public Service Delivery in India: Selected Case Studies*, ed. Vikram K. Chand (New Delhi: Sage, 2006): 376–8, especially Tables 11.1 to 11.4. There is considerable analysis on anti-incumbency in India. See Yogesh Uppal, 'The Disadvantaged Incumbents: Estimating Incumbency Effects in Indian State Legislatures', *Public Choice* 138 (2009): 9–27; Leigh Linden, 'Are Incumbents Really Advantaged? The Preference for Non-Incumbents in Indian National Elections' (unpublished paper, University of Texas-Austin, 2004); Gaurav Sabharwal, 'National Spillovers of Local Elections: Evidence from India' (PhD Diss., Princeton University, 2017).

[14] Mohak Gupta, '54 Demonetisation Changes in 42 Days: Here Are 9 Major Ones You Need to Keep Up With', *India Today*, 20 December 2016, accessed 20 June 2017, http://indiatoday.intoday.in/story/demonetisation-changes-8-major-currency-announcements/1/839305.html.

[15] The BJP formed governments in Goa, Manipur, Uttarakhand, and Uttar Pradesh but lost power in Punjab. Going into the poll, the BJP was the incumbent party in Goa and part of the ruling coalition (along with the Shiromani Akali Dal) in the state of Punjab.

he hit the rich in two eyes.'[16] Another feather in Modi's cap was that demonetization made clear where the prime minister stood on the issue of graft—in stark contrast to the opposition. Modi shrewdly portrayed those who opposed demonetization as being pro-corruption, arguing that they were 'brazenly standing in support of the corrupt and the dishonest'.[17]

In pushing for reform, a number of other actors could be important players. Large, multi-state industrial conglomerates could be allies in the political finance reform process because they need to maintain working relationships across party lines with different governments in various states and in New Delhi. If reform efforts succeed, the demand for 'donations' would see a reduction. Civil society groups and the media are also natural partners because they have often acted as watchdogs against corruption, using instruments like public interest litigation and the Right to Information (RTI) Act to address opaque government and party functioning.

Admittedly, this is highly optimistic. The opaque system of political finance is inextricably interlinked to weak governance and this equilibrium favours many powerful actors from politics to business and even in civil society. But if a political opening were to materialize, what might be the core elements of election finance reform in India?

REFORM AGENDA

The preceding discussion makes clear that reforming political finance is an increasingly pressing concern for India's long-term future, and may even be politically rewarding in the short run. However, this begs the question: What reforms *should* India adopt to improve its system of regulating money in politics? There are no easy answers here. While many commentators have advocated for instituting a system of public funding, our firm belief is that a public financing system only makes sense as

---

[16] Amy Kazmin, 'Modi Tightens Grip on Power with Uttar Pradesh Poll Win', *Financial Times*, 12 March 2017.

[17] 'PM Modi Likens Parties Opposing Demonetisation to Pakistan Helping Terrorists', *Press Trust of India*, 22 December 2016, accessed 20 June 2017, http://indianexpress.com/article/india/pm-modi-likens-parties-opposing-demonetisation-to-pakistan-helping-terrorists-4439799/.

part of a 'grand bargain' that requires candidates and parties to adhere to much more stringent transparency and disclosure requirements, with concomitant severe penalties for transgressions. In exchange for such concessions, public funding might make sense for India. However, in the absence of such reforms, there is nothing to stop parties from having their cake and eating it too—accepting public funds *and* private, undocumented funds. We discuss both elements of this grand bargain below, starting with the steps political actors must take.

Contributions

As noted above, there is little or no transparency when it comes to party contributions. Even with the new rules stipulated in the 2017 Finance Act, there are numerous loopholes that parties can exploit to avoid disclosure. Requiring only donations under some (arbitrarily chosen) fixed ceiling to be declared practically invites cheating.

Going forward, there should be complete transparency with respect to each and every rupee of political giving. The best way of ensuring this is for parties to go completely digital. In the wake of demonetization, many Indians turned to digital payment methodologies and away from cash (even if this switch was not completely voluntary). Arguably, parties are much better equipped to make this change, and doing so would ensure a record of all contributions they receive. To deter those who would want to game the system, would-be donors could be required to submit either their Permanent Account Number (PAN) or Aadhaar numbers, which conclusively link a specific individual with a specific contribution. Indeed, given the strong thrust towards digitization on programs for the poor, it is unclear why what is good for the poor is not good for political parties, which cry themselves hoarse in the name of the aforementioned poor. If a complete migration to digital payment systems is a bridge too far, there should be a cap both on the absolute amount of funds parties are allowed to raise in cash, as well as a share of their overall contributions.

Spending

If parties are willing to adhere to greater transparency, it might be time to substantially loosen limits on candidate spending (with periodic revisions to take inflation into account). Candidates openly flout the strict limits in place, and the administrative effort required to monitor the limits is considerable; data suggest that candidates report spending just over half of the prescribed limit, which politicians and regulators alike describe as ludicrous. As a result, the whole exercise of candidate expenditure reports has become a wasted effort; nobody takes these disclosures seriously.

Candidates have a point when they gripe about the rigid limits on candidate spending. Given the competitiveness of elections, the ballooning number of voters, and the expectations placed on campaigns, there is considerable room for revisiting the issue of spending limits. Unreasonable rules will justifiably lead even reasonable people to flout them and the ECI has much blame to shoulder in this regard. But, again, this should only be done if candidates agree to submit complete expenditure statements in a timely manner, with clear penalties, such as being debarred from holding any political office in case of severe transgressions. This will require enhanced enforcement; candidates are already required to submit their expenditure statements within 30 days of an election, but many openly flout this deadline (since election authorities—state and local officials deputized by the ECI— have often moved onto the next thing). The ECI must plug this enforcement gap and insist on strict punishment for those who break the rules. It should also consider instituting random audits to deter fuzzy accounting.

Political Parties and Their Accounts

Political parties are the essential link between voters and candidates. While they serve a public purpose, they are private associations of citizens who come together to advance their interests. But despite their necessity for democratic politics, their internal workings have always left much to be desired. As the British statesman Benjamin Disraeli put it, 'There is no act of treachery or meanness of which a political party is not capable; for in politics there is no honor.'

Political parties were not mentioned in the original Indian Constitution. The 52nd amendment passed in 1985—known as the anti-defection amendment—both recognized parliamentary political parties and regulated shifts in the affiliations and votes of their elected members. From 1989, a new provision (Section 29A) in the Representation of the People Act, 1951, framed rules for the 'registration' of political parties requiring that a party's rules 'contain a specific provision that the association shall bear true faith and allegiance to the Constitution of India as by law established, and uphold the principles of socialism, secularism and democracy and the sovereignty, unity and integrity of India'. But, once registered, there is little regulation on the functioning of political parties; in 2002, the Supreme Court ruled that the ECI does not have the explicit power to deregister a political party.

With regard to political finance, there are no limits placed on the spending of political parties. Indeed, they can expend an unlimited amount on a candidate's campaign, as long as the party uses those funds to promote the party programme without invoking the individual candidate by name. On the contributions side, there are restrictions on foreign contributions (although these were weakened by recent amendments to the FCRA law) but, as of the 2017 Finance Act, no limits on corporate giving.

Looking ahead, the biggest action item for reform insofar as parties are concerned has to do with auditing their books. While political parties must file audited income tax returns on an annual basis, there is no requirement of an independent, third-party audit. While the 2017 Finance Act strengthens the requirement that parties submit these returns within a defined time period, it is silent on the issue of auditing. In the future, party accounts should be subject to independent scrutiny either by the Comptroller and Auditor General (CAG) or a slate of respected auditors the CAG recommends. After all, the disclosure of false accounts is not much better than no disclosure.

While there is little doubt that political parties need greater regulation and accountability, specifying the nature of this accountability and identifying who would be the regulator are far more difficult than might appear. Are political parties private or public entities? In 2013, the Central Information Commission held that the RTI Act applied to political parties on the grounds that they were 'public authorities'. The rationale stated in its order was that, 'it would be odd to argue that transparency is good for all state organs, but not so good for political parties, which, in reality, control all the vital organs of the state'. The order was fraught since private entities can discharge a public function and conversely, 'merely because an entity is public does not mean a public law remedy should apply to it'.[18]

At the time of writing, a Public Interest Litigation (PIL) suit in support of the CIC's ruling was pending before the Supreme Court. While we do not yet know how the Supreme Court will act, it is ironic that private firms are far more regulated than political parties under the status quo. Indeed, just because a firm is private does not mean that it is not subject to corporate governance standards. Given their tax-exempt status, political parties should be subject to higher standards, but who would enforce those standards? While the ECI would be the logical body, it faces its own set of challenges.

Election Commission Powers

The ECI is widely recognized as one of the most powerful elections agencies in the world. Its constitutional mandate gives it broad powers over the conduct and superintendence of the electoral process. Having said that, it is hardly all-powerful. Many of its powers to regulate money in politics stem from the Representation of the People Act (RPA), and this legislation is badly in need of an overhaul. Even when politicians flout rules on campaign spending, the ECI has struggled to take punitive action due to gaps in, or legal ambiguity about, its enforcement powers.

New disclosure and reporting requirements will only be effective if the ECI has well-defined tools at its disposal to take action when these rules are broken. For instance, there is a legal question about whether the ECI can punish politicians who engage in the practice of 'paid news' (that is, colluding with media houses to provide positive coverage in exchange for a fee) since 'paid news' is not actually specified as a predicate offense in the RPA. Similarly, the ECI has requested the government to bring legislation that would grant it the explicit authority to nullify an election if there is evidence of widespread bribery of voters. While the commission has cancelled polls on such grounds before, it has done so under its broad constitutional authority (which leaves it subject to litigation).[19]

---

[18] Pratap Bhanu Mehta, 'Party Fixing', *Indian Express*, 6 June 2013.

[19] Anubhuti Vishnoi, 'Government Moves on EC Proposal to Cancel Election Over Bribery', *Economic Times*, 5 May 2017.

While it is tempting to invest much greater powers in the ECI, a note of caution is warranted since it also creates greater temptation for political parties to try and weaken the institution through other means (such as selection of its commissioners). The idea of independent institutions with Solomonic judgement is often a chimera. Indeed, one could argue that the ECI has contributed to the problem of mounting election costs, in some part at least, by increasing the duration of the electoral cycle. While multi-phase elections might increase the integrity of the electoral process at the booth level, they undermine integrity at a higher level and may well be a case of the best being the enemy of the good.

Public Funding

Only when there is a political consensus about the need to embrace the aforementioned reform agenda should the government contemplate establishing a system of public funding. Assuming that such a consensus materializes, state funding could be provided by combining three elements: a basic slab, an amount based on vote share in the previous election, and a matching grant to the amount raised by the party. The matching grant component should *only* be provided to match donations by cheque or digital payment with donor identities disclosed. The idea is to incentivize parties, through the carrot of matching grants, to raise donations transparently. To encourage small donations, the government could consider increasing the matching amount for donations under a certain size.[20] For instance, Gowda and Santhosh recommend a larger matching 'multiplier' for small donations under Rs 20,000 that are linked to a PAN card of a registered voter (which now could be extended to an Aadhaar number).[21]

Donors could claim tax benefits by contributing by cheque, and, in the process, create a legal, transparent system for adequate flows of

---

[20] Baijayant 'Jay' Panda, 'Now Reform Political Funding', *Times of India*, 23 November 2016.

[21] M.V. Rajeev Gowda and Varun Santhosh, 'A Proposal for Public Funding of Elections and Political Parties in India', *Ideas for India* (blog), 21 April 2017, accessed 17 October 2017, http://www.ideasforindia.in/article.aspx?article=A-proposal-for-public-funding-of-elections-and-political-parties-in-India.

party funds. At today's per capita income levels, parties like the Indian National Congress, which claims 30 million members, and the BJP, which claims over 100 million, should not find it difficult to raise adequate funds from large and small sources both. A matching grant system of state funding could help incentivize donations from a large number of members and supporters, which might also have the benefit of making parties more responsive and, thus, reinforcing intra-party democracy. State funding will have to be administered by the ECI to ensure a level playing field.

There is, of course, the outstanding question of how public funding would work in a context of highly centralized political parties. Revitalizing membership (through the fundraising mechanism) will help create pressure from below, but the ECI might need to weigh in more heavily to encourage internal democracy by laying down conditions of holding regular internal elections. It will be important for any public financing system to ensure a smooth flow of funds to candidates, not just at the national level, but also at the state and local levels. This would provide funds to lower-level political functionaries to nurse their political networks and finance elections campaigns, while maintaining some degree of independence from the party high command by providing a financial floor. The quantum of state funding, however, should be adequate, or it will not be effective in checking illicit fundraising. One option, raised by Gowda and Santhosh, is to mandate that a percentage of public funds be spent only at a constituency-level bank account to ensure that a significant share of money is spent at the local level to strengthen grass-roots party organizations.

There is, however, an additional wrinkle arising from the fact that local elections are playing an increasing role in election finance and their superintendence is vested with state election commissions and not the ECI. Should public financing be extended to local elections as well? If the grass roots are so important to the foundations of democracy, then it becomes even more important to have healthy roots if the plant is to thrive. But public funding for the quarter of a million panchayat elections is a formidable task. After all, elections at the most local level (the gram panchayat) are supposed to be party-less. Public funding of candidates would be massively complicated, both in the terms of the volume of funding and the logistics.

We wish to emphasize that it is important to tread carefully on matters of party regulation. Additional regulation of political parties requires significant public debate given that regulatory behaviour in India has historically erred on the side of too much, rather than too little. Political parties need to operate according to some broad parameters, but the state's role should be limited, since in principle, these are private associations with a public purpose.

THE 'AAP MODEL'?

Recently, a promising political finance model emerged from the Indian polity in the form of the Aam Aadmi Party. Initially, the AAP was the only major political party to have consciously adopted transparency in fundraising and expenditure.[22] The party, which formed in November 2012, emerged from a widespread, spontaneous, but also well-organized, anti-corruption movement led by a broad coalition of activists called India Against Corruption (IAC). IAC was founded by Arvind Kejriwal, a former civil servant and anti-corruption and RTI activist, with the well-known social activist Anna Hazare as its public mascot.

The movement eventually split with one faction, led by Arvind Kejriwal, taking the electoral plunge. To distinguish itself from existing political outfits, AAP initially adopted a number of structural innovations, including an apparent assurance of internal party democracy. It promised to hold elections at all levels of the party every three years, with an executive committee of the party being elected by local council members and an internal *Lokpal* to investigate allegations of

[22] See AAP's website for fundraising details: http://aamaadmiparty.org/. For detailed accounts, see Prashant Sharma, 'From India Against Corruption to the Aam Aadmi Party: Social Movements, Political Parties and Citizen Engagement in India', *International IDEA Political Parties and Citizen Movements in Asia and Europe* (2014), 39–54. Also see Mayank Jain, 'AAP's Fund Raising: Six Charts about How Much They're Getting and Where It's Coming From', *Scroll.in*, 14 January 2015, accessed 20 June 2017, http://scroll.in/article/700261/aaps-fund-raising-six-charts-about-how-much-they're-getting-and-where-its-coming-from; 'AAP Funding Takes Centre Stage in Delhi Elections', *Business Standard*, 4 February 2015; and 'How Aam Aadmi Party is Feeding Its Coffers', *Economic Times*, 12 January 2015.

wrongdoing against any office bearer. And prior to the 2013 Delhi assembly elections, the party leadership established a process of citizen engagement in order to select its slate of electoral candidates.[23] This system of internal party democracy is necessary context for what the party decided to do on the issue of electoral finance. Initially, the party pledged to function in a fully transparent manner, placing every donation and all expenditures on the party's website, and promising to update in real time with details of donations by date, amount, and location. In the Delhi assembly elections of February 2015, which the party won handsomely, AAP accepted donations in cash only up to Rs 20,000; donations between Rs 20,000 and Rs 1,000,000 were accepted by cheque or online transfer, while large donations over Rs 10 lakhs were acceptable only via cheque and subject to the party's PAC for verification.[24] The PAC supposedly scrutinizes each large donation by checking the validity of the company and its taxpayer identity information, whether it is listed on the Registrar of Companies, and whether the donation is channelled through a registered bank. It also does a simple Internet search to ascertain whether the individual or company stands accused of any criminal wrongdoing. What AAP claims it cannot do is independently verify the donor's private detail; in other words, it has to trust that donor filings are authentic.[25]

Can the AAP model last and can it survive geographical expansion? Sadly, it did not take much time for the sheen to begin wearing off; indeed, there are clear signs that the new model is struggling. Politically, AAP increasingly resembles most other parties in India: run from the top-down and organized around a single charismatic leader (Kejriwal, in AAP's case). Shortly after the Delhi victory, two senior members

[23] At the time, it required every aspirant to a party ticket produce signatures from 100 voters in his/her constituency, which are then scrutinized by a screening committee, resulting in a short list of five names which were released for public feedback before party volunteers rank the candidates via a secret ballot using a preferential voting system. The party's Political Affairs Committee (PAC), taking the result of the ballot into account, held a final set of interviews before choosing the party nominee. In the 2013 election, AAP used this system to select 33 of the party's 70 assembly candidates.

[24] 'AAP Funding Takes Centre Stage in Delhi Elections.'

[25] 'How Aam Aadmi Party is Feeding Its Coffers.'

of AAP—Prashant Bhushan and Yogendra Yadav—were expelled for engaging in 'anti-party activities'. Prominent individuals who have left the party complain that AAP has absorbed all of the trappings of a 'high command culture' that it once railed against.

Data compiled by ADR on the backgrounds of electoral candidates filed by AAP in recent elections also suggests that there are signs that the party has sacrificed probity and a clean record in exchange for 'winnability'. When it comes to fundraising, AAP has taken a 180-degree turn from its initial position touting full transparency; the last balance sheet on the party's website dated back to 2014 and the webpage containing a list of donors has long been listed as 'under construction'. During the 2017 Punjab assembly elections, in which the AAP made a strong push, one of its senior leaders claimed that it could no longer place the names of its donors online because they were being continuously harassed by opponents.[26] The AAP's partisans might defend this U-turn as indicative of the broader challenge of marrying transparency and scalability when it comes to fundraising: large donors, whose support will likely be needed for AAP's expansion, are not easily amenable to transparent funding. On the other hand, one could make an equally compelling case that principles are the first casualty of ambition and, in this case, the ambitions of one person (Kejriwal) pushed the party to expand more rapidly than its original model of fundraising based on probity would allow. In other words, the fundraising model adapted to the ambition rather than the other way around.[27]

FUTURE RESEARCH

A book like this raises as many questions as it answers. Given the limited scholarly work on money in politics in India (and in the developing world, more broadly) and the numerous hurdles that stand

[26] Chitleen K. Sethi, 'Punjab Polls: AAP Asks for Donations, but Donors to Remain Incognito', *Hindustan Times*, 22 December 2016.

[27] It should be noted that, in its 2014 campaign, the BJP ran into the problem of donor reluctance to disclose identities in its relatively successful online fundraising campaign. Online funds, however, only accounted for roughly 10 per cent of the BJP's raised funds in that election—with the other 90 per cent coming from traditional fundraising methods. Arvind Gupta (BJP online campaign head), in conversation with one of the authors, 11 December 2015.

in the way of empirical work in this area, the issues requiring future exploration are too many to count. Rather than providing a comprehensive list of all of the outstanding questions we can think of, we instead focus on some of the unresolved issues that we found to be of greatest interest.

Variation in Election Spending

One of the most visible puzzles when it comes to election expenditure is the enormous heterogeneity across states. Anecdotally, elections in the southern states of Andhra Pradesh and Tamil Nadu seem to be orders of magnitude more expensive than elections in states such as Gujarat or Delhi. Tamil Nadu, in particular, has gained international notoriety for the staggering amounts of money that are allegedly spent in pursuit of elected office.

In April 2017, ECI authorities cancelled a by-poll to be held in the state's R.K. Nagar assembly constituency on the grounds that the widespread pre-election distribution of money and other gifts had 'vitiated' the atmosphere. Media reports indicated that a faction of the ruling AIADMK allegedly handed out Rs 89 crores to voters in the run up to Election Day.[28] Documents recovered by tax authorities suggest that the party aimed to reach 85 per cent of voters in the constituency; if the money were divided evenly, this would amount to roughly Rs 4,000 per eligible voter.[29]

This is not the first time Tamil Nadu has found the spotlight thanks to the flood of election money sloshing around. In the 2016 state assembly polls, the ECI was forced (for the first time in its history) to cancel polls in two constituencies on account of the large-scale distribution of cash and other handouts during the campaign. Seven years earlier, Tamil Nadu made the headlines when the son of DMK president M. Karunanidhi, M.K. Azhagiri, supposedly flooded a parliament

[28] J. Sam Daniel Stalin, '"89 Crores Paid, 4,000 Per Voter": How Minister Planned Chennai By-Poll', *NDTV*, 9 April 2017, accessed 20 June 2017, http://www.ndtv.com/tamil-nadu-news/89-crores-paid-4000-per-voter-how-minister-planned-chennai-by-poll-1679015.

[29] J. Sam Daniel Stalin, '"89 Crores Paid, 4,000 Per Voter": How Minister Planned Chennai By-Poll.'

by-election in Thirumangalam with a torrent of cash.[30] The episode gained notoriety when Wikileaks made public a US diplomatic cable that provided sordid details of the scheme, which soon became known as the 'Thirumangalam formula'. According to the cable, an aide to Azhagiri confessed that the DMK leader distributed Rs 5,000 to every voter in the constituency using an innovative delivery mechanism: an envelope tucked into the morning newspaper delivery (along with a DMK voting slip).[31]

Anecdotal evidence suggests that candidates standing for parliamentary elections in Tamil Nadu often spend between Rs 25 and 50 crores on their election, while aspiring candidates in Delhi spend between Rs 10 and 25 crores (numbers current as of 2013–14). These are not hard numbers, but suggestive figures based on available fieldwork and reporting. Similarly, an assembly election in Delhi could set a major party candidate back between Rs 1 and 5 crores while a regional poll in Andhra Pradesh could cost twice as much (if not more).[32] The costs of elections also seem to vary within a locality in a given state. Chauchard's work in this volume on state elections in Mumbai reports election spending by major party candidates between Rs 1 and 16 crores.

But the variation in election spending across states does not, on first glance, appear to be about income alone. Delhi's per capita income is almost double that of Tamil Nadu's and Maharashtra's almost 50 per cent greater than Andhra Pradesh's. What are the factors behind this variation, across and (possibly) even within states? Are the stakes different and, if so, what are they? For instance, is the 'prize' of winning Tamil Nadu greater than Maharashtra? Even if one restricts attention to the major parties in a given state, do different parties employ

[30] Dharani Thangavelu, 'Tamil Nadu's History of Cash for Votes', *Mint*, 10 April 2017.

[31] U.S. Consulate Chennai, 'Cash for Votes in South India', diplomatic cable, 13 May 2009, accessed 10 January 2015, https://wikileaks.org/plusd/cables/09CHENNAI144_a.html.

[32] Vaishnav narrates the story of a first-time candidate standing for state election in Andhra Pradesh who spent Rs 10 to 12 crores on his campaign, an amount 30 to 40 times the expenditure ceiling mandated by the ECI. See Vaishnav, *When Crime Pays*, Chapter 4.

different political finance strategies? Or is there pressure to conform to the behaviour of others? If so, how does information regarding election spending travel and is there room for misperception, deliberate or otherwise?

The Stakes in Politics

If we accept that candidates and parties spend a lot of money, the question becomes why politicians are prepared to spend so much to win elections. What is at stake in winning elections? Clearly, the stakes must be high if aspiring politicians are prepared to spend so much. If that is the case, controlling election finance may well be a Sisyphean task akin to plugging the holes in a leaking dike when one should really be focusing elsewhere.

The stakes in politics can be symbolic, material, or ideological. Spending in campaigns might be a case of 'conspicuous consumption', symbolically similar to lavish weddings or splurging on religious festivals. The semiotics of conspicuous consumption are rooted in status-seeking behaviour. In a status-conscious society with different groups vying for social mobility, high spending on elections in India may have a 'signalling' function to members of the community. There is considerably more wealth in India than in the past, and conspicuous consumption now requires greater resources than earlier, since what was conspicuous two decades ago is passé today.

Alternatively, the stakes in politics may simply be more crassly material. Investing in election campaigns might be akin to an investment decision where there are material pay-offs for the winner. As long as the material pay-off (conditional on winning) is greater than the probability of winning times the campaign investment, campaign spending is simply a case of an investment under uncertainty.[33] The material pay-offs are, of course, a reflection of rent-seeking behaviour, which is possible because of weak governance institutions. Unfortunately, this behaviour creates a self-enforcing dynamic, since elected officials would hardly want to improve governance and limit their own rent-seeking opportunities.

---

[33] The pay-off of winning could, of course, include avoiding the long-term losses of losing.

Finally, it is possible that the stakes may be ideological. This clearly has been a driving factor in escalating election expenditures in the United States. However, in India, the greater prevalence of rent-seeking behaviour has attenuated the ideological drivers of electoral politics. While there are differences in political platforms, politicians in India are relatively promiscuous in shifting their positions and joining alliances in the pursuit of power—and the rents that come with it. One could argue that party ideologies are crucial in presenting citizens with different visions of the future and are at the heart of electoral competition. But when the differences become deeply polarizing, they begin to threaten democracy itself.

Reforming electoral finance will be more difficult unless the stakes in acquiring political power are reduced. India's first-past-the post electoral system creates a winner-take-all high stakes game. A greater weight to proportional representation might attenuate the stakes, but might also make governments more difficult to form. Strengthening public institutions would reduce rent-seeking opportunities and, with it, the attendant financial stakes of capturing power. Moving certain polarizing issues out of politics into the realm of law could reduce the political stakes.[34] And finally, if politics is the only road to achieving societal goals, the stakes in controlling that road will be that much higher. Civil society, markets, and social movements all offer complementary pathways and strengthening them are likely to (at least modestly) diminish the stakes of politics—and rein in the galloping demands of electoral finance.

Measurement

One impediment to studying election expenditure, especially as it relates to gift giving (which is believed to account for a large percentage of election budgets), is following the money trail. Kapur and Vaishnav's chapter in this book, which leverages fluctuations in cement consumption, and Sukhtankar's work on sugar mills are both examples of how researchers can use novel, indirect methods of tracing how

---

[34] William N. Eskridge Jr., 'Pluralism and Distrust: How Courts Can Support Democracy by Lowering the Stakes of Politics', *Yale Law Journal* 114 (2005): 1279–328.

campaign funds are channelled.[35] While neither offers precise data on the quantum of funds spent, they both help elucidate the mechanisms through which money is raised and spent.

Another recent entry in this literature is a paper by Anirban Mitra and colleagues.[36] The authors devise an ingenious method of studying vote buying: examining the consumption patterns of households using survey data. Using National Sample Survey (NSS) rounds on household consumption expenditure (which has detailed data on the date on which the survey was fielded) and state assembly elections data from 2004 to 2011, the study compares a household's consumption immediately prior to an election with consumption several days before and after the election in a state. Because of the staggered nature of state elections, the researchers can compare consumption patterns in a state that is going to polls with a 'control group' of households in neighbouring, non-election states. Working with fine-grained data on hundreds of commodities, the authors find that household consumption, including the consumption of staples, local liquor, and saris, exhibits a substantial spike just prior to the day of elections. While these findings largely confirm what we already know—that the distribution of material inducements (commonly dubbed 'vote buying') is rampant—the uniqueness of the methodology provides a level of detail on this distribution that has not previously been available.

The use of large-scale sample survey data represents an important innovation that can be leveraged in the future. Surveys, more generally, could be usefully employed to develop estimates of the sources, methods, and uses of money in politics. Bussell's contribution in this volume, based on survey data collected in three north Indian states, is a good example of one such effort. Researchers interested in electoral opinion surveys might also consider adding a module on the flow of money around elections as there is arguably less measurement error in

---

[35] Sandip Sukhtankar, 'Sweetening the Deal? Political Connections and Sugar Mills in India', *American Economic Journal: Applied Economics* 4, no. 3 (July 2012): 43–63.

[36] Anirban Mitra, Shabana Mitra, and Arnab Mukherji, 'Cash for Votes: Evidence from India on Election Financing and Dynastic Politics' (working paper, International Growth Centre, 28 December 2016).

what individuals or households report receiving from politicians than what candidates or parties claim to be spending on voters.

Adverse Effects of Greater Competition

The consensus in the political science literature is that electoral competition is, by and large, a positive attribute when it comes to democratic accountability and fostering better governance. Where competition is weak or absent, incumbents face little incentive to improve the level of responsiveness to their constituents because voters have no credible exit option. As competition increases and exit options grow, incumbents must step up their game or risk being voted out of power. This dynamic results in better governance outcomes, as several empirical studies have shown.

However, the effects of competition may not be unambiguously positive. In India, one could reasonably argue that there is a severe downside to greater competition: namely, the surging costs associated with elections. As Kapur and Vaishnav argue in the conclusion to their chapter on builders and politicians, 'more competition might also trigger greater electoral expenditure, as parties look to gain an advantage over their competitors.' Competition is typically measured in terms of the number of viable political parties in the fray, but another aspect of competition the authors highlight is the frequency of polls. With the advent of the 73rd and 74th Amendments to the Constitution, which ushered in a three-tier structure of local body elections across rural and urban India, there are nearly three million elected positions in India. Due to the staggering of local, state, and national elections, in any given state, it seems that another election is always around the corner. Political actors at all levels are mobilized for elections at every level to raise funds for their candidates.

In principle, greater political competition, decentralization (that is, greater number of elected sub-national bodies), and more frequent elections can enhance citizen accountability of elected representatives. But each of these benefits also comes with a financial cost with respect to increasing electoral expenditure. While competition may have a great many positive repercussions for democracy and governance, researchers also need to ask whether too much democracy can be a bad thing. Indeed, this appears to be one of the motivations behind Prime

Minister Modi's call for the ECI to consider the merits of conducting simultaneous as opposed to staggered elections in India.

Elections, Elections Everywhere ...

With all the attention showered on local, state, and national elections, other varieties of electoral politics often get short shrift. In the Indian case, student politics represents a fascinating venue for future research since it is in India's universities that many political leaders often get their start. Because campuses often serve as the proving ground for the politically inclined, the stakes are high—which means that they too are subject to the influence of money and muscle. With few exceptions, there is little empirical work on the role of money in these political fora. One exception is ethnographic work by Craig Jeffrey, who studies the political strategies of Jat student leaders in Meerut, Uttar Pradesh.[37] Jeffrey reports that Jat student leaders typically spent between Rs 150,000 and 300,000 (in 2004–5) on election-related expenses such as posters and handouts, vehicles, and feasts for students. For the student leaders Jeffrey studied, politics also functioned as a business; student union leaders at one local university could earn between Rs 800,000 and Rs 10 lakhs in a year working as a broker/fixer on campus.

The role money plays in student politics is an area crying out for research. Student politics in some way is a microcosm for the nation's politics, so it is inherently interesting to study. But it also sheds light on two other issues: the first is how politics becomes a vocation, even for college-aged youths in India, in a country where employment opportunities in the formal sector are few and far between. Relatedly, the influx of money in student politics also has ramifications for the larger endeavour of higher education in India itself, which is in a state of disrepair.[38]

But more broadly, money and elections are pervasive in a wide variety of nominally apolitical settings. Elections for leadership selection in numerous sports bodies in India are afflicted by large amounts

---

[37] Craig Jeffrey, *Timepass: Youth, Class, and the Politics of Waiting in India* (Palo Alto: Stanford University Press, 2010).

[38] Devesh Kapur and Pratap Bhanu Mehta, eds, *Navigating the Labyrinth: Perspectives on India's Higher Education* (New Delhi: Orient Blackswan, 2017).

of money (of which the Board of Control for Cricket in India is a prime example); the same is true of most professional bodies (the Medical Council of India is an especially egregious example). Indeed, from institutions of civil society to institutions of market governance (such as *mandis* that regulate local agriculture markets), and from dairy cooperatives to urban housing societies, elections are the principal mechanism of leadership selection. And in many (if not most) instances, money plays a role. Just how much of a role and with what consequences is poorly understood.

FINAL THOUGHTS

This book represents some of what we have learnt about how money in Indian politics is regulated, sourced, and spent, why such large sums are spent, and what impact this money has on the political system more broadly. But there is much we do not know about the interplay between money and politics in India—and there could hardly be a more pressing issue for social scientists. While there is a shared consensus that money is important, there is (probably) too much of it, and policymakers should be seized by the influx of money, there is no clear agreement about some of the basic facts that guide the routine flow of money. The aim of this book is to shine a light on the areas where researchers and policymakers can begin looking—in the quest for a more comprehensive and informed understanding of one of democracy's critical ingredients.

Index

Editors and Contributors

EDITORS

Devesh Kapur is director of Asia Programs and the Starr Foundation Professor of South Asia Studies at the Paul Nitze School of Advanced International Studies (SAIS) of the Johns Hopkins University, Washington D.C., USA. He is the coauthor of *The World Bank: Its First Half Century* (1997); *Public Institutions in India: Performance and Design* (2005); and *Defying the Odds: The Rise of Dalit Entrepreneurs* (2014). His three books on international migration examine the effects at a global level (*Give us your Best and Brightest: The Global Hunt for Talent and Its Impact on the Developing World* [2005]); on the country of emigration (*Diaspora, Democracy and Development: The Impact of International Migration from India on India* [2010] which received the 2012 Distinguished Book Award of the International Studies Association); and the country of immigration (*The Other One Percent: Indians in America*, co-authored with Sanjoy Chakravorty and Nirvikar Singh [2016]). He has two new co-edited books—*Rethinking Public Institutions in India* and *Navigating the Labyrinth: Perspectives on India's Higher Education*—both published in 2017. In addition to numerous academic articles he has published widely in the popular media. Prior to joining SAIS, he held appointments at the Brookings Institution, Harvard University, University of Texas, Austin and the University of Pennsylvania, USA.

Milan Vaishnav is a senior fellow and director of the South Asia Program at the Carnegie Endowment for International Peace. His primary research focus is the political economy of India, and he examines issues such as corruption and governance, state capacity, distributive politics, and electoral behaviour. He is the author of *When Crime Pays: Money and Muscle in Indian Politics* (2017) and co-editor (with Devesh Kapur and Pratap Bhanu Mehta) of *Rethinking Public Institutions in India* (2017). Previously, he worked at the Center for Global Development, where he served as a postdoctoral research fellow; the Center for Strategic and International Studies; and the Council on Foreign Relations. He has taught at Columbia, Georgetown, and George Washington Universities. He holds a PhD in political science from Columbia University.

CONTRIBUTORS

Lisa Björkman is assistant professor of urban and public affairs at the University of Louisville, Kentucky, USA. Her work studies how global processes of urbanism and urban transformation are redrawing lines of socio-spatial exclusions and inclusions in Mumbai, animating new arenas of political mobilization, contestation, and representation. Her book *Pipe Politics, Contested Waters: Embedded Infrastructures of Millennial Mumbai* (2015) is a political ethnography about the encounter in Mumbai between market-oriented urban development reforms and the material politics of the city's water infrastructures. *Pipe Politics* was awarded the American Institute of Indian Studies' 2014 Book Prize in the Indian Social Sciences. Lisa received a PhD in Politics from the New School for Social Research in New York in 2012.

Jennifer Bussell is assistant professor of political science and public policy at the University of California, Berkeley, USA. She studies comparative politics with an emphasis on the political economy of development, democratic representation, and governance outcomes, principally in South Asia and Africa. Her book *Corruption and Reform in India: Public Services in the Digital Age* (2012) examines the role of corrupt practices in shaping government adoption of information technology across sub-national regions and is based on fieldwork in sixteen Indian states, as well as parts of South Africa and Brazil. Her current research examines the provision of constituency service by high-level elected officials in patronage democracies, using elite and citizen surveys, interviews, qualitative shadowing, and experiments to explore the implications of citizen–state relations for public service delivery. She also studies the politics of natural disasters in developing countries and the incentives of governments to invest in preparedness. She received her PhD in political science from the University of California, Berkeley, and prior to returning to Berkeley taught in the LBJ School of Public Affairs at the University of Texas, Austin, USA.

Simon Chauchard is assistant professor in the government department at Dartmouth College, USA, and a faculty affiliate in the Asia and Middle Eastern Studies programme. He received his PhD in 2011 from New York University, USA. His research focuses on ethnic politics, voting behaviour, clientelism, political representation and politicians–citizens relations in India. Recent works have appeared in *Political Opinion Quarterly*, *American Political Science Review*, and *Comparative Political Studies*. His book, *Why Representation Matters: The Meaning of Ethnic Quotas in Rural India* (2017), combines qualitative work and a series of innovative surveys to explore the impact of caste-based reservation policies on everyday intergroup relations in India's villages. Ongoing projects rely on qualitative and experimental methodologies to explore political brokerage and the role that money and other forms of influence play in Indian elections.

Michael A. Collins is a postdoctoral fellow at the Centre for Modern Indian Studies (CeMIS) at the University of Gottingen, Germany. He received his PhD in 2017 from the University of Pennsylvania. His ethnographic research examines democratic politics, elections, and minority representation in emerging democracies, evaluating how the recent political mobilization of socially marginalized groups, particularly Dalits (ex-untouchables) and religious minorities, affects democratic practice in modern South Asia. The research presented in this volume was supported by a Fullbright-Hays Doctoral Dissertation Research Abroad (DDRA) Award and conducted in affiliation with the French Institute of Pondicherry.

Neelanjan Sircar is a senior fellow at the Centre for Policy Research, New Delhi, India. His research interests include Indian political economy and comparative political behaviour with an eye to Bayesian statistics, causal inference, social network analysis, and game theory. Sircar's recent work focused on state-level elections in India through both data work and ethnographic methods. He is particularly interested in understanding theoretic principles that undergird the decision-making processes of voters in India, which can shed light on democratic practice in the developing world more generally. He also works on projects characterizing the social connections between citizens in India and their local brokers and leaders, as well as how these local brokers and leaders, both rural and urban, make decisions. Sircar is also a non-resident fellow at the Center for the Advanced Study of India at the University of Pennsylvania, USA. He received a bachelor's degree in applied mathematics and economics from UC Berkeley in 2003 and a PhD in political science from Columbia University, New York City, USA, in 2014.

Eswaran Sridharan is the academic director and chief executive of the University of Pennsylvania Institute for the Advanced Study of India (UPIASI), New Delhi, India. He is a political scientist with interests in Indian politics and international relations and is the editor, most recently, of *Coalition Politics in India* (2014). He has published over 70 journal articles and chapters in edited volumes, and lectured and made conference presentations extensively in India and abroad. He has held visiting appointments at the University of California, Berkeley, London School of Economics, Institute for Developing Economies, Tokyo, Institute of South Asian Studies, Singapore, and the Center for the Advanced Study of India, University of Pennsylvania, USA. He is the Editor of *India Review*, a pan-social science refereed quarterly dedicated to India, and on the Editorial Board of *Commonwealth and Comparative Politics*. He holds a PhD in political science from the University of Pennsylvania.

Jeffrey Witsoe is the author of *Democracy against Development: Lower Caste Politics and Political Modernity in Postcolonial India* (2013), an ethnographic study of 'backward caste' politics in Bihar. He is associate professor of anthropology at Union College, New York, USA. He completed his PhD in social anthropology from the University of Cambridge, UK, in 2006.